Retiring to

Italy

Victoria Pybus

Published by Vacation Work,
9 Park End Street, Oxford
www.vacationwork.co.uk

RETIRING TO ITALY
by Victoria Pybus

First edition 2006

Copyright © Vacation Work 2006

ISBN 13: 978-1-85458-359-8
ISBN 10: 1-85458-359-X

Publicity by Charles Cutting

Cover design by mccdesign

Typeset and text design by Guy Hobbs

Cover photograph: cypress trees in Tuscany.

Printed and bound in Italy by Legoprint SpA, Trento

Contents

PART I – BEFORE YOU GO

Setting the Scene

Basics

PART II – A NEW HOME IN ITALY

Where to Retire To

Your New Home in Italy

Housing Finance

PART III – A NEW LIFE IN ITALY

Adapting to Your New Life

Quality of Life

Personal Finance

Healthcare

Crime, Security and the Police

Returning Home

MAPS

NOTE: the author and publishers have every reason to believe in the accuracy of the information given in this book and the authenticity and correct practices of all organisations, companies, agencies, etc. mentioned; however situations may change and telephone numbers etc. can alter, and readers are strongly advised to check facts and credentials for themselves. Readers are invited to write to Vacation Work, 9 Park End Street, Oxford OX1 1HJ or e-mail info@ vacationwork.co.uk with any comments or corrections.

TELEPHONE NUMBERS

Please note that the telephone numbers in this book are written as needed to call that number from inside the same country. Italian numbers are easily distinguished from UK numbers. The first two, three or four numbers are the area code (e.g. 06 for Rome, 050 for Pisa, 0584 for Viareggio) followed by a gap or dash, and the subsequent numbers are written without spaces. Italian telephone numbers can be eight or ten digits, which is why some numbers look 'odd'. All area codes start with a zero. You must dial the two- three- or four-digit area code, even when you are dialling a local number.

To call Italy from the UK: dial 00 39 and then the Italian number including the first zero.

To call the UK from Italy: dial 00 44 then the UK number minus the first zero of the area code.

FOREWORD

For the discerning, Italy has it all: more historical, classical and artistic treasures than any other nation, one of Europe's most delicious and healthy cuisines, a beautiful language, warm and friendly people, exquisite landscapes, 8000km of coastline, architectural gems of cities, colourful medieval traditions, hundreds of arts festivals and so on. Italy used to have some of the cheapest property, but the demand from the *cognoscenti* has long outstripped supply in areas such as Tuscany, Liguria and now Le Marche, where suitable property for sale has all but dried up. And there have been big increases in prices, which usually means lack of choice for anyone hoping to find the kind of super cheap property that was available twenty years ago. You now have to venture deeper into the lesser-known regions to find your dream property at the price you can afford. Fortunately no frills international flights have made once remote areas accessible and ripe for consideration.

Bear in mind also, that retirees coming from the Anglophone world are liable to experience culture shock, not least from the notorious time wasting bureaucracy which Italians rage against as much as foreigners do. For initial and ongoing support you cannot beat the émigré grapevines, either the local one in Italy, or the cyber ones on expatriate websites. Particularly useful are online forums where subscribers swap useful information about dealing with aspects of daily life and Italian bureaucracy. These can be invaluable and informative.

In Italy, expats living outside Tuscany and the grand cities, tend to be more scattered than in the English-speaking 'colonies' of the Dordogne or the Costas of Spain making interaction with neighbouring Italians essential; and Italian is considered less difficult to learn than many languages. It is said that foreign retirees in Italy integrate better with their local community than retirees to many other countries, and that they are less likely to become disillusioned and want to return to the UK. This speaks volumes about the wisdom of making Italy your retirement choice.

Victoria Pybus
Oxford
May 2006

ACKNOWLEDGEMENTS

A book such as this can only come about through the co-operation and assistance of other people with specialist knowledge. Grateful thanks are given to **Gordon Neale** whose expertise on Italy generally and house purchasing in Italy and gardening in Italy in particular, are scholarly and unrivalled. His contributions on these subjects are included in this book. I would also like to thank the obliging and helpful retirees whose stories of retirement in Italy form such an integral part of *Retiring to Italy*: Carole Oram, Carole Means, Harris Freedman, Mel and Kate Holmes and Freddi and Vince Ferrigno; may they all continue to flourish in their respective domains and encourage others to do what they have done. In addition, thanks to Christina Cornish for her photograph of Trulli houses in Alberobello.

Part one

Before
You Go

Setting the Scene

Basics

Setting the Scene

CHAPTER SUMMARY

o Italy has a well-deserved reputation for being a secure place to live and retire to.

o Many Italians adhere to traditional values and quality of life at any age is taken very seriously there.

o The average age for retirement in Italy used to be 55, but the government reforms of 1995 began a gradual raising of the retirement age in line with the rest of Europe.

o Social security and healthcare provision are likely to deteriorate in the future as the population ages and becomes top heavy with retired people.

o Italy's fitness as a place to retire is due to its people, sunshine, culture, beautiful landscapes and historic architecture though there are considerable differences in lifestyle and wealth between north and south.

o Italy tends to attract true Italophiles who are prepared to integrate into the local community, rather than form colonies of English-speakers as often happens in Spain and France.

o In Italy, probably more than in any European country, it is who you know that ensures your smooth passage in Italian life.

o Italians seem genuinely fond of the British and there is no great historical antagonism between the two nations as there is with France and England, and Britain and Spain (over Gibraltar).

o Italy has the reputation of being the most bureaucratically frustrating country in Europe.

THE NEW 'OLD': CHANGING ATTITUDES TO RETIREMENT

At the start of the twenty-first century we are in the midst of a major social transformation. The post-war notion of retirement as a time to put your slippers on and settle in front of the telly with a nice cup of tea is fast becoming obsolete. The very word 'retirement', not to mention the images of encroaching decrepitude that it conjures, no longer fits the reality of how people are living their lives post full-time employment. Today's retirees are often younger, fitter and wealthier than their forebears and together they are reshaping the very meaning of 'old age' and 'retirement'.

Many social commentators suggest that these changes are being wrought by the baby boomer generation. Born between 1945 and 1965, they are a force to be reckoned with, making up almost a third of the UK population and responsible for nearly 80% of all financial wealth. The baby boomers grew up in an era of postwar optimism and new social freedoms, and as such, have always represented a force for social change. Indeed, they have spent a lifetime reconstructing social norms. In 2006 the first wave of this generation is approaching retirement age, and with such political and financial clout their approach to growing old is profoundly different. As *The Times* recently put it: *'the pioneers of the consumer society are unlikely to settle for an electric fire and a can of soup'.*

One of the main reasons that the concept of retirement is changing is that people are living far longer. Life expectancy in the twentieth century rose by 20 years due to better healthcare and greater health awareness. Around 18 million people in the UK are over 60. This is creating something of a crisis in the British economy and if the government had its way, then we would all work until we dropped, easing the pressure on the already over-burdened state pension fund. The new generation of retirees however, are not prepared to do this. Not only are people living longer, they are also leaving the workforce younger. Many are giving up work in their early fifties when they are still fit and active, in order to enjoy a new stage in life – not their 'retirement', according to the American website www.2young2retire.com, but their 'renaissance'.

A recent report by *Demos*, a democracy think tank, claims that the baby boomers are intent on having their time again; of creating a

new life phase in which they can revisit their own desire for personal fulfilment, free from the pressures of overwork and childrearing. The report identifies a new 'experience economy' of travel, food, learning and lifestyle. The baby boomers do not want to retreat from the world as the word 'retirement' suggests, but to head out into it with renewed vigour.

The new retirement is all about finding a better life balance. This may not necessarily include giving up work – around half of the people who leave permanent 'career' jobs before state pension age move initially into part-time, temporary or self-employed work, be it in the UK or abroad. It would seem that people are no longer happy to compartmentalise their lives into linear stages – school, work, parenthood – with retirement at the end of the line. Retirees these days are demanding greater flexibility; preferring to see life as a never-ending cycle, in which they can choose to dip in and out of periods of work, education and leisure. Others have the funds behind them to pursue a hobby or interest full-time. And an increasing number of people have realised that they can do either of these things in a climate far removed from the dreary British winter.

Almost a million Britons already draw their state pensions abroad, and this figure does not include the many more who have retired early. According to a report from Alliance and Leicester, one in five older people (an extra four million) will be living outside the UK by the year 2020, lured by the warmer climate, a slower pace of life, health advantages and a lower cost of living.

It would appear that the prevailing gloom that people once felt about the ageing process is slowly being replaced by a sunny optimism. People no longer dread reaching retirement age, but eagerly anticipate a new life stage, in which, released from the shackles of full-time work, they can seek out new cultural experiences.

ITALIAN ATTITUDES TO RETIREMENT

As with other developed nations Italy is coming to terms with the facts of an ageing workforce and low birth rates. This change of attitude is more traumatic for Italy than other countries as for years Italy has had a very strong tradition of early retirement with a full pension from the age of 55 (for state workers) followed by an average of 35 years of *la dolce vita* after that. By the end of this decade a quarter of Italy's population will be aged over 60; by 2040 experts say the figure will be nearer 40%. Over the period 1980 to 1997 the number of people over 55 increased by 20% while the number of employees aged over 55 decreased by the same percentage. Italy currently has more pensioners than workers. Clearly, the current generation of workers will no longer be able to retire so early, as the Italian government would be bankrupted. The pension reforms of 1995 mean that by 2008 the minimum age for retirement, which is being gradually phased in, will be 57 with 40 years of contributions. Many Italians study until their late twenties, and this would raise their retirement age even higher to 65 in order to meet the contributions criteria.

As mentioned, this is an extreme change for Italy, because a long retirement is so ingrained in the culture, and the adjustments will take some time to work through the national mindset as well as the pension system. One of the ideas being promoted is 'active ageing' which is being trialed in Lecco province, where elderly workers are being reintroduced into the workforce. Other likely reforms include reducing working hours at the end of a career and encouraging people to stay in work longer. This shows that Italy is prepared to tackle the pensions timebomb, but the workers will need some convincing as their protests show; they brought down the government in 1994 when Berlusconi made the first attempts to overhaul the system.

REASONS FOR RETIRING TO ITALY

According to a recent article in *Woman's Own* there are more retired British people living in Italy than there are in France (but not more British property owners or workers) proving that the Italian lifestyle has a special appeal. Research done into the ease with which British émigrés settle into their adopted countries, shows that amongst the popular countries for retirement, Italy is the one where foreigners are most likely to integrate into the local community. This is probably because there are fewer foreigners living in Italy overall, than there are in France and Spain, where generally, foreigners tend to settle in enclaves and socialise mainly with other expats.

Britons Freddi and Vince Ferrigno were absolutely amazed by the welcome they got from their Italian neighbours when in 2003 they moved into a neglected seaside villa on the edge of Brindisi:

We have lovely neighbours including an English lady who arrived here when she was 18, married an Italian and has been here for over 30 years. For the first few months after we moved here we didn't need to buy any fresh fruit or vegetables at all. Our neighbours arrived with quantities of garden produce on a daily basis. One of them actually brought us a complete breakfast; I think they thought we must be lacking cooking facilities.

Those who might be concerned that they are moving to a country where living standards and infrastructures leave a lot to be desired and where the government is inherently unstable will find only a few of their worst fears justified. Italy is a highly developed country where even the farmers have the latest model Alfa Romeo or Audi tucked away in a barn, and where workers know the exact market value of their skills in the work place. The Italian postal system, especially for internal services, was generally regarded as very inefficient, but in recent years has been completely modernised as has the telephone system, and the Italians have embraced the mobile phone like no other nation. The national road system, which owes its origins to the Romans, Mussolini and in modern times, the charging of staggeringly high tolls, is one of the best in Europe and is constantly being upgraded.

PROS & CONS

Pros

- Easy access thanks to cheap flights from regional UK airports to over 30 Italian cities; this means you can afford to visit the UK, encourage visits to your Italian home, or get back to the UK in a hurry if there is an emergency.
- Italy has a generally reliable and extensive train network and trains are extremely cheap compared with the UK.
- The Italian lifestyle is more laid back and geared towards the art of living than the British one (The Slow Food movement began in Italy)

- Land and property are much cheaper than in the UK (though more expensive than in France and Spain) and you may be able to retire to Italy early if you are lucky enough to have a valuable UK property that you can sell to fund your retirement .
- Italy has the greatest concentration of cultural heritage of any European country and this is its biggest draw along with the Italians themselves.
- There is very little historical antagonism between the British and the Italians.
- It is relatively easy to get good advice (in English), about Italian conveyancing from the British and Italian legal firms and companies used to dealing with Brits buying in Italy.
- Superb local food and wines are available at a fraction of the cost you would pay in the UK and the weekly markets are a cornucopia of fresh local produce.
- Italian bureaucracy *vis-à-vis* foreigners from the EU living in Italy has been simplified in recent years (but daily bureaucratic dealings are notoriously frustrating and time consuming).

Cons

- Retiring to Italy means creating a new social life and meaningful human interactions, which can be difficult if you don't speak Italian (though you can always learn).
- Italian doctors are generally excellent and they are not sparing of the latest medical technology, but state hospitals may come as a shock especially in terms of provision of basic personal care. Northern hospitals are considered better than most southern ones though there are exceptions. Private medical insurance may be essential depending on where you are located.
- Eating out and fresh food may be cheaper but other daily consumer costs in Italy have risen by 20% in the last ten years.
- Some of the cheaper regions in which to buy property are cheap for a reason: they may be remote and slightly backward and difficult or prohibitively expensive to connect to utilities.
- While Italians have a more relaxed lifestyle Italian bureaucracy is the bugbear of Italians and foreigners alike.
- Italy is given to regular government crises and resignations as well as public worker strikes that cause great inconvenience.

INTRODUCING ITALY

Introducing Italy might seem unnecessary, since most people have an idea of Italy and Italians. However, there is more general awareness of key events in French history than in Italian ones. For instance, until 1861 Italy did not exist as a united country. Before that, the lands of what we know as Italy, were several different kingdoms. Likewise, the Papacy has not always been based in the Vatican in Rome, but was located in Avignon, France during the 14th century. The wider history of Italy is fascinating and extremely complicated not only because of the many kingdoms of which Italy was made up, but especially because of the legacy of Greeks, Etruscans and Romans who all colonized the area, and in the case of the Romans dominated the known world of the time.

Ancient Italian history and the Renaissance are not only pertinent to that country, but also the key to understanding the civilization of the Western World. After the feudal times of the Middle Ages, blinkered by religious aspirations and preparation for the afterlife, the astonishing burgeoning of creativity that characterised Italy during the Renaissance hearkened back to Classical literature, art and philosophy and developed the scientific understanding of the world, heralding a return to humanistic values. It would take more than several retirements' worth of reading to exhaust all the subjects of Italy's past. There are hordes of Italian historical and cultural titles and Amazon.co.uk or local libraries are good places to start. Below is a chronology of some pivotal events in Italian history, which may help to set the scene and put into context the country you have adopted for retirement.

Key Periods and Dates of Italian History

8th Century BC By this period the Etruscans from Asia Minor have established a cultured and prosperous empire in central Italy.

4th Century BC The Celtic tribes invade Italy and oust the Etruscans from the Po Valley in the north. In the southern central region of Campania, Etruscan civilization is being squeezed out by the more aggressive Samnites, who have assumed many of the cultural traits of their Greek colonial neighbours.

5th Century BC The Greeks establish colonies in Magna

Graecia (southern Italy and Sicily). Beginning of the rise of Rome and the Latin tribes.

5th Century BC to 5th Century AD Rise, expansion and fall of the Roman Empire and the spread of Christianity. Any free man within the empire was entitled to Roman citizenship.

5th Century AD Italy (and the rest of the Roman Empire) begins to be invaded by waves of barbarian tribes of which the German Visigoths, the Huns and the Ostrogoths are prominent.

402 Ravenna becomes capital of the Western Roman Empire.

476 Romulus Augustus, the last Roman Emperor of the Western Empire is deposed. This is usually regarded as the end of the Roman Empire, but the Eastern Roman Empire, based in Byzantium (Constantinople), continued until 1453.

C.482-565 Reign of the Eastern Emperor Justinian I reunites East and West and restores Roman power in Italy and Spain. Known as The Legislator, he collects and codifies the Empire's laws into a Codex, the original Body of Civil Law for Europe.

569 Lombards from northern Italy under Alboin, displace the rule of Byzantium and form a new kingdom.

751 Lombards take Ravenna. Their advance on Rome was halted by Pepin of the Franks who expelled the Lombards.

754 Pepin gives Ravenna to the Pope. Rise of the Papal States.

800 Charlemagne, son of Pepin is crowned Emperor of the West at Rome. This event shaped much of later history in Italy as successive Holy Roman Emperors claimed Italy while the rise of the temporal power of the Papacy increased.

882-962 Italy was ruled by several weak kings notable mainly for their feuding. The Magyars (from Hungary) raided northern Italy.

917 Arabs seize Sicily and plunder the Italian mainland.

961 After an appeal by the Pope for protection, German King Otto 1 invaded Italy and was crowned Holy Roman Emperor in 962 by the Pope. Italy and Germany were united and this marked the beginning of the Holy Roman Empire.

10th & 11th Centuries – Northern and Central Italy: The beginning of this century sees the rise of the city states, as the commercial leaders of the cities banded together into city-leagues against the power of the nobles. At the same time Italian merchants were becoming the middlemen in the hugely lucrative trade between the Muslim world and the rest of Europe. The prosperous city leagues warred against each other and this disunity prevented any kind of consolidation of a larger Italian state. Certain cities gave rise to family dynasties such as the Visconti and Sforza of Milan. Meanwhile the Holy Roman Emperors continued titular claim to all of northern Italy.

11th Century – Southern Italy: The southern regions of Apulia and Calabria were occupied by the Normans under Robert Guiscard. He and his successors also took Sicily from the Arabs and created the Norman kingdom of Sicily. The Normans imposed feudalism in their kingdom, in marked contrast to central and northern Italy where petty lords defied imperial rule and the cities defied the petty lords. The marked difference in the social and economic conditions between North and South which lingers into the 21st century have their origins in this time.

1348 Black Death ravages Italy.

1378-1417 The Papacy moves to Avignon in France (the so called Babylonian captivity of the Popes at Avignon) as local tyrants become too powerful in the Papal States of Italy. The church loses a lot of its moral authority during this period and is challenged by the new 'heresies' of Europe. Meanwhile the great flowering of Renaissance art and culture is well underway, changing the civilization of Western Europe.

1494 Beginning of the Italian Wars. Charles VIII of France invades Italy.

15th Century By the end of this century the map of Italy showed the following divisions: the Kingdom of Sicily and Naples in the south, The Papal States of central Italy, the republics of Siena, Florence and Lucca and the city states of Bologna, Forlì, Rimini and Faenza; in the north the duchies of Ferrara, Modena, Mantua, Milan and Savoy and the two great, cosmopolitan merchant republics of Genoa and Venice. The Renaissance reaches its peak.

1559 Italian wars end with most of Italy under Spanish rule or influence. Treaty of Cateau-Cambrèsis is signed by Spain and France. Spain gets kingdoms of Sicily and Naples and Duchy of Milan.

1748 After three centuries of political weakness and of being the target of European power struggles, accompanied by economic decline as the commercial activity of Europe moved elsewhere, Naples, Sicily and the duchies of Parma and Piacenza were ruled by Spanish Bourbons; Milan, Mantua, Tuscany and Modena were under the rule of Austria. Independent pockets of Italy remained: the Papal States, the declining republics of Genoa, Lucca and Venice, and the Kingdom of Savoy and Sardinia created in 1720 under the house of Savoy.

18ᵗʰ Century Throughout the 18ᵗʰ Century Italy continued to exert strong influence on the arts throughout Europe, particularly architecture and music, whilst being politically a shambles. No longer able to dominate commerce or wield power, Italians at first saw The French Revolution and the rise of Napoleon as an inspiration for their own nationalist aspirations.

1795-1812 Savoy, Piedmont, Liguria, Tuscany, Parma and the Papal States were annexed by France under Napoleon.

1796-97 Napoleon's Italian campaign was welcomed by the Italians because he defeated the armies of Sardinia and Austria. Napoleon redrew the map of Italy more than once, creating the Cisalpine Republic from the regions of Lombardy and Emilia-Romagna.

1802 Cisalpine Republic is renamed 'Italian Republic' and renamed again the 'Kingdom of Italy', and Venezia is added to it. Napoleon is crowned King.

1806 Joseph Bonaparte made King of Naples. Succeeded by Murat, Napoleon's brother-in-law in 1808. Sardinia remains under the Savoys and Sicily is ruled by Spanish Bourbons.

19ᵗʰCentury Napoleon's failure to unite Italy under self-government causes wide discontent amongst the growing band of Italian nationalists. They form secret revolutionary movements such as the Carbonari to plan the unification of Italy, which came to fruition later in the century.

1814-15 Congress of Vienna generally relapsed Italy back to pre-Napoleonic divisions under the old ruling families, but Venezia united with Lombardy became the Lombardo-Venetian Kingdom under Austrian rule and Liguria became part of the Kingdom of Sardinia.

1816 Naples and Sicily become The Kingdom of the Two Sicilies.

1848 The Austrians find it impossible to crush aspirations of the unification movement, the so-called Risorgimento. Revolutionary unrest occurs in Naples, Venice, Tuscany, Rome and the Kingdom of Sardinia.

1861 Unification achieved under the House of Savoy. Heroes of the hour include Cavour, Garibaldi and the new nation's king, Victor Emmanuel II who was crowned in 1861. The new Italy does not include Venezia, Rome and a portion of the Papal States .

1866 Austro-Prussian War. Italy supports Prussia and gets Venezia added to the new nation.

1870 Italy annexes Rome, which was a Protectorate of Napoleon III. Austria still retains some Italian-speaking areas: parts of the south Tyrol plus the city of Trieste.

1861-78 Reign of Victor Emmanuel II.

1878-1900 Reign of Humbert I. Moderate social and political reform instituted. Beginnings of northern Italy's industrial expansion.

1882 Italy joins alliance with Germany and Austria (the Triple Alliance and the Triple Entente).

1889-1890 Italy's belated colonial expansion. Acquires part of Somaliland and part of Eritrea.

1896 Ethiopians rout Italians at Adwa preventing further colonial expansion.

1900-1946: Reign of Victor Emmanuel III, the last king of Italy. Continuing expansion of industry in the north causes social and economic problems and massive emigration from the impoverished undeveloped south, to the northern industrial areas. And then, with economic depression, emigration to the Americas.

1911-12 Italo-Turkish War. Italy acquires Libya and the Dodecanese islands of Greece.

1915 Italy enters the First World War on the Allied side.

1918 Battle of Vittorio Veneto won by Italians against Austria-Hungary which surrenders.

1919 At the Paris Peace Conference, Italy gets southern Tyrol, Trieste, Istria, part of Carniola (in Slovenia) and several of the islands off the Dalmatian Coast and is allowed to keep the Dodecanese Islands in the Aegean. However not as much is given as was promised by the Allies.

1922-43 Rise of Fascism in Europe, which is partly due to the unemployment and the resulting breakdown of social order, which causes increasing unrest and results in the rise of the Italian Fascist leader Benito

Mussolini, 1922 Mussolini successfully marches on Rome and assumes directorial powers with the blessing of the king. Carries out programme of reforms, which include draining the Pontine Marshes and construction of a motorway system.

1935-36 Italy invades and conquers Ethiopia and forms a pact (Axis pact) with Germany.

1937 Italy withdraws from League of Nations and draws closer to Nazi Germany and Japan.

1939 Italy seizes Albania.

1940 Italy declares war on France and Britain after a year of remaining neutral in World War II.

1945 Mussolini is captured and summarily executed by partisans. Germany surrenders. The first Christian Democrat premier is appointed.

1947 Italy's postwar borders established. The small alpine regions of Brigue and Tende became French, the Dodecanese Islands were returned to Greece, while Trieste, Istria, part of Venezia Giulia and some Dalmatian islands were returned to Yugoslavia (as was). Italy also lost its colonies as a result of the war.

1996 In the elections of this year, a centre-left government under Romano Prodi was elected. Far-reaching austerity measures were taken to bring Italy up to financial scratch for EU monetary union.

1997 Prodi's government collapses.

2001 Parliamentary elections produced victory for Berlusconi's conservative coalition and he becomes premier for a second time (the first time was in 1994).

2003 Berlusconi's government passes a law making the premier and other top political figures immune from prosecution while they are holding office. This was widely seen to be aimed at ending Berlusconi's own trial for corruption.

2004 The constitutional court overturned the new indemnity for serving politicians and Berlusconi's trial proceeds, only to end in acquittal. He was unable to put a good spin on this unbelievable result despite owning nearly half the media.

2005 Berlusconi's self preservation manoeuvres provoked outrage and crippling losses in local elections, forcing him to resign and reform his government to survive another day.

2006 In the April general election Romano Prodi's centre-left coalition wins by a hair's breadth. At the time of press Berlusconi was disputing the result.

ECONOMY

Italy's post-war economic aims are to a large extent responsible for today's massive division between north and south. The powers of the time decided to open up Italy's economy and go for an international export market rather than concentrate on restructuring production for self-sufficiency at home. This was about the extent to which the Italians went to plan a post-war economy and up until quite recent times policy in this area can best be summed up as *laissez-faire*. In other words, production was allowed to rally to the demands of the open market with virtually no controls or restraints. Such an economic 'policy' was to a great extent dictated by circumstances, namely that Italy possesses few of the resources (e.g. iron, coal & oil) essential for most industrial processes. Italy's main markets have traditionally been Western Europe and North America. Rather than pour money into quickly modernising agricultural production methods, which would have resulted in mass unemployment in the south, most resources were directed into expanding the industries of the north. As agriculture slowly modernised and therefore required a smaller labour force, the unemployed farm-workers of the south were used as a cheap source of labour for the expanding factories of the north – which helped offset the cost of importing the resources necessary for the manufacturing processes.

The years between 1958 and 1962 were years of thriving economic growth for Italy. However, with their economy so closely linked with the USA, the lira, which was pegged at 625 per dollar until 1971, collapsed along with the whole system of fixed exchange rates when America devalued the dollar. Italy's economy stayed weak up to the beginning of the 1980s and Italy was well known as the poorest of Western European countries. In the 1980s the economy took off again at breakneck speed. However, there was a downside to the rapid economic growth. As a result of having had no clear discernible economic policy for years, the national debt had now grown to the extent that it exceeded Gross Domestic Product and stood at 123% of GDP. By raising VAT (sales tax) rates in 1997 and exercising great budget discipline, which verged on austerity measures, the budget deficit, which was running at 6%, was reduced to 2.8% and Italy managed to meet the strict requirements of the European Union for entry into European Monetary Union.

Italy's economy grew faster than most others in Europe in 2000 and early 2001, but its growth had stopped by the middle of 2001. The growth in the economy has raised the per capita GDP to around US$21,000, but this figure is misleading as to the general wealth of the country because of the disparity between the north and south of the country. This slowdown, coupled with increased public spending (big pay rises for public servants) and a cut in income taxes in 2005, meant a rise in the budget deficit for 2005 to 3.8%, which is above the EU guidelines for Eurozone members. Berlusconi's government was noted for providing a lot of fluff but few hard details on how they would fulfil their election promises and it remains to be seen how the Italian economy will fare under the new regime of Romano Prodi. GDP growth is predicted to rise to just under 2% in 2006.

Stringent budgets are the solution to one of Italy's economic problems and the Berlusconi government was forced into a modicum of crisis management in this direction, but there is another great problem. In economic terms, Italy claims to have done better at reducing its budget deficit than either France or Germany – though this seems to be an optimistic claim. If it were true about the budget deficit, then it means that Italy is in a better state to succeed in the single currency than either France or Germany, which does not bode well for the euro. However, such a claim is belied by the size of the national debt, 9% unemployment and the enormous drain on government resources caused by the demands of the welfare system. Inflation is running at 2.2% – higher than the EU average.

One factor that is not usually taken into account when assessing the state of the Italian economy is the amount of revenue lost through tax evasion. This is despite the fact that taxation accounts for approximately 43.4% of GDP – second only to France at 44.2% and compared to the US at 25.4%. The Italian tax authorities also have the power to levy taxes on perceived wealth – such as the Ferrari parked in the garage of a poor tradesman.

Italy in the Future

Despite the difficulties with its economy already mentioned above and a decline in Italians' optimism about their future, the country continues to attract a steady amount of foreign investment and to encourage business

and commerce in the regions through its Sviluppo Italia programme.
The amounts of foreign investment are however miniscule compared
to the UK which attracts around 30% of all inward EU investment.
Italian economists have traditionally been pessimistic; in their view the
economy was like the Titanic – heading full steam toward disaster. This
is probably why the Italians were so enthusiastic about European monetary union and the stabilising effect of the European Union generally.
There is no doubt that the new government faces economic problems
including a large amount of debt and the fact that one mainstay of the
economy, the Italian fashion industry, has been greatly undermined by
the upsurge of designers in countries which have traditionally bought
Italian clothes (i.e. Germany). The undercutting of the fashion market
by designers who have clothes made up in the Far East will continue to
be problematic for the Italian economy and the opening up of Chinese
textile products has been disastrous to the Italian textile industry. But
some of the old problems have at last been tackled: lack of transpar-
ency and the massive bureaucracy have both been improved; corruption
possibly less so. However, Italy still imports 80% of its oil while having
voted in a national referendum to phase out the entire Italian nuclear
power programme. Also, the separation between the highly developed
north and the poor south will continue to be exacerbated by the ongoing economic success of the north at the expense of the south, unless
action to encourage investors (both foreign and domestic) to look at
areas they have previously discounted continues to show progress.

POPULATION

Italy's population numbers approximately 58.1 million, slightly smaller
than that of the UK, and approximately a quarter of the US. However,
the Italians have more elbow-room than Britons with 190 persons per
square kilometre compared with 232 in the UK. Until the 1980s Italy
had been a country of emigration rather than immigration. The waves of
emigration were: from the 1890s to 1930s to Argentina and the United
States; from the 1950s to 1970s to Australia, Canada, Germany and
Switzerland. From the end of communism around 1989 there has been
huge immigration into Italy from old Eastern Bloc countries. Surpris-
ingly for a country traditionally associated with large families, Italy has

one of the lowest birth rates in Europe with many couples choosing not to have children and those that do having a single child. This low birth rate and restrictions on immigration from outside the EU has led to fears that the population will shrink so much that there will be a severe labour shortage in the future that will ruin the economy.

THE LARGEST ITALIAN CITIES

City	Population
Rome (Roma, Capital)	2,628,000
Milan (Milano)	1,724,557,
Naples (Napoli))	1,214,775.
Turin (Torino)	1,181,698,
Palermo	996,000,
Genoa (Genova)	787,011,
Bologna	493,282,
Florence (Firenze)	441,654,
Venice (Venezia)	305,000,
Verona	255,000

Immigration from Outside the EU. Already, the population includes a large number of immigrants; some are from ex-colonies, including Somalia, Libya and Eritrea. Most of the immigrants have arrived within the last twenty years as a result of Italy's liberal entry regulations. These have, however, been tightened up under the Schengen Agreement because of fears from other EU countries that Italy would become a stepping stone for massive numbers of immigrants. There are also significant numbers of Eastern Europeans, Filipinos and Brazilians in the country. There is no official census of the number of immigrants, though around half a million have arrived through official channels. The majority of immigrants remain illegal (aided by Italy's 8000 km long and difficult to patrol coastline) and the vicinity of Italy to the coasts of Albania and Tunisia. The total number is believed to exceed two million. Naples now has a large African population while Rome has become home to people with a wide variety of ethnological backgrounds amongst its population of nearly three million. The most recent influx of immigrants and refugees to Italy has come from the stricken country of Albania. An estimated 316,600 Albanians have entered Italy both legally and illegally, amongst them a ruthless criminal element, who are rumoured to be more deadly than the Mafia whom they are replacing in some areas, particularly Milan.

GEOGRAPHICAL INFORMATION

Mainland and Offshore Italy

Italy occupies an area of 116,000 square miles (301,278 sq km). As well as the long peninsula which, as most schoolchildren learn, is shaped like a boot, Italy's offshore elements include the island of Sicily situated off the toe of the boot across the Strait of Messina, the islands of Pantelleria, Linosa and Lampedusa which lie between Sicily and Tunisia, the island of Elba located off Tuscany, and the rocky, barren island of Sardinia which lies west of Rome and south of Corsica. The Tyrrhenian Sea bounds the south west of the peninsula, with the Ionian Sea under the sole of the boot. The Adriatic Sea lies on the eastern side between Italy and former-Yugoslavia. Italy shares borders with France, Switzerland, Austria and Slovenia.

Main physical features include the Alps, which form much of the northern border with Slovenia, Austria, Switzerland and France. Also in the north are Italy's main lakes: Garda, Maggiore and Como. An offshoot of the Alps curves round the Gulf of Genoa and runs spine-like down the peninsula to form the Appenines. The longest river, the Po, lies in the north and flows from west to east across the plain of Lombardy and into the Adriatic. On Sicily, the still active volcano, Mount Etna rises to 10,741 feet (3,274 m).

Earthquakes and Volcanoes The European fault line runs right through Italy from north to south. The main risk areas for quakes are central and southern Italy where about 70% of the region is susceptible. Tremors are quite common in Umbria and the Appenines. Seismologists claim that the number, strength and frequency of quakes hitting central Italy is increasing. Following an earthquake there is usually a drop in tourism and house buying by foreigners. Over 2000 minor tremors a year occur in Italy, the majority of them below Magnitude 4 (on a scale of 10). Italy's last epic earthquake flattened

Messina in 1908, killing 84,000 people and causing the shoreline to sink by half a metre overnight. Other serious ones were Friuli (1976), Irpinia (1980), and Umbria (1997) – the most memorable recent quake caused severe damage to the Church of Asissi in front of the television cameras. Despite the well publicised risk in certain areas such as Umbria, and the fact that 90% of Italy is seismic, most retirees are unlikely to consider earthquakes when buying a property. This could be to their cost as Carole Means, whose home in Umbria was destroyed in the 1997 earthquake, explains:

> *We lost everything except some furniture, which we salvaged from the ruin. We rented somewhere nearby to live. The alternative was to stay in the emergency portakabins provided by the region; some people were still living in these five years later. Because we took care of ourselves we received no compensation from the state. We didn't think it was worth waiting for them; we wanted to get on with our lives, so we went back to work and bought another house in Apulia.*

As if this were not geological excitement enough, Italy has three well-known active volcanoes. The most famous of these is Vesuvius near Naples, which buried 2,000 inhabitants in their hedonistic city of Pompeii in AD79. These days the volcano's rumblings are under continuous monitoring so there should be plenty of warning before it pops again. The other volcanoes are off the mainland: Etna on Sicily (which was very active in 2001) and Stromboli on a small island off the western coast of southern Italy. Up-to-date information on seismicity in Italy can be found at the US Geological Survey site (www.neic.usgs. gov/neis/world/italy/).

Climatic Zones

The climate of Italy shows the kind of regional variation one would expect from a country with its head in the Alps and its toe in the Mediterranean. At the foot of the Alps in the north is the flat and fertile Plain of Po, which is also one of the main industrial areas. Cold and wet in winter, those who find themselves living and working in the north can escape to different climatic regions to rejuvenate themselves.

REGIONAL DIVISIONS

For administrative purposes Italy is divided into twenty regions, five of which have special autonomy, 106 provinces and more than 8000 comunes. The regions (listed northwest to south) and their respective provinces are as follows:

AOSTA VALLEY (Val d'Aosta) Aosta.
PIEDMONT (PIEMONTE) – Alessandria, Asti, Biella, Cuneo, Novara, Torino, Verbano-Cusio-Ossola.
LOMBARDY (LOMBARDIA) – Bergamo, Brescia, Como, Cremona, Lecco, Lodi, Mantova, Milano, Pavia, Sondrio, Varese.
TRENTINO-ALTO-ADIGE – Bolzano, Trento.
VENETO – Belluno, Padova (Padua), Rovigo, Treviso, Venezia (Venice), Vicenza, Verona.
FRIULI-VENEZIA GIULIA – Gorizia, Pordenone, Trieste, Udine.
LIGURIA – Genova, (Genoa), Imperia, La Spezia, Savona.
EMILIA ROMAGNA – Bologna, Ferrara, Forli-Cesena, Modena, Parma, Piacenza, Ravenna, Reggio Emilia, Rimini.
TUSCANY (TOSCANA) – Arezzo, Firenze (Florence), Grosseto, Livorno, Lucca, Massa-Carrara, Pisa, Pistoia, Prato, Siena.
UMBRIA – Perugia, Terni.
MARCHE – Ancona, Ascoli-Piceno, Macerata, Pesaro-Urbino.
LAZIO – Frosinone, Latina, Rieti, Roma, Viterbo.
ABRUZZO – L'Aquila, Chieti, Pescara, Teramo.
MOLISE – Campobasso, Isernia.
CAMPANIA – Avellino, Benevento, Caserta, Napoli (Naples), Salerno.
APULIA (PUGLIA) – Bari, Brindisi, Foggia, Lecce, Taranto.
BASILICATA – Matera, Potenza.
CALABRIA – Catanzaro, Cosenza, Crotone, Reggio Calabria, Vibo Valentia.
SICILY (SICILIA) – Agrigento, Caltanissetta, Catania, Enna, Messina, Palermo, Ragusa, Siracusa, Trapani.
SARDINIA (SARDEGNA) – Cagliari, Nuoro, Oristano, Sassari (and four new provinces Sulcis-Iglesiente (main town Iglesias), Medio Campidano (main town Sanluri, Ogliastra (main town Lanusei) and Gallura (Ollbia).

There are the cold, dry Alps further northwards for winter sports. The Italian Riviera (Liguria), which is pleasantly mild in winter. Or there is the south, including Sicily, where the winters are even milder and typically Mediterranean. In summer and winter, the middle regions of Tuscany and Umbria, which are home to many expatriates, have the best of both worlds: neither too cold in winter nor too parched in summer. However, the higher areas of even these favoured regions can be cold and snowbound in winter. The far south and Sicily are generally considered too hot for comfort in summer.

AVERAGE TEMPERATURES				
City & Province	**Jan** °F/°C	**Apr** °F/°C	**July** °F/°C	**Nov** °F/°C
Ancona (Marche)	42/6	56/14	77/25	55/13
Bari(Puglia)	46/8	57/14	77/25	59/15
Bologna (Emilia Romagna)	37/3	56/15	78/26	50/10
Florence (Tuscany)	42/6	55/13	77/25	52/11
Genova (Liguria)	46/8	56/14	77/25	55f/13
Milan (Lombardy)	36/2	55/13	77/25	48/9
Naples (Campania)	48/9	56/14	77/25	59/15
Palermo(Sicily)	50/10	61/16	77/25	50/16
Rome (Latium)	45/7	57/14	78/26	55/13
Trieste (Friuli-Venezia)	41/5	55/13	75/25	52/11
Venice (Venetia)	39/4	55/13	75/24	52/10

CULTURE SHOCK

(Some comments listed by an Englishwoman living in Italy)

- No one dreams of respecting a zebra crossing. If, as a motorist, you stop at one the pedestrian looks at you with amazement and refuses to cross.
- In the restaurants vegetables come on separate plates. The romantic candle-lit dinner is very rare. Most restaurants have bright fluorescent ceiling lights and a TV blaring.
- In the country, men in camouflage carrying shotguns, i.e. hunters, seem to trespass everywhere. The hail of shot on roofs makes the foreigners indignant, (but this used to be much worse).
- The degrading of women on TV, such as women dancing on a

table-top with newscasters behind them wearing suits. Every pro-gramme seems to present women in the same way, as sex objects. Yet there are no men in the same situations, and why are all male presenters fat and bald? Italian TV is just crap!

o Black prostitutes on the roadside, black madams in the middle of the country.

o You seldom see drunks or drunken brawls outside bars. Pubs dedicated exclusively to the consumption of alcohol do not exist. Bars are open to all, with all ages welcome.

o Men sitting in bars not drinking but playing cards.

o The beggars in Rome, bands of them especially around the Vatican, hassling people.

o The way people walk through the town in the evening all dressed up (the *passeggiata*).

o The *festas* (celebrations), which bridge the generations, are delight-ful, e.g. mothers teaching their young boys how to dance a mazurka. A big community spirit, perhaps because of their old way of life, when everyone had to club together to harvest the grapes and olives.

o The long lunch hour; you have to get used to being able to do nothing between 12.30 and 4pm or later. But in compensation all the shops are open until eight o'clock in the evening.

o The high status of the working man. You see workmen and truck drivers eating at tables with freshly laundered white tablecloths. A shock to see their healthy choice of food such as vegetable soups, fresh salads, and grilled fish etc.

o Hospitals: In the hospitals there may be nowhere to have a shower. They come and give you a bowl of warm water. The bathroom facilities in a modern hospital may not be adequate. They may not put screens round you when the doctor examines you. They expect relations to bring food; they only give you gruel. But they are not sparing of the latest medical technology and treatment and medical attention. What was most shocking of all was the sight of a chain-smoking radiographer.

o The *carabinieri* are not so approachable as our police. If you talk to them they bark back and ask what's wrong? It is not the custom to ask the carabinieri anything.

○ Italians' lives are very ordered and organised, they always have their wood stacked up, their apartments are so neat. In England they are knocking down high-rise apartment blocks because people couldn't live in them. Here they are flat dwellers. They take a pride in their homes. Their policy of community housing is to put relations near to each other.

○ Young children and babies are welcomed and made a fuss of everywhere, especially in restaurants.

○ Old people are looked after by their children and respected by the young.

○ The ambulance service – the *Misericordia* is run by volunteers, a free service which dates back to the Middle Ages, available day and night.

Basics

CHAPTER SUMMARY

○ The cost of living in Italy varies depending on where you live. The biggest differences are between north and south. The south being much cheaper for property, rents, bus travel and eating out among other things. On average though, Italy is still slightly cheaper than the UK, apart from Milan, which compares directly with London in terms of prices.

○ Knowledge of how to use the internet and other computer services will make your life in Italy, and staying in touch with friends and relatives much simpler; knowledge of the Italian language is also very important.

○ It is advisable to have a trial period living in Italy for a few months to make sure that you really want to make the move and to get to know the locality where you will be moving.

○ Alternatives to moving to Italy include extended renting and homeswaps.

○ Any non-Italian planning to stay in Italy for more than 90 days must apply for a *permesso di soggiorno* (stay permit). EU citizens have an automatic right to stay but must still have a permit .

○ Before you depart the UK permanently, you should arrange to have your UK pension paid into your bank account in Italy.

○ If you are taking dogs and cats to Italy they must be micro-chipped and vaccinated against rabies.

○ The cardinal rule before arranging removals is to have a massive house turnout and reduce the items for removal to Italy to a minimum.

THINGS TO CONSIDER

Is It Affordable?

The basic point here is that if you can afford retirement (i.e. a non-income generating activity) in the UK, then you will be able to afford it in Italy. However it may be a mistake to assume that it will be cheaper to live in Italy as it depends on your lifestyle and how much you spend on goods and services to create and maintain it, how regularly you want to make trips back to the UK, whether your pension and any other income amounts to a secure, regular long-term income and what happens if your funds are linked with the fate of the euro, which is likely to fluctuate in value. Also, a major factor influencing living costs in Italy is location. Not only is there a big difference between north and south, with the south being much less expensive, but there are also wide variations within the same area. Living in a Tuscan city is much more expensive than living in its rural hinterland. The further south you are the cheaper it gets.

The economic pundits and official purveyors of statistics tell us that the cost of living is slightly lower in Italy than in Britain. Eating out, fresh produce in markets and land and property are all cheaper, but essential tradesmen's services such as plumbing, repairs and renovations, tend to be more expensive. Public transport is excellent value, but many retirees are living in rural areas where at least one car is a necessity to reach an embarkation point for public transport.

Prices have gone up faster in Italy (by 20% since 1996) than anywhere in the EU other than Ireland, Portugal and Greece. There were big increases in 2004 in the duties on alcohol and tobacco, and price rises on food and drink and recreation (particularly holidays and transportation) were also substantial.

The Bare Necessities of Life: Comparison of UK and Italy

○ **Alcohol.** Of course it depends what you are drinking but local wines are usually very good value from €3-€10 (£2-£7) per bottle so there is not a huge difference in price between Italy and the UK supermarkets; the difference is that in Italy cheap doesn't mean bad. Alcohol and tobacco are items showing the highest rise (because of tax) in the Italian Consumer Price Index in the last five years, but tobacco is still much cheaper than in the UK.

o **Books and Newspapers.** More expensive than the UK. In the case of books because they carry VAT at 4%.

o **Cars.** Car expenses are nearly as high as the UK and a car is not a luxury item but a necessity if you are not city based. Road fund tax and insurance costs are similar to the UK and petrol is slightly cheaper (per litre: €1.24 unleaded; €1.13 diesel). However, buying a second-hand car in Italy is much more expensive than in the UK, as are the re-registration costs for the logbook and owner details which can cost over €400.

o **Clothing and Footwear.** Mostly more expensive; think chic and good quality. Factory outlets and other cut-price outlets exist but are more geared to the young and very young. Probably cheaper to stock up in the UK on trips back there.

o **Food and Drink.** While fresh produce markets are still a cheaper way to shop than supermarkets, food and beverage prices rose 10% in 2000 and 20% in 2003, so the once cheaper food basket of Italy is catching up with the UK.

o **Furnishings.** Secondhand furniture can be excellent value as Italians prefer new. A leftover perhaps from the tradition of Italian New Year's Eve, which involved chucking out all the old furniture from the home into the street. Furniture sales are also good sources as they offer huge markdowns.

o **House Taxes.** Property tax (ICI) is the Italian equivalent of Council Tax in the UK but is far less financially punitive, usually amounting to a couple of hundred pounds a year. There is also a modest rubbish collection tax, the TARSU. Although property taxes are much lower, Italy is overall a country of high taxation (even after the Berlusconi tax reforms) and if your income is being taxed in Italy this may cancel out the difference in lower property taxes.

Leaving Family and Friends

In the excitement of realising that you can afford to retire in Italy as you have always dreamed of doing, it is easy to forget that moving to another country means leaving your circle of friends and family behind; close families can find the idea of this quite daunting. On the other hand you may be giving family and friends a whole new dimension to their lives in the form of a unique holiday home, which they can visit as often as commitments permit for as long as they like. Potentially more problematic, is leaving behind elderly or frail relatives especially elderly parents. The consequences of you moving to Italy in this instance need to be considered carefully as they may be too frail to visit you in Italy, or they may have to come and live with you there.

Main Considerations Before Moving Abroad

- You will need contingency plans to stay in touch with and assist close friends, children, grand-children elderly parents and relatives, and to deal with any emergencies that may arise in the UK when you are living in Italy and to have somewhere for any of the above to stay with you when they want or need to.
- Are you familiar with computer technology? If not, you should attend a computer course before leaving the UK in order to familiarise yourself with the internet, e-mail and computer linked gadgets that will help you maintain your links with the UK and enable you to run your life in Italy smoothly.
- Are you going to take your right-hand drive car to Italy or are you going to buy one there? It is generally considered safer to have a left-hand drive in Italy, especially for overtaking.
- Are you going to be dependent on Ryanair or other budget airline operating to a small airport in proximity to your Italian property? If so, it is important to bear in mind that routes can be axed or fares rise, so you will need to ensure that you are within easy access of alternatives or can bear the increased prices.
- Are you going to sever all your financial links with the UK and become wholly liable to Italian taxes? This is something that requires expert advice as it may not be financially beneficial. At the very least, most people find it useful to maintain a UK bank account for ordering supplies from UK outlets, and for use on their regular trips back to the UK.
- If you are a couple, have you considered what will happen if one of you dies? Will the other one want to stay on or return to the UK?

This ties in with whether or not you sever all links with the UK tax and national insurance system. If you have wholly left the British system and then want to return to it, you may find it financially punitive to do so, unless you have made plans for this contingency.

o Who will you leave your Italian property to? You will need to consult a law firm with expertise in both English and Italian inheritance laws as it may be necessary to have two wills (an Italian and an English one) to avoid any complications later on (see *Wills and Inheritance*) in the *Personal Finance* chapter.

ALTERNATIVES TO RETIRING TO ITALY

If you are not quite sure whether permanent retirement to Italy is for you, but you plan to spend a large part of your retirement in Italy without actually severing your ties to the UK, it is not essential to own your own Italian property. There are several possible alternatives including extended renting of holiday homes, timeshare and home exchanges. The advantages or disadvantages of each of these possibilities compared with each other and compared with buying and having your own retirement property will have to be weighed up in order to ensure that you make the right choice for your circumstances.

The obvious advantage of any of these alternatives is that it relieves you of the worry of having to buy and maintain your own property. It could also allow you to stay in an expensive region such as Tuscany or Liguria, where you might not be able to afford to buy, or if you did buy you would worry a lot about leaving the property empty for longish periods.

Main Points of Extended Renting

o Holiday rentals are charged by the week and longer rentals are regarded as any period longer than a month. Some rental companies only rent up to a maximum of three months, others will consider a year or longer though contracts are usually reviewed annually.

o Expensive if done through a rental company. Many Italian properties have been renovated by foreign owners with rental income in mind and have been finished and furnished to the high standard this demands, including having a swimming pool. The cheapest low season rent for an apartment in the Umbrian town of Orvieto is €350 per week and typically the cheapest is €400-€450 per week for Tuscan farmhouses etc. Discounts on longer rentals are not huge, usually 10% but in the low season it is worth trying to negotiate.

○ Renting from an Italian landlord is a possibility but you will probably need help to find a suitable place and with the contracts and negotiations (if you don't speak Italian) and there will be the usual Italian run around of paperwork. This is probably a cheaper way to rent, but more complicated and time consuming. The tenancy agreement for a furnished property rented for three or more months is a *Contratto di Locazione*.

○ Longer rentals are much more common in Spain than in Italy where spending retirement wintering there and returning to the UK in summer, is firmly established, but there has been a rising interest in Italy, mostly for rural properties of character.

○ The best deals are likely to be obtained by negotiating with the owner direct and to do this you will probably have to trawl the small adverts on expat websites and the Italian section of Slow Travel (www.slowtrav.com/italy) and in Italian property magazines. However, if a rental property is not being managed by an agency it may not be fitted up to the highest standards. You would have to be as thorough as possible in finding out exactly what you were getting. The owners will probably want to meet and interview you. The rental agreement will be an Italian one governed by Italian law the same as for renting from an Italian landlord. The cost of drawing up the contract is usually split between the tenant and the landlord.

Long-Term Rental Contacts

www.lifeinitaly.com: covers all of Italy.

www.slowtrav.com/italy: See Slow Travel's long-term rentals section.

www.umbria-rentals.com/long-term.html: Long-term rentals in Umbria

Italian Property/Lifestyle Magazines

Italia!*:* www.Italia-magazine.com. Monthly.

Italy: www.italymag.co.uk. Monthly.

The Italian Magazine: www.magazine-group.co.uk. Monthly.

The Mostly Lows of Timeshare

○ Timeshare has a bad reputation, particularly in Spain, but in Italy owing to strict laws governing its sale there is very little timeshare property available, although there are some ancient hilltop hamlets which have been restored and converted to timeshare apartments.

○ The principal behind timeshare is that you buy a share in a timeshare company, which gives you a lifetime's use of the property for a fixed number of weeks per annum. The catch is that you never own a brick of it; it is merely a rental right, which other people who have bought into the company also have; so it is in fact a multi-rented property. As there are other people using the property throughout the year, it will never feel yours.

○ Under the Italian system, you are buying shares in a timeshare company. You can sell these shares on if you wish (which may or may not be at a loss); or you can leave the timeshare to your heirs. You can rent out the property for the weeks that you have bought which could make you a profit over time.

○ If the timeshare company goes bust, you lose not only your right to the property, but you may also be liable for a part of the timeshare company's debts.

○ In addition to the usually very poor investment potential that a timeshare offers, there will be costs involved with the day-to-day running of the property which will be passed on to you as management fees; probably in the region of £200-£300 per year.

Main Points of Home Exchanges

○ Although one of the oldest home exchange organisations, Homelink, was established over 50 years ago, the internet has opened up the possibilities for home exchanges (also called home swaps) enormously with instant communication, virtual tours and thousands of homes worldwide offered for holiday and longer-term slots.

○ Most home exchange organisations charge an annual fee for posting your details and a photograph of your home and for use of their database. Fees vary, but start at £21 per annum.

○ Differences in style of housekeeping can make or break a home-swap, so it is best to swap with someone who shares a similar life-style or who is at a similar stage of life to you. It is also essential to get to know your exchange partner via email, telephone and if possible a meeting, before agreeing to the exchange. Also ask for references (business and personal).

○ If you decide to buy a home in Italy, you can then exchange yours with other homes in Italy and spend your retirement in Italy visiting other parts of it on a no cost basis.

○ Most (but not all) home exchanges come with a car, which is essential if you are planning to explore or even look for a property to buy.

HOME EXCHANGE ORGANISATIONS

Website	Members	Cost
www.homelink.it	13,500	£100 per year.
www.intervac.it	15,000	€99 per year
www.homexchange.com	7,000	$49.95 per year
www.scambiocasa.org	5,000	€50 for 1 year, €75 for 2 years
www.gti-home-exchange.com	1,600	£21 (€31.50) per year
www.4homes.com	1,000	$40($40) per year

A TRIAL PERIOD

There will always be people who decide on the spur of the moment after a two-week holiday to retire to Italy, but the majority of us are better off treating this as a project and approaching it in a methodical way. One possibility is to have a trial period, so that all the disadvantages and advantages can be weighed up having been experienced at first hand. Or it can even be a way of easing yourself into retiring to Italy as the first step. A trial period can take the form of several 'reconnaissance trips' staying in different regions for more than the usual holiday length of one to three weeks. Ideally, you should plan to stay for several months continuously by renting either in one location or several different ones. It is also essential to spend part of a winter in the place where you intend retiring, as many areas undergo a complete change of character in the cold months; coasts may be desolate and deserted, and countryside liable to winter periods of bone numbing cold; even Tuscany and Rome have freezing cold nights. You also need to see if you can survive with minimal Italian language skills, or better still you can use the reconnaissance period to brush up and improve your Italian so that you are ready to handle dealing with every day bureaucratic and financial matters in a foreign language. It also gives you the time to get to know the facilities and attractions of the region where you intend living. You can also use a trial period to meet the neighbours so that you have a network of contacts in place before you take the final plunge.

LEARNING ITALIAN

If you don't speak Italian you are forced to rely on the expatriate community for your survival; few Italians speak English. Learning Italian can be a rewarding and therapeutic experience. Most Italians are flattered if you make an attempt to speak it. They will encourage you in your efforts; and it is a beautiful and not too difficult language to learn. Roger Warwick who is in his fifties has lived in Italy for more than twenty years and stresses the importance of speaking the language:

> *I speak fluent Italian, which is essential. I know foreigners who have lived in Italy for twenty years and can only mumble a few words in Italian, which severely limits the possibilities of making friends with Italians as hardly any of them speak English well enough to have an interesting conversation.*

Standard Italian evolved from Tuscan, the language of Dante (*la lingua di Dante.*) It was forged by the poets Dante and Petrarch in the Middle Ages, and consolidated by writers like Alessandro Manzoni in the nineteenth century. Manzoni's novel *The Betrothed* (*I Promessi Sposi*), familiar to generations of Italian schoolchildren, was set on the shores of Lake Como, but instead of speaking the Comasco dialect the characters were made to speak in Tuscan. Manzoni washed his language in the river Arno 'rewriting' the book in 1840. In 1861 only 2.5% of Italians spoke standard Italian, in 1955 the figure was 34%, in 1988 it was 86%. By 1995, 93.1% Italians were speaking standard Italian, 48.7% were bilingual dialect Italian speakers and only 6.9% spoke in dialect alone. Television has accelerated the standardisation of the language, especially among young people. Nowadays a teenager from

Naples and a teenager from Como, whose grandparents would not have understood each other, speak the same standard Italian. This is the language for foreigners to learn.

Apart from the variations in Italian spoken around the country, some of the inhabitants of the border and outlying regions do not, in fact, use Italian at all. Various forms of French are spoken by a large percentage of the population in the Val d'Aosta and a strongly Germanic minority in the Trentino-Alto-Adige region uses German. The majority of the island population of Sardinia speaks a mixture of Italian, Latin, Punic and Spanish while in Calabria and Sicily, entire villages still speak Albanian and Greek.

Learning Italian Before You Go

Part-time Courses. Local colleges of education and community or adult studies centres are the best option as they often run day and evening courses catering for a variety of standards. Italian cultural organisations also offer courses

Intensive Language Courses with International Organisations. One real advantage of an international organisation is that it offers language courses which, begun in your home country, can be completed on arrival in Italy. See Berlitz and Linguarama below.

Useful Contacts
Berlitz School of Languages: 2nd Floor, Lincoln House, 296-302 High Holbourn, London WC1V 7JH; ☎020-7611-9640; fax 020-7611 9656; www. berlitz.com for international centres.

Linguarama: Quality Cobden Hotel, 166, Hagley Road, Birmingham B16 9NZ; ☎/fax 0121-455 6677; www.inlingua.com; for information about US inlingua schools visit www.inlingua.com/usa.html.

Self-Study Courses. This is the most flexible option but you need to give yourself goals otherwise learning can be dilatory. You can start before you go, and then continue to learn while being totally immersed in the language all around you. Various well-known organisations produce whole series of workbooks, CDs, audiocassettes and videos for learning a wide range of foreign languages. The BBC no longer produces language courses for adults, but the excellent (1982) series *Buongiorno Italia* is still available to buy and the BBC Education website provides interactive language tutorials online.

The Italian Bookshop (7 Cecil Court, London WC2 4EZ; ☎020-7240 1635; Italian@esb.co.uk) is a well-known stockist of Italian language books and courses. Grant and Cutler, the UK-based foreign language bookseller stocks a range of over 30 teach yourself courses for Italian (www.grantandcutler.com/catalogues/Italian/main/b04i103.htm). A very comprehensive reference list of course books, dictionaries, grammar books and and exam preparation books can be found at www.liv.ac.uk/ulc/independent%20learning/catalogue/ItalianCat2.htm and also at www.wannalearn.com/Academic_Subjects/World_Languages/Italian/.

Learning Italian in Italy

The most famous Italian language schools are at Perugia and Siena universities, at the British Institute in Florence and at the Scuola Leonardo da Vinci in Florence, Rome and Siena. But all major Italian cities have schools of Italian. A list of courses in Italy can be found at www.goto4me.com/pages/it/Italian-school.php and also at www.studying-italian-in-italy.tinusi.com and www.studyabroaditaly.org and www.italianlanguagecourse.com. A typical university course in Italian e.g. at the University of Trento, costs 400 euros (about £275), for outsiders for 40-50 hours of lessons in total. American freelance writer Roger Norum recommends learning in a small town rather than a city popular with tourists where you are likely to end up speaking English outside the classroom and he says ' you probably won't find the intimate cultural experience that you might in a village or small town.' Writer Harris Freedman who is old enough to retire, but says writers never do, learned Italian in Perugia in his late fifties, after buying his Italian home in 2001:

I spent four months going to basic Italian classes in Perugia; after that it got too difficult driving back and forth to my house, which is 40 minutes from Perugia, so I gave up the classes and just carried on learning by talking to Italians.

The first step in learning Italian is to understand that it is phonetic: the words are pronounced exactly as they are spelt. Once you have mastered the phonetic rules you can make yourself understood, immediately, by learning a few key phrases and idioms. Mel Holmes who moved to Calabria in 2000 is much encouraged by Italians' response to his use of their language:

We didn't learn before we came, but we brought tapes with us. We pick it up as we go along. I learnt a lot of Italian words from dealing with builders. I can get by. The thing about Italians is that they are genuinely delighted if you try to speak Italian. I don't think the same can be said of the French.

To acquire the sound and the cadence of the language it is worth listening to Italian radio or TV. Quiz programmes are particularly educational in that they show words and their spelling on screen.

Useful Contacts

An extensive list of language schools can be found on the websites mentioned above and at www.intoitaly.it.

Centro Lingua Italiana Calvino: ☎055-288081, www.clicschool.it. School open all year. Residential summer courses are organised in Calabria.

The Centro Linguistico Italiano Dante Alighieri: ☎055-210 808; ☎06-8320184, www.dantealighieri.com; e-mail study@clida.it.

CESA Languages Abroad: ☎01872-225300; www.cesalanguages.com. Organises language courses in Florence Venice, Rome and Siena.

Istituto Europeo: ☎055-2381071; e-mail info@istitutoeuropeo.it. Language courses; also cultural, professional and music courses.

Istituto Italiano: ☎06- 704 52138, www.istitutoitaliano.com. Contact in the USA: Lingua Service Worldwide: ☎1-800-394 5327 or 1-631-424 0777; www.linguaserviceworldwide.com/IsItalia.htm

It Schools: an online directory of Italian language schools in Italy and around the world: www.it-schools.com.

Italiaidea: ☎06-6837620; www.italiaidea.com; e-mail.italiaidea.com.

Italian for You: (online course); www.italianforyou.it.

Scuola Leonardo da Vinci: Schools in Rome, Florence and Siena; ☎055-290305; www.scualoaleonardo.com.

RESIDENCY REGULATIONS

All Nationalities

For stays of longer than 90 days all nationalities of visitor require a *permesso di soggiorno* (permit to stay), which must be applied for within eight days of arrival. EU nationals, whose passports are not usually stamped on arrival, will not have to worry quite so much about this time limit as non-EU visitors, whose visas will be checked and their passport stamped at the port of entry.

Up to date information on residency regulations can be found on the Italian Embassy website (www.ambitalia.org.uk). Visas for non-EU nationals must be applied for at the Italian consular office whose jurisdiction covers the region or country in which the applicant lives.

European Union Nationals

Any EU national, has a basic right to live permanently in other EU countries. However, there is still red tape to get through for EU nationals (but not nearly as much as there is for non-EU nationals) who want to stay longer than 90 days in Italy. The difference for EU nationals is that there is an obligation to allow them to remain in Italy long-term, even though they still have to apply for a residence permit. The possession of a residence permit *(permesso di soggiorno)* is essential to get access to public services such as health care and utilities contracts. The bureaucratic rigmarole involved with residing in Italy is almost without exception complicated and time consuming. The main thing to bear in mind as you struggle with bureaucratic insanity, is that it is as much a bugbear for the Italians themselves, as it is for the foreigners staying in their country.

Non-European Union Nationals

For non-European Union nationals the process is much more involved as their right to stay and work in Italy is not assumed from the outset. A non-EU national must apply for their long stay visa from the Italian consulate in their country *before* entering Italy.

Getting a Permesso di Soggiorno

EU Nationals: EU nationals apply at the *ufficio stranieri* (foreigners office) of the *questura*, (police station) or the *comune* in smaller towns, for their *Permesso di Soggiorno* (sometimes also known as a *Carta di Soggiorno*), within eight days of arrival. Reports vary as to how long it takes for the *Permesso di Soggiorno* to be issued, but three months is the official delay.

Requirements for the *permesso di soggiorno* vary. You will be required to produce proof of financial solvency, or income and your intended profession while in Italy, if this is relevant. The *soggiorno* is free of charge and has to be renewed periodically, however long you have lived in Italy. Note that failure to renew can result in a substantial fine. Renewals are made through the *comune*, or the *questura* in large towns and cities. All renewals must be made on special document paper, *carta bollata*, which can be purchased from most tobacconists (*tabaccherie*) currently for €11.

Non-EU Nationals: non-EU nationals *(extracomunitari)* intending to live in the country must have received the necessary visas before arrival otherwise they will have little or no chance of regularising their paperwork with the authorities.

Documents Required When Applying for a Permesso di Soggiorno

- A valid passport. Most countries require your passport to be valid for six months or more beyond your intended stay and Italy is no exception. A photocopy of the relevant information pages, including your visa (if applicable), will also be required.
- Up to four black and white passport-sized photos.
- A tax stamp *(marca da bollo)* of the correct value (check what is required at the local *questura*).
- For the self-employed, proof of registration with the Chamber of Commerce and VAT certificate (or exemption) is required.
- For retired/non-working people proof of financial resources is needed.

○ Proof of health insurance or coverage by social security system of
  Italy or another country.
○ Marriage/divorce certificate (if applicable).

It is necessary to have notarised translations of certain documents
and have others provided in Italian – check with the office where the
application will be made for current requirements. Official translations of marriage, divorce and birth certificates in Italian will probably be required. Translations should be done by an official translator
and enquiries should be made at an Italian Embassy or at the *questura*
where an application is to be made.

Autocertificazione (di Residenza)

Once you have obtained a *permesso di soggiorno* and moved into your
new Italian home, you can use the new *autocertificazione* system to
self-certify your residence status. You achieve this by signing a declaration (bearing in mind it is a criminal offence to falsely self-certifi-
cate yourself). You sign this when you apply for health care, a driving
licence, open a bank account and ship your personal effects to Italy.
This replaces the previous requirement to apply for a residence certificate, *certificato di residenza* and also cuts down on the bureaucracy.
Now all you need is the permesso di soggiorno, a *codice fiscale*, and a
declaration of residency to gain all the vital privileges that you previously had to have a certificato di residenza for.

Codice Fiscale (Tax-code Number)

After getting a permesso di soggiorno, all nationalities have to have a
tax-code number, whether or not they are retired, or liable for Italian
taxes. The reason for this is that the codice fiscale is essential for most
of the activities that living in Italy entails including opening a bank or
postal account, signing any official contract (e.g. lease, utilities, insurance), buying a Vespa or motor vehicle, or of course, working. You will
have to visit the Provincial Tax Office (taking your stay permit and
passport/ID) to get your tax-code number, which should be allocated
on the spot.

The Carta d'Identità

All residents, native and foreign, are required to carry an identity card (*Carta d'Identità*) with them at all times. Permanent residents are issued with an identity card that includes the holder's nationality and is valid for five years. The card should be bought from the *comune*. However, only Italian nationals can use their Italian identity card as a travel document in lieu of their passport.

Registering with the Embassy

Expatriates are advised to register with their Embassy or Consulate in Italy – US, Canadian and British offices are listed below. This registration enables the Embassy to keep their nationals up to date with any information they need to be aware of and also enables the Embassy to trace individuals in the event of an emergency. The Consulates can also help with information regarding their nationals' status overseas and advise with any diplomatic or passport problems. They may also be able to help in an emergency such as the unfortunate event of the death of a relative. Some embassies run social clubs for their nationals.

Sources of Information

Before getting too far into planning any move to Italy, all information should be checked and double-checked – including information in this book. Italian Embassies and Consulates in whose jurisdiction you live and your own Embassy in Italy are the best places to get information, though they might not always respond quickly.

Inhabitants of Rome, its province or region can try one of the websites aimed at expats in Italy such as The Informer (www.informer.it), which operates by subscription with basic information available free to all, www.expatsinitaly.com and expatsinitaly@groups.msn.com message board, or http://virtualitalia.com/forums which is free and also www.romebuddy.com. These are online guides to living in Italy,which carry useful information and online discussions on how to handle the paperwork involved in getting various *certificati* and *permessi*, which you now find you need. www.intoitaly.it is a Yellow Pages for Italy and a useful resource for Anglophones living in Italy.

Useful Contacts: Information & Help with Italian Bureaucracy
Italian Bureaucratic Help Service Centre; ☎/fax +39 (0)6 7236559; mobile
+39 347 0603556; e-mail cristina.nucci@tiscali.it; www.icaro.it/bureaucratic.
service/. Will get all kinds of bureaucratic papers from permesso di soggiorno,
and help with opening a bank account and much more. ☎020-7312 2200; fax
020-7499 2283; www.embitaly.org.uk.

www.stranieriinintalia.it: website portal for foreigners in Italy that gives
useful information for everyday life including updates on Italian legislation and
practical advice.

www.clandestinos.itdocumentitaliani.it.asp: site giving details of all the
main *documenti italiani* and how to get them and renew them (in Italian). Other
useful information about Italy including embassies, universities and *comunes*
and everything required to legalise your stay.

Italian Embassies and Consulates in the United Kingdom:
Italian Embassy: 14 Three Kings Yard, Davies Street, London W1Y 2EH;
☎020-7312 2200; fax 020-7499 2283; www.embitaly.org.uk.
Italian Consulate General: 38 Eaton Place, London SW1 8AN; ☎020-
7235 9371; fax 020-7823 1609; e-mail itconlond_visti@btconnect.com; www.
ambitalia.org.uk/visainfo.htm.
Italian Consulate General: Rodwell Tower, 111 Piccadilly, Manchester M1 2HY;
☎0161-236 9024. Easier to get through to than the London Consulate. For
latest regulations send a request and a stamped addressed envelope to the
Visa Department.
Italian Consulate General: 32 Melville Street, Edinburgh EH3 7HW; ☎0131-
226 3631 and 0131-220 3695; e-mail consedimb@consedimb.demon.co.uk.
Italian Vice Consulate: 7-9 Greyfriars, Bedford MK40 1HJ; ☎01234-356647;
e-mail consulat@netcomuk.co.uk. Open 9.30am-12.30pm Monday to Friday.

GETTING THERE AND AWAY

By Air

Over the last few years new air services between the UK and Italy have
been created and it is possible to fly direct between the UK and over 25
Italian cities. easyJet flies between the UK and ten Italian cities, while
Ryanair manages fourteen. If you change to a domestic flight at Milan

or Rome, you can reach still more destinations. Low cost airlines also fly between Italian cities and the rest of Europe; newcomer My Air (http://web4.myair.com) has flights all over Italy with maximum fares of €19.99 on domestic and €29.99 on international routes and is definitely worth a look. Due to the constantly changing nature of the airline industry and the spreading network of the budget airlines, it is likely that origin and destination airports will change, and some budget airlines will disappear like Buzz, which was taken over by Ryanair in 2003. Italy's original budget airline Volare is in administration, and may be bought by Alitalia but is still trading at the time of press. The information below is therefore for guidance only and should be checked on the internet, or direct with the airline before you make any plans. A useful website for checking budget flight airlines is www.attitudetravel.com/italy.

Internet tools that regularly scan airlines' websites and download details of fares from different airlines and compare them can be useful. www.skyscanner.net and www.aerfares.net and www.easyvalue.com are such tools, and cover most budget airlines, while Austrian Airlines website has a comprehensive interactive flight planner that allows travellers to find details of most scheduled flights, on any airline, in the world: www.aua.com. It is getting hard for Americans to find cheap flights direct to Italy. Promising websites for bargains include www.airtravelcenter.com and the Dutch-based website www.etn.nl. Americans also have the option of getting a cheap flight to London and then picking up an ex-UK, no frills fare, to Italy from there.

Milan Linate is 10 km east of the city and Milan Malpensa is 46 km north-west of the city. Malpensa to Milan is by Malpensa Express (train) and the Malpensa Shuttle coach.

Most of the airlines listed below allow passengers to book flights online.

Useful Contacts: Budget Airlines & Charter Flights

Avro: ☎0870-458 2841; www.avro.co.uk. Charter flights to Italy.

Aer Lingus: ☎0818-365000; www.aerlingus.com. Flies direct from Dublin to Bologna and Milan from £34.

Air Malta: ☎0845-607 3710; www.airmalta.com. Flies London Gatwick to Catania via Malta.

Alpie Eagles: ☎899-500058; www.alpieagles.com. Italian Internal budget flights between fourteen airports.

Alitalia: ☎0870-544 8259; www.alitalia.co.uk and in Ireland ☎01-677 5171. Flies from main UK cities to most cities in Italy. Not budget but may acquire Volare, Italy's original budget airline.

Air Berlin: ☎0870-738 8880; www.airberlin.com. German airline that flies direct from Stansted to Milan and Rome and Manchester to Milan.

BMI: ☎0870-607 0555; www.flybmi.co.uk. Flies from Heathrow to Milan, Naples and Venice.

British Airways: ☎0870-850 9850; www.ba.com. Uses Heathrow and Gatwick. Sample fares: Gatwick to Turin and Bari from £64.40 return.

Charter Flight Centre: ☎0845-045 0153; www.charterflights.co.uk.

easyJet: ☎0870-600 0000; www.easyjet.com. Flies from Bristol and East Midlands to Venice and Rome; Newcastle to Rome; Gatwick to Milan, Venice, Rome and Olbia; Luton to Cagliari and Turin; Stansted to Bologna and Naples.

Excel Airways: ☎08709-989898; www.excelairways.com. Flies to Rome.

Globespan: ☎0870-5561 522; www.flyglobespan.com. Low fares operator based in Scotland flies Glasgow Prestwick to Rome (Fiumicino) and Edinburgh to Rome (Fiumicino) and Venice. Fares from about £60. Also flights from Canada to Scotland.

Jet2: ☎0871-226 1737; www.jet2.com. Flies from Manchester to Pisa and Venice.

Meridiana: ☎020-7730 3454; www.meridiana.it. Italian domestic carrier but also flies from London Gatwick to Cagliari, Olbia and Florence. Special offer flights from £29 (London to Florence without taxes).

My Air: ☎899-500 060; http://web4.myair.com. Budget flights all over Italy and Europe.

Ryanair: ☎0871-246 0000; www.ryanair.com. Based at Stansted. Flies to many Italian destinations including Alghero, Ancona, Bari, Brescia, Brindisi, Cagliari, Genoa, Milan, Palermo, Pescara, Pisa, Rome, Trieste, Turin and Venice.

Thomsonfly: ☎0870-190 0737; www.thomsonfly.com. Flies from Coventry to Naples, Pisa and Venice and from Doncaster and Bournemouth to Pisa. One-way flights from £16.

Virgin Express: ☎0207-744 0004; www.virgin-express.com. Belgian airline that flies from Brussels and Amsterdam to Rome (Fiumicino) and Milan (Linate).

By Rail

For those who don't care to fly, getting to Italy from Northern European stations such as Paris and Calais can be a doddle on a direct through train. It is however expensive compared with no frills airfares. Eurostar and European train tickets including Italy (rail passes and tailor-made travel to and within Italy from the UK can be booked through www. railbookers.com. A list of Trenitalia agents in the UK can be found at www.trenitalia.com/home/en/international_travel/agenzie/uk.htm   and they include Railchoice (☎0870 165 7300; fax 020-8659 7466; sales@ railchoice.co.uk) There are also sleeper services from Paris and Calais (contact Citalia ☎0870-9014013; www.citalia.co.uk or Rail Europe ☎0870 5848848).

If you want to take the car but not drive it to Italy, you can use the Motorail service from Denderleeuw in Belgium. Denderleeuw is about a 100-mile drive from Calais and the route goes through Belgium, eastern France and Switzerland. Once in Italy the route goes through Milan and terminates at Bologna. A useful contact is Railsavers; ☎0870-750 7070; www.railsavers.com.

By Road

You can enter Italy by road from France, Switzerland and Austria. The routes from Austria and France are open year round. From Switzerland access is via the Mont Blanc tunnel from Chamonix (France) to Cour-mayeur in Italy. If you have a tunnel phobia then from Switzerland access is via the St. Bernard pass, which can be dodgy in winter when you will almost certainly need snow chains on your tyres.

Route planning is especially easy if you have internet access as there are websites can supply you with route details starting from your own street in the UK all the way to your Italian destination. Some also provide town plans and estimate the time and the cost of your journey.

Route Planner Websites

www.mappy.it	www.theaa.com
www.viamichelin.co.uk	www.rac.co.uk

PREPARATIONS FOR DEPARTURE

Making a permanent move to Italy requires preparations which will normally entail weeks, or months as you contemplate every aspect of daily life and decide what has to be cancelled in the UK and what has to be transferred to Italy and how it should be done. For such an arduous undertaking checklists are virtually essential in order to bring a degree of organisation into the process. How your checklists pan out depends on your personal requirements. The items below are the essential ones.

Banking

At some stage it will be appropriate and necessary to open a bank account in Italy, but not necessarily before you go. Estate agents usually advise you to open an account when you are looking for a property to buy so that the financial part of the process can take place quickly and smoothly. The drawback is that it is best to know where you will be living first, so that you can deal with a local branch. If you are spending a trial period in Italy, you can withdraw money from your UK bank account with a cashpoint card with the Visa or Cirrus symbol but there is a charge and you may not get a good exchange rate. You will need to know your PIN number or you may not be able to use your card.

For details of banking in Italy including Post Office banking services see the banking section in the chapter *Settling Into Your New Life*.

Arranging to Have Your Pension Paid in Italy

You should arrange for your occupational and state pension payments to be paid into your bank account in Italy. To do this you need to contact the pensions service in the UK (www.thepensionservice.gov.uk; ☎0845 60 60 60) and search/ask for details of Overseas Direct Payment in local currency. For occupational pensions contact your provider. For more details see *Pensions and Exportable UK Benefits* in the *Personal Finance* chapter.

Medical Matters

You are not usually allowed to have all your UK records to take with you to Italy. However access to these records by a medical practitioner in Italy can be arranged. Once you have a doctor in Italy, you can contact your UK doctor/medical practice and ask for your records to be sent to your new doctor there. The same applies to dental records. You may be asked to pay for this.

Medical records in Italy are in the process of being computerised so the system for sending medical records around the EU may be simplified in future. For more information about Italian healthcare and entering into the Italian health system, see the chapter *Healthcare.*

You should also ensure that you know what the Italian equivalents are of any regular prescriptions that you are taking. Ask your doctor for advice before you depart.

Main Points – Medical Matters

○ If you are on a reconnaissance trip to Italy, which lasts for less than three months, or you have just moved there you should take an EHIC (European Health Insurance Card) with you. Application Forms (ask for a T6 leaflet) are available at UK post offices. The EHIC entitles you to 90% of the costs of emergency treatment. It is advisable to take out health insurance to cover the remaining 10% of costs as these could be considerable. The EHIC runs out after three months by which time you should have entered the Italian health system.

○ It could be financially disastrous if you fall ill in Italy before you are integrated into the Italian health system if you do not have an EHIC.

○ If you forget to apply for an EHIC before departure, the Department of Work and Pensions will send it to you, or you can download the forms from their website www.dh.gov.uk.

○ If you are retiring to Italy and are entitled to UK state benefits (pension, invalidity, bereavement) ask for form E121 from the UK Department for Work and Pensions before you leave so that you can register with Italian social security and receive the same benefits as the Italians in Italy.

○ If you retire early from the UK to Italy and have paid Class 1 or 2 NI contributions up to the time you leave (or at least up until some months before you leave), then you will be entitled to benefit from the same entitlements as an Italian resident for an extended period (the length of time is not entirely clear). If there is too long a gap between the time you stopped paying NI contributions and your application for E106, then you will be turned down. This type of E106 is obtainable from the Medical Benefits Section of the DWP and you should do this before you go.

> **DWP and Private Health Insurance**
> **Department for Work & Pensions:** The Pension Service, International Pension Centre, Medical Benefits Section, Tyneview Park, Whitely Road, Newcastle-uponTyne NE98 1BA; ☎0191 218 7547; www.dh.gov.uk.
> **Expacare:** ☎01344 381663; www.expacare.net

Mail Forwarding

You may need to have ordinary mail forwarded to you in Italy. If you are keeping your UK home and therefore address, this is likely to generate more post than if you have sold up your UK assets and left the UK entirely. If you have a trusted neighbour, or your tenants are friends you can ask them to check your post, throw away obvious junk and readdress any important looking mail to you in Italy. If you have no UK address you should arrange to have your post redirected by The Royal Mail via airmail. You can arrange this at any post office. The time limit for redirecting mail is two years and it costs £60 per surname, per year. Special Delivery and signed for mail cannot be forwarded. A more flexible service can be provided by having an Accommodation Address. Your mail is forwarded to a commercial address provider and you can customise the service to your requirements. Obviously, this is going to work out far more expensive than Royal Mail. There are dozens of accommodation address mail forwarders and you can find them via an internet search.

Pets

All cats and dogs entering Italy must first be micro-chipped and then vaccinated against rabies, (which periodically makes an appearance in

Italy, usually arising from illegally imported animals). The vaccination has to be given at least 21 days and not more than 12 months before leaving the UK. Your vet will give you an EU pet record book which you must have with you when you enter Italy. The Italian authorities do not require cats and dogs to be treated for ticks and tapeworm before they enter the country. This is however a requirement for Pets entering the UK from Italy.

If you want to bring in pets other than cats and dogs, there are other rules. If you want to bring in a parrot or similar you will have to swear that you are not going to resell it in Italy and agree to a veterinary inspection. The local Italian consulate will advise you of formalities for other types of animals. The UK Department of Food Environment and Rural Affairs/DEFRA (www.defra.gov.uk) can provide forms for Italy. If you are thinking of exporting animals other than cats and dogs the PETS Helpline (☎0870 241 1710) will give you the section you need to call.

Removals

The cardinal rule for removals is to take as little as possible with you. This means having a massive turnout of your whole house from basement to attic. If you are renting initially in Italy then the same rule applies for storage. Removals by land are very expensive and will cost over £1000.

There are numerous removal firms: many of them advertise in Italian property magazines. Membership of the BAR/British Association of Removers (www.bar.co.uk) provides a guarantee that you are dealing with a reputable company that is not likely to go bust suddenly. This is an important point as you normally have to pay the company up front for the removal. BAR has set up International Movers Mutual Insurance so that any clients of any of its member companies will be compensated for loss or damage, or in the case of bankruptcy, the removal will be completed by another BAR member. A list of members can be obtained from the website or telephone 01923-699480.

The website www.etbrokers-removals.com/ claims that it can save you up to 60% on your removal costs to Italy. You give them all your removal details, and for a flat fee of about £35 they will hunt down the best quote. You can also phone them on 0870 800 3880.

Removals Checklist

o Before moving you should make an inventory of all the possessions and household effects that you think you should take with you and then reassess it and pare it down (several times if necessary).

o You should dispose of all items that you will probably never use again if you have not used them for years. You can give them to charity shops, local homeless shelters, sell them on e-Bay, have a garage sale or participate in car boot sales, give them to your relatives or take them to the council tip as appropriate. If you are not selling your UK home then you can probably skip this step, though not if you are renting it out.

o Furniture and other large items from your English home might not be suitable for your chalet in the Savoy Alps or your farmhouse in Le Marche. Bear in mind that it is easy to buy cheap second-hand furniture in Italy.

o UK electrical appliances should work in Italy with adaptors, but it may be difficult to get spare parts for them in Italy. On the other hand electrical equipment is generally more expensive in Italy.

o If you want to be ultra cautious choose a removal company with an office in Italy as well as in the UK as they will be the safest bet, if more expensive.

o Decide what smaller items you want to transport yourself by car to Italy.

Odds and Ends Checklist

o Cancel any regular subscriptions to newspapers, magazines, book, wine etc clubs, or arrange to have them redirected if this is possible and appropriate.

o Cancel gym or other UK club memberships.

o Return library books.

o Cancel any regular deliveries of groceries etc.

o Cancel contracts with gas, electricity and telephone companies and settle accounts.

o If you are renting out your UK home take meter readings for gas and electricity and settle bills before tenants move in and make an inventory of items left in the house to be attached to the tenancy agreement.

Part two

A New Home in Italy

Where to Retire
Your New Home in Italy
Housing Finance

Where to Retire

CHAPTER SUMMARY

O It is important for potential visitors that you are within easy reach of an airport or train station. More than an hour's drive from any of these and your visitor rate drops by 25%; more than an hour and a half and it drops by 50%.

O Unfortunately, land and property with proximity to airports and railway stations is invariably pricier than property off the beaten track but it is probably worth making sacrifices to get a location with good access.

O Property in Tuscany is very expensive and the supply of individual properties on the market is very limited. However, many hilltop hamlets are being restored and converted into holiday apartments.

O Lake Garda (Lombardy), is attracting settlers from Britain because of its lifestyle possibilities, but it has the highest population density of any Italian region.

O Liguria (the Italian Riviera) has the second highest population density in Italy and its people the longest life expectancy in Italy. It has a large population of older people.

O The city of Udine in Friuli-Venezia-Giulia came out top in an Italian poll on the best place to live.

O In general, the region of Emilia-Romagna (north east) is the real working Italy, where 'happy valleys' of expatriates are not a feature.

O In Umbria, large numbers of desirable derelict country properties have been bought up and converted by Anglophone buyers, and the supply has dried up.

O In Le Marche you can find property bargains in the countryside and the villages and towns. Property in rural areas is cheap because access roads can be a problem.

CHOOSING THE RIGHT LOCATION

Many countries are potential retirement places, but Italy is one with a long track record of foreign retirees, and many advantages. If we choose Italy, we do so because it has a good climate, lovely people, good food, plenty of culture etc. and it is an attractive country with beautiful scenery. Perhaps we know it through holidays or visits to friends or relations. But where in Italy exactly is a good place to retire to?

It could be argued that Italy is the most historically interesting country in the western world thanks to its Classical heritage. Italians themselves are keen on their local history. Most towns have a local group called the *Pro Loco* (for the place). Whereas in Britain, successive governments have robbed Britain of some her local county identities, quite the opposite tendency is at work in Italy. Regional identity and autonomy are respected and guaranteed by constitution. Historical differences are celebrated, and it is good for you, as an outsider, to become aware of the nuances.

Some regions are more homogeneous than others. Tuscany for example, which was once a country in its own right. Others are disparate, like Campania, where the Neapolitans again, are quite different from the people of Benevento. Other regions, such as Veneto, have been cut off from their historical partners; Brescia and Bergamo are in Lombardy, but you can see the influence of Venice in the architecture and hear it in the speech.

The regions that have become congenial to both English-speaking and German-speaking residents within the last 40 years are: Tuscany, Umbria, Le Marche (The Marches), and now Puglia. But rumours have been heard from Umbria: a saturation point might have been reached: the supply of suitable houses has practically dried up. So you could try Abruzzo and Molise, which have the same old-fashioned charm of Umbria and the Marches, but have not been 'discovered.'

Or, if you still want to be in Tuscany or Umbria – you can forget the countryside and opt for a town house or apartment. These are still comparatively cheap. This would nullify the inconvenience of driving long distances when you live in the country and give you the pleasure of town life and public transport and make your visitors more frequent.

Further afield, if you like mountains, you have the magnificent range of the Dolomites, which straddle the regions of Trentino Alto-Adige and Veneto, enjoying sunny winters and wet summers. They are much frequented by Italians, who appreciate the delights of the Tyrolean ambience on their own doorstep.

Another option that beckons strongly is the island of Sardinia. This has the same Mediterranean feel of Majorca or the Spanish Costas, but without the crowds. It has to be high on any list of desirable Italian locations. The island has not yet been spoilt by indiscriminate development. Sardinia is well served by cheap flights; it is no longer the preserve of the super rich.

Finally, for the intrepid and pioneering there is the southern part of Italy or Sicily. These regions are not bland and anodyne and predictably European, like the north and centre of Italy. You are confronted by a radically different mindset, which is stereotypically Italian to the prejudiced Anglo-Saxon eye. Power and swagger are respected here, and organised crime can still be a problem. This is the part of Italy, which produced the bulk of Italian immigrants to the USA, Australia and Britain...since the 1890s. Unfortunately, uncontrolled illegal building development has defaced much of the coastline throughout Sicily and Calabria. However, awareness of the environment has coincided with the advent of the internet. The tide has turned, and splendid thriving resorts are growing throughout the regions of the South, which attract mainly Italian visitors at the moment, but could easily appeal to a more international clientele.

THE NORTH-WEST

PIEDMONT

Capital: Turin (30 metres above sea level)

Area sq km: 25,395; *Population:* 4,231,334 (density 167 per sq km)

Foreign visitors: 1,124,686; *Italian visitors:* 1,526,317

Regional website: www.regione.piemonte.it

Climate: Temperatures: Summer 21C; Winter 7.2C; mean 12.3C.
          Average annual rainfall 893mm; 146 days of rain per year.

Airports: Turin: Caselle International airport, Cuneo airport

Unesco world heritage sites: 1997 Residences of the Royal House of Savoy.

National parks: Gran Paradiso/Val Grande

Piedmont gets its name from its position at the 'foot of the mountains'. It is surrounded by Alpine ranges, with famous skiing resorts such as Sestrière, Bardonecchia and Limone Piemonte. The regional capital, Turin, is situated in the centre of the region on the River Po, and is a city of baroque art and architecture. As well as having a wide spread of industries Piedmont is also famous for its wine production and gastronomy (especially the white truffle).

Piedmont borders with France to the West (the Maritime Alps and the Cottian Alps), with Switzerland to the north (the Pennine and Lepontine Alps), with Lombardy to the east, with Emilia-Romagna to the southeast, and with Liguria (the Ligurian Apennines) to the south.

There is a clear contrast between the encircling mountains and the plain, which can be divided into two areas, the upper plain at the foot of the Maritime Alps (the towns of Cuneo, Mondovì and Saluzzo) and the lower plain round the cities of Novara and Vercelli.

The other provinces in Piedmont after Turin, in a clockwise direction are:

○ **Biella** – pre-eminent for its wool and textiles since ancient times, and proud to be a province since 1996.
○ **Verbania** – on the western shore of Lake Maggiore, which includes Stresa and Pallanza. The mild microclimate and the beautiful steep lakeside setting have made this a favourite retirement spot for centuries. There is another lake, Orta, 10 km to the west of Lake Maggiore, which is equally romantic and less crowded.
○ **Novara** – in the Po valley, near Milan, rich in manufacturing industries (such as bathroom fittings).
○ **Vercelli** – the 'rice capital', paddy fields and superb Gothic architecture.
○ **Alessandria** – a hub for road and rail communications; this province includes the spa resort of Acqui Terme
○ **Asti** – the most attractive hilly vineyard area famous for wine and truffles, with hill towns like Canelli, Nizza, Monferrato and Cocconato.
○ **Cuneo** – the breathtaking gateway into the Maritime Alps, full of art and gastronomy, with summer and winter resorts. Among its towns are Alba, and medieval Mondovì.

Property

18th and 19th century farmhouses and villas, both ruined and restored, can still be found in Piedmont, as well as large wine estates, and old village houses for restoration everywhere. Town houses abound in the grand *umbertino* (Victorian) style. Piedmont excels also in 19th century industrial archaeology. A trend has started for the conversion of the old, mostly brick-built, warehouses and factories. The horrendous tenement blocks of the 20th century, which housed the workers, are still in evidence, as homes now for new immigrants.

Location	Type	Description	Price
Cocconato (Asti) 1km from town.	Semi-detached restored country house.	250sq m. 2 bedrooms, 2 bathrooms, verandah, garden and meadow.	€450,000
Canelli (Asti)	Ruin with cellar	3-storey ruin in idyllic vineyards	€80,000
Cavagnolo (Turin 35km)	1890s Art Deco Villa in need of renovation.	305sq m plus servants' quarters. Panoramic views. Formal garden and orchard.	€350,000

Agents for this region: www.casedicampagna.com; www.smith.gcb.demon. co.uk; www.casatravella.com; www.homesinitaly.co.uk, www.piedmont.co.uk; www.houses-in-italy; www.italy.realestate-dreams.com; www.homesinitaly.co.uk.

LOMBARDY

Capital: Milan (221 metres above sea level)

Area sq km: 23,861; *Population:* 9,108,645 (density 382 per sq km)

Foreign visitors: 3,927,618; *Italian visitors:* 4,645,189

Regional Website: www.regione.lombardia.it

Climate: Temperatures: Summer 21.8C; Winter 6.6C; mean 12.7C.
            Average annual rainfall 1,191mm; 80 days of rain per year.

Airports: Milan-Linate, Milan-Malpensa, Bergamo.

Unesco world heritage sites: 1979 Rock Drawings in Valcamonica, Dominican Convent of Santa Maria, Delle Grazie with *The Last Supper* by Leonardo Da Vinci, 1995 Crespi d'Adda.

National parks: Stelvio Val Grande

Lombardy covers the Po Valley and the middle of the Italian Alps, bordering Switzerland to the north, Emilia Romagna to the south, Piedmont to the west and Trentino Alto-Adige and Veneto to the east. It is the most densely populated Region (382 inhabitants per square km) especially the province of Milan, which has a fourteenth of the country's entire population and a density of 1,442 inhabitants per square km. 47% of the region is plain, 40.6% mountainous and 12.4% hilly.

The mountains and lakes, and their towns, from east to west are: Varese on Lake Maggiore, Campione on Lake Lugano (an Italian enclave with a casino), Como, Brunate, Lecco and Bellagio on Lake Como, The Lago d'Iseo is a lake east of Bergamo in the Franciacorta wine area. East of Brescia is Lake Garda with its towns of Salò, Desenzano, Sirmione and Limone. To the northeast are the Orobian Alps and the town of Sondrio in the valley of the river Adda and the Valtellina wine area. Further up is the resort of Bormio and the Tonale pass through to the Stelvio national park. North of Milan are the Brianza hills and in the south are the provinces of Pavia, Cremona and Mantua.

Industrially and commercially Milan and its hinterland is the capital of Italy and is recognised as the design capital of the world. Bergamo and Brescia are rich entrepreneurial industrial provinces. The presence of Lake Garda to the north of this area is fortunate. It is a well-deserved lung for the hardworking population of the Po Valley.

Property

The lake towns are much sought after by Italians, and Varese and Como are popular with expatriates because of their Mediterranean microclimate; there are superb gardens in the area. The mountains of Sondrio, the Valtellina and parts of the provinces of Brescia and Bergamo are thinly populated and cheap. The lake Garda area is attracting settlers from Britain because of its lifestyle possibilities – sports are well catered for. The lake is ideal for windsurfing and public services and hospitals are good. There are ski-resorts nearby and golf courses at hand, and the food and wine are of course exquisite.

Location	Type	Description	Price
Argegno – Cernobbio (Como)	New detached house with lake view	170sq m. Garden and double integral garage.	€388,000
Ranco (Varese)	Restored town house near town centre.	150sq m. 3 bedrooms, 3 bathrooms, verandah, garden with double parking space. Lake view.	€330,000
Viadanica (Bergamo)	Detached hillside suburban house	One-storey. Two bedrooms, garden, double parking space.	€330,000

Agents for this area: www.tecnocasa.it; www.homesinitaly.co.uk, www.Italian-network.it (Sothebys); www.ibossi.com (Varese); www.immobiliarelombardia.com.

LIGURIA

Capital: Genoa (3 metres above sea level)

Area sq km: 5,421; *Population:* 1,572,197 (density 290 per sq km)

Foreign visitors: 1,184,946; *Italian visitors:* 2,241,310

Regional website: www.regione.liguria.it

Climate: Temperatures: Summer 24.5C; Winter 9.2C; mean 16.5C.

Average annual rainfall 1,057mm; 101 days of rain per year.

Airports: Genoa, Cristoforo Colombo International Airport; also Nice in France.

Unesco World Heritage Sites: 1997 Portovenere, Cinque Terre including the islands of Palmaria, Tino and Tinetto.

National Park: Cinque Terre.

Liguria has the highest population density in Italy after Campania and Lombardy. Although not one of the richest regions, the people of Liguria have one of the longest life expectancies in Italy, and the area has a large population of older people. Liguria is also one of the smallest regions and is often referred to as the Italian Riviera. It lies between the mountains and the Ligurian Sea (*Mar Ligure*) and is backed by the Maritime Alps (*Alpi Marittime*) and the Ligurian Apennines (*Appennino Ligure*). Its coast is divided into the harsh and steep eastern riviera (*Riviera di Levante*) from Genoa to La Spezia, and the more open landscapes of the western part (*Riviera di Ponente*), which has many sandy beaches and small seaside resorts, and towns including Ventimiglia, Sanremo, Imperia and Savona. Liguria reaches from the border with France to the west,

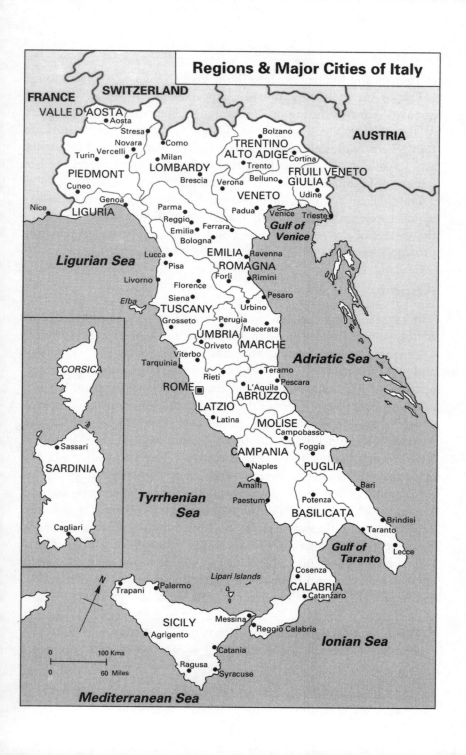

Regions & Major Cities of Italy

to Tuscany and Emilia Romagna in the east. To the north is Piedmont.

The largest industry is tourism, especially on the coast where the population triples during July and August. The famously smart resort of Portofino lies east of Genoa. Other established resorts include Bordighera, Sanremo, Alassio, Finale Ligure, Nervi, Santa Margherita and Rapallo. The Cinque Terre national park is the end strip of the Riviera di Levante.

The chief city of the region is also Italy's largest port, Genoa (*Genova*) which sprawls along the coast for 25 km and inland for 15km up the valleys of the rivers Polcevera and Bisagno. The region has four provinces: Genoa, Imperia, La Spezia and Savona.

Property

The Ligurian coast is chaotic and overcrowded in the summer, thanks to the ribbon development that boomed from the 1950s onwards. Old fishing villages, such as Portofino and Bogliasco, are very pretty and well preserved, and throughout the region grand villas, hotels and apartment mansions, especially in Santa Margherita Ligure, Rapallo and Sanremo, bear witness to the wealth and fashion of the Victorian epoch. A sea view (*vista mare*) comes at a premium. The prices are highest in the old English colony of Alassio, where a three-bedroom house with a garden and a sea view costs €730,000. Condominium apartments in converted period hotels, as at Sanremo, are going for €400,000. Prices decrease dramatically the further inland you go, and houses are 25% cheaper in the west of the region (Imperia) than in the east. Medieval hill-towns like Triora (Imperia) have finished two bed-room apartments for €80,000, including 500sq.m of garden. Abandoned farmhouses and fertile land can still be found, never far from the convenience, and noise, of an arterial *autostrada*. Gardeners will feel at home here; so will yachtsmen, gamblers, and gourmets.

Agents for this region. www.tecnocasa.it; www.villecasali.com; www.brianfrench.com; www.gabettionline.it; www.italy-riviera-realestate.com; www.casatravella.com; www.liguriaestates.com; www.realinvest.co.uk; www.homesinitaly.co.uk.

Location	Type	Description	Price
Diano Marina (Imperia) 500m walk from sea, in olive grove.	Annex of villa (55sq. m) tastefully converted	1 bedroom, kitchen, bathroom, terrace, sea view 95sq m garden	€209,000.
Montalto Ligure (Imperia). 20km from sea.	Attached stone-built village house (55sq m)	One bedroom. Small garden. 2 cellars. Habitable.	€65,000
San Colombano Certenoli (Genoa) 15km from sea (Chiavari)	Abandoned farmhouse (140 sq m + 2500 sq m of land)	3 storeys. For complete restoration. Good access. Sunny position. Fertile valley of Fontebuona.	€110,000

VALLE D'AOSTA

Capital: Aosta (583 metres above sea level)

Area sq.km: 3,263; *Population:*120,909 (density 37 per sq.km)

Foreign visitors: 234,938; *Italian visitors:* 547,453

Regional Website: www.regione.valdaosta.it

Climate: Temperatures: Summer 20.5C; Winter 0.8C; mean 10C.

Airports: nearest, Milan and Turin.

National park: Gran Paradiso

The Valle d'Aosta is the smallest and most thinly populated region in the Italian Republic, bordering with Switzerland (north) and France (west) and Piedmont (east and south). It became an autonomous region with special statute in 1948.

It is entirely mountainous, extending across the Graian and Pennine Alps. The head of the Valley is closed by Mont Blanc, the highest peak in Europe (4,810m), and by glaciers feeding the sources of the River Dora Baltea. To the south is the Gran Paradiso massif (4,061m) and to the north is the Monte Rosa group (4,633m). The climate is affected by the high altitude, averaging 8°C at Courmayeur below Mont Blanc, 10°C at Aosta in mid-valley, and 12°C at St. Vincent lower down. About one sixth of the area is covered by the Gran Paradiso national park.

Commerce and finance are concentrated on **Aosta** (583m), the regional capital, lying on the important Mont Blanc tunnel arterial through route, is in an attractive position on the crossroads for France and Switzerland, encircled by the Alps. There is a railway line up the valley from Turin to Mont Blanc. The official languages are French and Italian.

Property

The mountain areas have become depopulated since the 19th century, except for the major tourist centres in the lateral valleys. Tourism has replaced poor mountain agriculture. Old stone houses dot the landscape in the Val d'Aosta. Ruined dwellings are plentiful and cheap. Modern houses follow the style dictated by the traditional ones. The property market here has gone up nearly 10% in the last couple of years. Properties become more expensive near the ski resorts. Courmayeur and Breuil-Cervino being the most fashionable of these, although smaller places like 'sun-drenched' Torgnon have a greater charm.

Agent for this region: www.immobiliare-la-tour.com.

Location	Type	Description	Price
Torgnon	Restored two-room chalet	60sq m with balcony, cellar, central heating and garden.	€160,000
Courmayeur	New house in traditional style.	200sq.m on various levels in own park 3000sq.m. Panoramic, tranquil position.	€995,000
Verrayes	Small stone house for renovation.	70sq m. Two floors. Altitude 1200m. 14km Torgnon ski resort.	€20,000

THE NORTH-EAST

TRENTINO ALTO ADIGE

Capital: Trento (187 metres above sea level)

Area sq.km: 13,607; *Population:* 950,495 (density 70 per sq km)

Foreign visitors: 3,947,662; *Italian visitors:* 3,156,473

Regional website: www.regione.taa.it

Climate: Temperatures: Summer 28C; Winter 0C.

              Average annual rainfall 724mm.

Airports: Nearest: Venice-Treviso, Verona, Brescia, Forli

National park: Stelvio

This is the most northerly region of Italy, bordering Switzerland to the northwest, Austria to the north, Lombardy to the south-west and Veneto to the east and southeast. It has been an autonomous region with special statute since 1948, consisting of the two autonomous provinces of Bolzano and Trento, which take it in turns to be regional capital every two years. Trentino means the territory of the ancient city of Trent or Trento. Alto Adige means Upper Adige (a river), a name adopted after World War I to replace the German Süd Tirol (South Tyrol). The area is mostly mountainous with the lowest population density in Italy after the Valle d'Aosta. The province of Trento is almost entirely Italian speaking with Venetian and Lombard dialects. Small pockets of the Rhaeto-Romansch or Ladin language survive in Val Gardena, Val Badia and Val Pusteria. It is a protected language, taught in schools.

The standard of living in the whole area is above the national average. The region has a superb rail and motorway system linking Verona with the Italian – Austrian Brenner pass. For sports, summer and winter, the Valgardena is the jewel of the Dolomites with skiing in the winter and beautiful hiking paths in the summer. The numerous lakes and torrents are well equipped for water sports and white water rafting. Pony trekking, tennis, golf and mountain biking are all catered for.

Bolzano (*Bozen*) (altitude 250m population: 95,400) is a Tyrolean German speaking town. Bolzano airport has flights to Rome, Naples, Cagliari, Olbia, and Lamezia Terme).

Trento (*Trent*) (altitude 194m, population 106,190) is a great Renaissance Italian town with imposing buildings and a famous university.

Property

This region has a low population density and a disproportionate number of *agriturismos* (over 2,500) – as many as in Tuscany. It is perhaps better therefore to rent than to buy here. If you are buying a house in this region it is wise to be aware of Radon gas. Consult with your *geometra* and refer to the Bolzano province environment website (www.provincia.bz.it) on which there is an 'at risk' map.

Agents for this region: www.casa.it; www.systemacasa.it.

Location	Type	Description	Price
Roncone (Trento)	Mountain house	120sq m. 2 floors. South facing. Solar panels. Mains water. 5,174sq.m of land.	€82,000
Riva del Garda (Trento)	Detached house for renovation	One storey at present in two apartments. Southwest facing panoramic terrace. 170sq m private garden	€450,000
Ortisei (Bolzano)	Modern apartment in quiet location	66sq m. 2 bedrooms. 2 bathrooms, cellar, garage.	€300,000

VENETO

Capital: Venice (0 metres above sea level)

Area sq.km: 18,391; *Population:* 4,577,408 (density 249 per sq km)

Foreign visitors: 7,155,425; *Italian visitors:* 4,528,321

Regional website: www.regione.veneto.it

Climate: Temperatures: Summer 22.6C; Winter 16.3C; mean 16.3C.

                 Average annual rainfall 428mm; 95 days of rain a year.

Airports: Venice: Brescia, Marco Polo, Treviso, Forlì.

Unesco world heritage sites: 1987 Venice and its lagoon, 1994 City of Vicenza,

    Palladian villas of the Veneto, 1997 Botanical garden (*Orto Botanico*) Padua,

    2000 City of Verona.

National parks: Dolomiti Bellunesi.

The region of Veneto is in the north-east of Italy bordering on Austria to the north, Trentino Alto Adige to the west, Lombardy to the south and west, Emilia Romagna to the south, Friuli-Venezia Giulia and the Adriatic sea to the east. It is 56.4% plain, 29.2% mountainous and 14.4% hilly. There are seven provinces in the region: Belluno, Padua, Rovigo, Treviso, Venice, Verona and Vincenza.

The transport system – rail, road, and air is excellent. Industries are favoured by the excellent communications infrastructure, which offers direct arterial links with Austria and Germany, Central Italy, the Balkans, Switzerland and France. Heavy traffic and industrial development is confined to the spacious Po plain, leaving the hilly and mountainous districts, with their historic towns, as desirable locations for living and recreational activities.

The health service in Veneto is excellent, but school leavers are less qualified here than the national average. Newspaper readership, TV viewing, and the crime rate are low. There are more church marriages and fewer divorces than in any other region. There is a strong smallholding tradition and part-time farming by industrial workers is a relevant factor in the economy.

Property

Veneto is a rich region with Venice at its heart with its wonderful architecture, including *palazzi* built of pink Istrian stone, which fetch astronomical prices and have clauses safeguarding their conservation. Treviso, Verona and Vicenza have villas for sale many of them in the Palladio style. There are about 5,000 Veneto villas (*ville Venete*) built between the 15th and the 19th centuries, of which 1,400 are declared to be of historical and monumental interest. Villas were built in great numbers in the 16th century to drive inland agricultural production, so, basically the villas are grand Palladian farmhouses. The Veneto region includes the east side of Lake Garda, where suburbs full of modern condominium blocks and villas are popular with German and Austrian renters. The winter resort of Cortina D'Ampezzo on the other hand caters to upmarket Italians, and the buildings there – mainly condominiums – are the height of chic, with such things as communal card rooms (devoted to bridge)

Location	Type	Description	Price
Pagnano d'Asolo (Treviso)	Modern, 3-storey house.	Spacious 430sq m. Traditional style with verandahs. 2000sq.m of garden.	€430,000
Venice Lido (Alberoni)	Ground floor apartment	80sq m. 2 bedrooms. Small terrace looks over communal garden. 50m from beach; 300m from golf course.	€280,000
Venice (Giudecca Island)	New, one bedroom appt.	55sq m. 3rd floor roof terrace and views of lagoon.	€267,000

Agents for this region: www.collinepiacentine.it; www.venice-sales.com; www.homesinitaly.co.uk; www.brianfrench.com.

FRIULI-VENEZIA-GIULIA

Capital: Trieste (20 Metres above sea level)
Area sq km: 7,855; *Population:* 1,191,588 (density 152 per sq km)
Foreign visitors per year: 755,715; *Italian visitors per year:* 978,302
Regional website: www.regione.fvg.it
Climate: Temperatures: Summer 24.1C; Winter 5.6C; mean 16C.
Average annual rainfall 873mm; 137 days of rain per year.
Airport: Trieste: Ronchi dei Legionari International Airport
Unesco World Heritage Sites: 1998 Archaeological Area and the Patriarchal
Basilica of Aquileia.

Occupying the northeastern extremity of Italy, Friuli-Venezia-Giulia is bordered by Austria to the north, Slovenia to the east, the Veneto region to the west and the Adriatic Sea to the south. The region is divided into four administrative provinces, two are Giulian (Trieste and Gorizia) and two are Friulian (Udine and Pordenone). As with remote mountainous regions in general, it is quite poor and under-populated.

Tourism is highly developed in the Adriatic seaside towns of Lignano and Grado, popular since the 1890s, during the Austria-Hungarian Empire. Grado is especially popular with families and over 50s and is attached to the mainland by a four-mile causeway. Trieste has its own extreme winter climate of bitterly cold and fierce northeastern winds (the *bora*). Rainfall is abundant.

The population of the Gorizia and Trieste provinces includes minorities of Slovenes (distributed mainly in the Natisone and Val Resia valleys). About three-quarters of a million people speak Slovenian.

Property

The varied cultural influences of Friuli-Venezia-Giulia and the climate have shaped the types of architecture: slate-roofed, stone chalets in the mountains, neoclassical and art nouveau style in Trieste, Venetian in the towns. The city of Udine, came out top in an Italian poll on the best place to live. Property is reasonably priced and modern villas and apartments in towns should be considered.

Agent for this region: www.tecnocasa.it

Location	Type	Description	Price
Trieste	Apartment	4 rooms + bath & kitchen. 2 balconies. Parking. Quiet area. Small wood in front.	€175,000
Trieste	Roof-top apartment in a prestigious palazzo	260 sq m Sea view. Terraces. Cellar and Garage with the property	€150,000
Pineta (Grado)	New terraced house.	200sq.m. Four storeys, garage, cellar, 3 bathrooms, 4 terraces, garden and sea views.	€265,000

EMILIA-ROMAGNA

Capital: Bologna (38 metres above sea level)

Area sq.km: 22,124; *Population:* 4,030,220 (density 182 per sq.km)

Foreign visitors: 1,957,074; *Italian visitors:* 5,660,099

Regional website: www.regione.emilia-romagna.it

Climate: Temperatures: Summer 25C; Winter 5.8C; mean 17.7C.

Average annual rainfall 351mm; 86 days of rain per year.

Airports: there are three: Bologna Marconi, Forlì and Rimini.

Unesco World Heritage Sites: 1995 Ferrara City of Renaissance – Po Delta,

1996 Early Christian Monuments of Ravenna, 1997 Cathedral Torre Civica,

Piazza Grande, Modena.

National parks: Appennino Tosco – Emiliano, Monte Falterona Campigna &

Foreste Casentinesi.

Emilia Romagna borders Piedmont and Liguria to the west, Lombardy to the north and north-west, Veneto to the north east, the Adriatic Sea to the east, the Marches and the Republic of San Marino to the south east, and Tuscany to the south. 47.8% of it is comprised of the wide, fertile alluvial plain of the Po Valley and about 25% is mountainous.

The mountains are thinly populated, with a few modest winter-sports resorts. The beaches of Romagna on the other hand are geared for mass tourism – mostly Italian, but a lot of Russians and eastern European visitors, particularly at Rimini. Cervia is the best yachting marina. There are wide sandy beaches in all the resorts: Milano Marittima, Cervia, Cesenatico, Bellaria, Rimini, Riccione, Cattolica, and the Ferrara and Ravenna beaches, which are packed. July and August are to be avoided because of overcrowding.

Population is dense along the axis of the Via Emilia – the old Roman road, which goes through Piacenza, Parma, Reggio, Modena, Bologna, Imola, Faenza, Forlì, Cesena and Rimini. There is an excellent communications network: the *autostrada del Sole* (Milan-Bologna-Florence-Rome), which branches off to Padua and Rimini at Bologna. The Bologna railway junction is the hub of the Italian railway system. All this activity leads to pollution and traffic problems. At Faenza and other towns odd and even number-plate days have been introduced to control the volume of traffic.

Property

The city centres of Parma, Modena, Ferrara, and especially Bologna are full of commercial and residential life. This pattern is echoed in the smaller towns like Bagnacavallo (Ravenna). Sadly the gracious *palazzi* of the local aristocracy, seldom come on to the market. Apartment conversions and architecturally homogeneous blocks of flats are common, however, in downtown areas. The countryside, is characterized by huge brick farmhouses and barns, often derelict. Romantics can find pretty ruins to convert in the Tusco-Emilian Apennines west of Parma and Piacenza, and in the hills around the concrete chaos of the Eastern seaboard. Beachside apartments are to be found in converted hotels in Rimini. The marinas and lidos north of Ravenna are crowded and expensive.

In general, the region of Emilia-Romagna is the real working Italy, where 'happy valleys' of expatriates are not a feature.

Location	Type	Description	Price
Bolgogna Centre	Penthouse flat	In elegant modern block. 2 bedrooms. Living room opens on to roof terrace.	€500,000
Comacchio (Ferrara)	New, 2-storey townhouse .	Traditional style. 2 bedrooms, 2 bathrooms. Yard/terrace.	€125,000
Bagnacavallo (Ravenna)	Country villa	Spacious (420 sq m). 2 storeys. Double garage. 1350 sq m of fertile garden.	€555,000

Agents for this region: www.appennninocasa.com; www.lacasaemilia.com; www.gabimm.it, www.secondacasa.com; www.tecnocasa.it

CENTRAL ITALY (NORTHERN)

TUSCANY

Capital: Florence (38 metres above sea level)

Area sq km: 22,997; *Population:* 3,516,296 (density 153 per sq km)

Foreign visitors: 5,218,189; *Italian visitors:* 4,792,560

Regional Website: www.regione.toscana.it

Climate: Temperatures; Summer 25.2C; Winter 6.7C; mean 16.9C.

Average annual rainfall 813mm; 154 days of rain per year.

Airports: Florence: Amerigo Vespucci international; Pisa: Galileo Galilei Airport.

Unesco world heritage sites: 1982 Historic Centre of Florence, 1987 Piazza del Duomo (Pisa), 1990 Historic Centre of San Gimignano, 1995 Historic Centre of Siena, 1996 Pienza Historic Centre. 2004 Val d'Orcia landscape and architecture, 'an icon of the renaissance... people in harmony with nature ...'

National parks: Appennino Tosco – Emiliano, Arcipelago Toscano: Monte Falterona, Campigna and Foreste Casentinesi.

If Britons have heard of anywhere in Italy, it is Tuscany, which is bordered by Liguria to the northwest, Emilia Romagna to the north, the Marches and Umbria to the east and Lazio to the southeast. To the west is the Tyrrhenian sea and the Tuscan archipelago including the islands of Elba, Capraia and Giglio. Outstanding nature reserves are in the Casentino, famed for its timber, and in the lower Maremma, in the Parco dell'Uccellina.

The population of Tuscany is heavily concentrated along the Tyrrhenian coastline between Carrara and Livorno, and in the lower Valdarno plain, where densities of 500 persons per sq km are recorded. This part of Tuscany is a sprawling industrious megacity, whilst the surrounding mountains and the less populated hills in the south are more rural and backward.

The road and rail networks are well developed and overcrowded. There is a railway line down the coast, through Pisa and Grosseto, and down the middle through Florence and Arezzo. The spinal *autostrada del sole* motorway, which connects the north and the south of Italy, is severely congested especially in the section between Florence and

Bologna (tight curves and narrow lanes through tunnels).

If the traffic on the autostrada has reached saturation, so has Tuscany's major industry, which is, of course, tourism. Tuscany's massive heritage of architecture and art and its glorious countryside continue to attract millions of visitors – even the centre of Lucca has become a tourist ghetto.

Chiantishire

'Chiantishire' is a journalistic expression invented in the 1970s to describe the perceived English colony that is supposed to have taken over Chianti, Chianti being a district in Tuscany between Siena and Florence. The area was 'discovered' in the 1960s. A founding father of this colony was the English writer Raymond Flower, who, with the assistance of the local mayor, procured dozens of farmhouses in the environs of Castellina-in-Chianti. The generation that enjoyed that idyll is now disappearing. Their houses now come up for sale in need of renovation a second time. The indigenous population, who breathed life into this countryside for 2500 years are only a memory now. An immigrant workforce, predominantly Albanian, has taken their place, as employees in the massive trophy vineyards that are transforming the landscape. A farmhouse near Pianella, which cost £4000 in 1968, is now worth over one million pounds, In 1968 it seemed to be in a remote wilderness. Now it is within earshot of four or five villas with swimming pools, and two or three Albanian and Kosovar families, some of them housed in converted pigsties. There are very few permanent English residents in Chianti, but a large number of increasingly luxurious rental properties that cater to the dream of Chiantishire.

Property

Rural properties are still reasonably priced in the more remote areas such as the Lunigiana, the Casentino, the Colline Metallifere, where sometimes you will hit on a village of charm or a colony of congenial compatriots to make up for the interminable driving up and down the tortuous mountain roads. Derelict farmhouses where everything is right (access, water, privacy, silence, sunset views, shelter from north winds, level walk to shops etc.) are impossible to find now (*introvabili*). Renovation enthusiasts are happy to make do with *rustici* in remote hamlets or awkward roadside situations, which are often mere hovels, particularly in the hills of Garfagnana and Lunigiana in the northwest and the Casentino in the northeast of the region. Ready developed units, on the other hand, sometimes whole hamlets (*borghi*), and up and running *agriturismos*, are for sale everywhere. Aristocratic villas and castles, with large estates, and monastic or ecclesiastical buildings, also come up for sale. Before you abandon the thought of retiring to Tuscany consider that a modest bolthole in a central location, a flat in a village, preferably with a garden, is all you might need.

Location	Type	Description	Price
Florence Centre, nr. Pitti Palace	One-bedroom flat	60sq m. Living room with fireplace.	€265,000
Lucca centre	Luxury apartment	120sq m in aristocratic *palazzo*. Fully restored. 2 bedrooms; 3 bathrooms.	€600,000
Pescia Hills (Pistoia)	Isolated two-storey house for conversion.	140sq m. 3 bedrooms, 1 bathroom. 9,000sq m of land.	€125,000

Agents for this region: annaredi@tin.it; www.brianfrench.com; www.casealsole.com; www.TuscanPropertySales.com; www.lunigianahouses.com; www.knightfrank.com; www.homesinitaly.co.uk.

UMBRIA

Capital: Perugia (205 metres above sea level)
Area sq km: 8,456; *Population:* 834,210 (density 99 per sq km)
Foreign visitors: 600,096; *Italian visitors:* 1,420,378
Regional website: www.regione.umbria.it
Climate: Temperatures: Summer 30C; Winter 0C; mean 11.8C.
  Average annual rainfall 796mm.
Airport: Perugia
Unesco world heritage sites: 2000 Assisi. The Basilica of San Francesco and other Franciscan Sites.
National park: Monti Sibillini

Umbria is in the middle of Italy, with no coastline, bordering with the Marches (Le Marche) to the northeast and east, Lazio to the south, and Tuscany to the west and northwest. It has the fourth lowest population of all the Italian regions. The density of the population is half the national average. It consists of 29% mountains and 71% hills, split by the Valley of the Tiber and the Valle Umbra. The river Tiber flows southwards through Umbria joined by various tributaries. Trasimeno on the Tuscan border is the fourth largest lake in Italy. Piediluco is another lake on the Lazio border. Umbria has seven nature reserves:

- **The Sibillini mountains**, shared with the Marches, whose slopes are dotted with watchtowers and castles, beautiful orchids, lilacs and fritillaries, and flowering meadows in the spring. There are rare gentians and huge beech forests. *The Gola dell'Infernaccio* is a spectacular canyon.
- **The park of Lake Trasimeno**. This includes the towns of Castiglione del Lago and Passignano, and three islands, one inhabited. Rich marsh vegetation, and wildlife, rare cormorants and raptors, survive here and the waters teem with carp, eel, tench, pike and perch.
- **Tiber River Park** (Parco fluviale del Tevere). In the south, this goes down to the hydroelectric dams of Corbara and Alviano, past Todi towards Orvieto, through the 'Forello' gorge into the Vallone della Pasquarella valley, linking up with an old droving trail.
- **Monte Cucco**, in the north east, is in the centre of the Umbra Valley, to which Assisi is the gateway; a mystical area associated with St Francis – Spello, Nocera Umbra and Gualdo Tadino are nearby towns.
- **Colfiorito Park**. An upland plateau east of Perugia with wetland flora and fauna and the ruins of a Roman city, *Plestia*.
- **The Nera river park (Valnerina)** to the east, with the reservoir of Piediluco, waterfalls, springs and gorges, and flourishing wildlife, including abundant trout and crayfish.

Umbria is an enclave of history preserved, a mystical home of saints and hermits. The gates of its medieval towns welcome pilgrims from everywhere. It is the most spiritual region of Italy.

Property

Large numbers of desirable derelict farmhouses, barns, convents, tobacco sheds and mills have been bought up and converted already by Anglophone buyers, ably assisted by efficient compatriot agents. The stock that remains belongs mostly to owners who are reluctant to relinquish their rising assets, leaving only the larger barracks and roadside properties on the market. The buildings are of similar architecture but generally more modest than Tuscan counterparts, and a large proportion is of monastic origin. Newly built suburban houses are worth considering; idyllic countryside is never far away, especially around Orvieto and Amelia. In the mostly hilltop towns such as Todi and Spoleto traffic congestion and parking has become a problem. Property developers and first wave buyers now offer ready converted units for easy buying, particularly in the Umbertide area, and the beautiful Niccone valley, which was one of the first to be colonised by foreigners. Tasteful rental properties are available in abundance, with a good English-speaking infrastructure. The Trasimeno area is popular – the lake is superb for sailing and water sports, there are Dutch and German colonies and an idyllic atmosphere, reflected in the price of the rare properties that come on the market there. Città di Castello in the north of Umbria is consolidating its appeal, as is Orvieto to the south, as a civilised livable city.

Location	Type	Description	Price
Spoleto (10km)	Modern country house	247sq m. Perfect condition. 3 bedrooms, study, garden and 6.5 hectares including 90 olives and small vineyard	€440,000
Near Perugia (S. Cristina)	Independent stone-built house.	180sq m. Well restored with 500 sq m garden + a hectare of woodland.	€340,000
Castello dell'Aquila, nr. Amelia (Terni)	Modern House in own grounds	Private drive and panoramic views. 2 bedrooms, 2 bathrooms	€210,000

Agents for this region: www.brianfrench.com; www.laportaverde.com; www.propertiesumbria.com; www.greenumbria.com; www.gabimm.it; www.casait.it; www.UmbriaPropertySales.com; www.homesinitaly.co.uk; www.welcomeservice.it.

LE MARCHE

Capital: Ancona (5 metres above sea level)
Area sq.km: 9,694; *Population:* 1,484,601 (density 153 per sq.km)
Foreign visitors: 362,468; *Italian visitors:* 1,668,796
Regional website: www.regione.marche.it
Climate: Temperatures: Summer 27C; Winter 1C.
             Average annual rainfall 1,157mm.
Airports: Ancona, Falconara
Unesco world heritage site: 1998 Historic Centre of Urbino
National park: Monti Sibillini: Gran Sasso-Monti della Laga

The region of the Marches in central Italy borders on Emilia-Romagna
and the Republic of San Marino to the North, Tuscany, Umbria and Lazio
to the west, Abruzzo to the south and the Adriatic Sea to the east. It is
68.8% hilly and 31.2% mountainous. Mount Vettore (2,476m), part of
the Sibillini range on the Umbrian border, is the highest mountain. It has
116 km of Adriatic coast. One sixth of the population is engaged in agriculture, particularly smallholdings. Craft businesses are also common.

Up-valley locations seem remote and landlocked. Socialising
expatriates get used to long drives on winding roads. But the coast
has excellent communications: The arterial Bologna – Taranto
autostrada relieves the flow on the shore road along the Adriatic. A
projected superstrada linking the Adriatic with the Tyrrhenian Sea
has reached the level of Urbino. Ancona has direct intercity rail links
with Bologna and Rome as well as an international airport.

The upland pastures and other inland rural areas – only eight hours
drive from Munich – are full of idyllic second homes belonging to
Germans. The British are also in evidence – a veritable colony now
– pioneered by refugees from Tuscany in the 1970s. But the secret came
out and property prices have gone up alarmingly in the last five years.

Property

You can find property bargains here, from hilltop castles to small apartments. Rural architecture is modest and unassuming: white stone farmhouses and cottages. The villages are attractive and interesting. Large

signorile 18th century town houses, which need a lot of work, are cheap. Similar places in the country are hard to find. You can buy an inexpensive apartment on the coast. A charming 2-bedroom flat with a balcony overlooking the sea on the sea-front at Senigallia (Ancona) will cost only €155,000. Property in rural areas is cheap, but access roads can be a problem. House-hunters in Le Marche are often disappointed by the low quality of the stock now on offer.

Location	Type	Description	Price
Marina di Montemarciano (Ancona)	One-floor modern house	Terrace with garden plus air con.	€85,000
San Severino Marche	Partly restored stone-built farmhouse	Two floors with 753 sq m of land.	€140,000
San Constanzo (Ascoli)	Renovated farmhouse	3000sq m. with 5000sq m of fenced land. 8 km to sea; 15km to yacht marina; 30km airport, 10km train station.	€420,000

Agents for this region: www.brianfrench.com; www.MarchePropertySales.com; www.mch.it; www.marcheshire.com; www.marchepropertyconsultancy.com; www.homesinitaly.co.uk.

CENTRAL ITALY (SOUTHERN)

LAZIO

Capital: Rome (35 metres above sea level)

Area sq.km: 17,207; *Population:* 5,145,805 (density 299 per sq.km)

Foreign visitors: 5,299,592; *Italian visitors:* 3,244,400

Regional website: www.regione.lazio.it

Climate: Temperatures: Summer 25.4C; Winter 11.8C; mean 18.1C.

Average annual rainfall 482mm; 142 days of rain per year.

Airports: Rome: Ciampino, Rome: Fiumicino

Unesco world heritage sites: 1999 Villa Adriana (Tivoli), 2001 Villa d'Este (Tivoli), 2004 Etruscan necropolises of Cerveteri and Tarquinia.

National parks: Abruzzo, Lazio and Molise, Circeo.

The region of Lazio is on the Tyrrhenian side of central Italy, bordering on Tuscany, Umbria and Le Marche to the north, Abruzzo and Molise to the east, and Campania to the south. It is 53.9% hilly, 29.1% mountainous, 20% plain and dominated by Italy's capital city and conurbation of Rome. It has five provinces: Rome, Viterbo, Rieti, Frosinone and Latina.

The coastal strip, north to south, is called the **Maremma** (a continuation of the Tuscan Maremma) as far as Tarquinia. After the interruption of the Tolfa hills (616m) and the Linaro promontory, near the seaport of Civitavecchia, the flatlands are called the Agro Romano – or the Roman Campagna – which is the site of Rome's international airport, Fiumicino at the mouth of the river Tiber. Southeast of this, near Latina, are the Pontine marshes, finally drained in the 1930s. The islands of Ponza, which belong to Lazio lie off the coast. Long stretches of the Lazio coastline are hideously disfigured by rampant 20th century building

Inland Lazio is hilly, the province of **Viterbo,** (known as Tuscia in recognition of its Etruscan origins) contains two volcanic mountain ranges, the Volsinian and Ciminian (1,053m), with huge craters, which hold Lake Bolsena and Lake Vico.

Northeast of Rome is the province of **Rieti** and the Sabine hills. The province of **Frosinone** east of Rome called Ciociaria, a rugged and hilly terrain with the Mainarde Alps (Monte Cairo 1,669m), in which the famous Abbey of Monte Cassino, rebuilt after its destruction in the war, stands sentinel. The province of **Latina** south east of Rome is partly reclaimed Pontine marshland, and partly mountains. Formia is an ancient seaport, originally Greek, with ferry services to the islands of Ponza and Santo Stefano.

Rome is above all the centre of the Italian communications network. It is the home not only of the government of Italy but also of the Vatican, a massive multinational, a state within a state. It therefore contains two sets of embassies from most nations in the world. It is a magnet for pilgrims and tourists, and crowded at all times of the year.

The centre of Rome is barred to traffic in certain areas, outside which, within the circle of the ring road (*il raccordo anulare*) is a nightmare of traffic jams, which are even worse than those of Paris. As a result, many Italians find Rome far too confusing for comfort and not 'livable' (*poco vivibile*).

Property

The humour and buzz of the street life attract foreigners to the centre of Rome, where apartments with roof terraces are prized investments. Papal dignitaries and aristocrats used to build their villas in the surrounding hills, places like Farnese, or Tivoli, once a favoured haven for English expatriates, but now engulfed by urban sprawl. The Alban Hills, to the south, around Frascati, are full of pleasant suburban homes amidst the vineyards and strawberry fields. The coast to the west, around Ladispoli, is badly degraded and now colonised by immigrants (20% of house-buyers there). Further south, the Circeo, Sperlonga, Gaeta are attractive areas with a wonderful climate, and a great range of houses for sale, from medieval to modern. But for peace and quiet, Romans themselves are heading for the hills inland, around Frosinone, or Rieti, where the Sabine Hills can supply foreigners with ruins to convert, and Italians with building plots, still cheaper than Tuscany although less than an hour from Rome. Lakes Bracciano and Bolsena, are Italian summer resorts, with empty tracts of Etruscan country in between, studded with venerable ancient towns like Tuscania and Vetralla. The sombre grey stone of the houses and the narrowness of the streets confer a melancholy air on places like Bomarzo, near Viterbo, which is a deterrent to foreign buyers.

Location	Type	Description	Price
Pisoniano, 57km east of Rome	18th century townhouse for restoration	200sq m plus 60sq m garden. Altitude 520 m.	€30,000
Cantalupo in Sabina (Sabine Hills)	New country villa	2-storey, ochre plastered. 3 bedrooms, 2 bathrooms, surrounded by a hectare of olive and fruit orchards. 8km from train station. 10km from autostrada.	€360,000
Sperlonga 50m from sea	Ground floor apartment	2 bedrooms. Small hedged garden.	€22,000

Agents for this region: www.dopropertysearch.co.uk; www.europropertynet.com; www.brianfrench.com.

ABRUZZO

Capital: L'Aquila (721 metres above sea level)
Area sq.km: 10,798; *Population:* 1,273,284 (density 118 per sq.km)
Foreign visitors: 189,254; *Italian visitors:* 1,154,796
Regional website: www.regione.abruzzo.it
Climate: Temperatures: Summer 25C; Winter 7C; mean 17.4C.
        Average annual rainfall 635mm; 128 days of rain per year.
Airport: Pescara
Unesco world heritage sites: Gran Sasso-Monti Della Laga, Abruzzo, Lazio &
    Molise, Majella.

Abruzzo, in the middle of the Italian peninsula, borders with Le Marche to the north (the river Tronto), Lazio to the west, Molise to the south (the river Trigno) and the Adriatic Sea, 129 km of coastline, to the east. It is 65.1% mountainous and 34.9% hilly, and one of the least populated regions in Italy. The peak of the Gran Sasso d'Italia massif (2,912m) is the highest in the Apennines. Of the four provinces, L'Aquila, inland, is completely mountainous, Chieti is hilly, whilst Pescara and Teramo are half hilly and half mountainous. A third of the whole region is protected by national or regional park or nature reserve status.

Winter sports have transformed many of the upland towns and villages, and there are 22 skiing resorts, mainly in l'Aquila province. The coastline is varied; broad sandy beaches and well-tended resorts, with night life, at Alba Adriatica and Pineto ('the pearl of the Abruzzo Riviera') give way further south to rockier small beaches.

San Giovanni in Venere is the site of an imposing Benedictine Abbey, where ancient fishing contraptions called *travocchi* are still in use. It is a recommended location for holidays or retirement – a few minutes from the lively seaport town of Pescara, from a golf and country club (at Miglianico), from beaches, ski resorts, autostradas, an international airport, and a direct rail link with Rome and Bologna.

Communications have been recently improved by the Pescara-Rome and the Teramo-Rome autostradas and the 10km tunnel under the Gran Sasso mountain, added to the Bologna-Bari coastal autostrada and the international airport at Pescara.

Property

The dream of an old-fashioned farmhouse in an old-fashioned Italy is still attainable in Abruzzo. All the *desiderata* are there: the old buildings, the olive groves, the vineyards, and, above all, the friendly, helpful neighbours. This is the region of Italy least corrupted by industry, developers, or the mafia. There is a large stock of ancient buildings, medieval hamlets and townhouses worthy of preservation: serious central Italian traditional masonry and fired clay, reminiscent of Tuscany and Umbria. Inland, an unrestored 3-bedroom farm or townhouse can cost less than €80,000 (add at least €100,000 for restoration). This price triples or quadruples as you near the coast or a large town. On the coast itself, habitable seaside villas, near Pescara, of the late 20th century can cost less than €200,000. **Agents for this region:** www.brianfrench.com; www.abruzzoproperties.com; www.homesinitaly.co.uk.

Location	Type	Description	Price
Roseto degli Abruzzi (Teramo) 4km from coast	Detached house in small village	270sq m. Fully modernised. Cellar, garage, 800sq m garden. View of sea and mountains	€440,000
Montepagano (Teramo)	15,000sq m agricultural land with ruined farmhouse.	Opportunity to build new house of 200 sq m, 4km from village. Superb views	€125,000
Loreto Aprutino (Pescara)	Country house in traditional architectural style.	350sq m. 4 bedrooms, 3 bathrooms, own grounds, panoramic views, cellar. Excellent finish	€250,000

MOLISE

Capital: Campobasso

Area sq.km: 4,438; *Population:* 321,047 (density 72 per sq.km)

Foreign visitors: 16,987; *Italian visitors:* 170,252

Regional website: www.regione.molise.it

Climate: Temperatures: Summer 26C; Winter 1C.

              Annual rainfall 628mm.

Airport: Pescara

National parks: Abruzzo, Lazio and Molise.

Molise is 55% mountainous, with a 38 km stretch of Adriatic coastline, bordering with Abruzzo to the north, Lazio to the west, Campania to the south and Puglia to the Southeast. The Apennines divide Molise into isolated mountains and a chaotic array of hills, which create a state of isolation and make communications difficult. There are several rivers, which are greatly affected by fluctuations in seasonal rainfall, heaviest in spring and autumn, longer lasting in winter, peaking in November and at its lowest in July. Inland the weather is extreme with up to 2,500mm annual rainfall. The coastal area is milder and drier. Agriculture is a major activity, often at subsistence levels. There is only one really industrialised area, near the port of Termoli; otherwise tourism and the coast are undeveloped. Ferries ply to the three Tremiti islands 25km offshore.

The Italian tourist board is urging people to visit Molise before it becomes fashionable. It has mountains with winter sports – and speleology – at Campitello Mates, but for many the most attractive area will be the benign foothills by the sea, the wide sandy dunes and the old droving trails (*tratturi*). These beaches are still wild – crowded in July and August – but delightful in the off-season.

Campobasso is the regional capital, with its historic purlieus and 15th century Montforte castle. Isernia is the second city and provincial capital high up between the rivers Carpino and Sordo.

Property

Molise is in an earthquake zone, which has deterred many prospective buyers. Indeed, many towns have been completely rebuilt several times. The prevailing architecture is now low-rise, antiseismic, reinforced concrete, often low on finish and upkeep. There are farmhouses on the plains, abandoned monasteries in the hills and castles hidden in the mountain forests, which cannot be found except by personal reconnaissance. This is the least discovered and one of the lowest populated Regions of Italy, like its neighbour Abruzzo in need of new pioneers. A good investment is a typical 3-4- room house for renting out in the university town of Isernia. Even better: a ruin or a building plot near the sea, surrounded by olive groves. The area between the medieval cathedral towns of Larino and Termoli is full of potential gems whose emigrant owners are often back home in July and August, who you must talk to in the company of a friendly *geometra*.

Agents for this region: www.casa.it; www.tecnocasa.it; www.casainrete.com.

Location	Type	Description	Price
Bojano (Campobasso) Central mountains.	New villa with fenced garden	High spec 250 sq.m, 3-storeys, 4 bedrooms, integral garage, covered pool, large garden. In need of renovation. Quiet location.	€400,000
Vinchiaturo (Campobasso) Central mountains.	Building plot with planning permission.	1,000 sq.m of land for 180 sq.m of dwelling.	€30,000
Petacciato (Campobasso) 5km from the sea.	New seaside apartment.	2 bedroom, terrace, sea view, integral parking.	€99,700

SARDINIA

SARDINIA

Capital: Cagliari (1 metre above sea level)

Area sq.km: 24,090; *Population:* 1,637,639 (density 68 per sq.km)

Foreign visitors: 556,150; *Italian visitors:* 1,341,023

Regional website: www.regione.sardegna.it

Climate: Temperatures: Summer 30C; Winter 6C.

            Average annual rainfall 585mm; 65 days of rain per year.

Airports: Cagliari (Elmas), Olbia (Costa Smeralda) and Alghero (Fertilia).

Unesco world heritage site: the Nuragic village of the Val di Noto

National Parks: La Maddalena/Asinara, Gennargentu e Golfo di Orosei

Sardinia is the second largest island in the Mediterranean after Sicily, 12 km from Corsica to the north, 120 km from Tuscany to the Northeast and 185 km from North Africa to the south. It has 1,849 km of coastline and very deep coastal waters, high rocky cliffs running straight for miles, often ending in promontories and surrounded by islands. Inland are ponds, marshes and extended barren hills. The northwest and northeast coastlines are jagged and impassable for long sections. The highest mountain, Gennargentu (1834m) is in the middle of the island and is part of the 40 km Marghine chain, which spreads towards the north. The valleys are deep and there is not much flat ground except for the great plain of Campidano, which extends across the south (the Gulf of Cagliari) for about 100km up to the Gulf of Oristano. Tracts of virgin forest have survived totalling one sixth of the whole surface of the island.

The climate is generally mild, influenced by the masses of air flowing from the Atlantic, Africa and the Arctic. The weather is fair – 300 days of bright sunshine in the year.

The Property Buyers' Perspective

At the moment Sardinia is regarded as a place to visit by the yacht-borne super rich who have a fabulous enclave on the Costa Smeralda in the Northeast. This development was the brainchild of the Aga Khan who has since sold out to a consortium. Private beaches accessible only from the sea, completely unpolluted water, a wild hinterland and an irresistible seafood cuisine, lure more than one million Italians to Sardinia every summer. A property anywhere near a beach or a village would be an extremely good investment – especially if you wanted to travel around in summer and let it out, and delightful to live in during the winter – bright sun and bracing winds – but above all, local people of great warmth and passion – a deep culture at the local folklore level, and also at the museum and archaeological level.

Drawbacks and myths. Sardinia is an earthquake-free zone, but there are drawbacks and myths to look out for:

- **Water shortages.** 1995-2000 were emergency years. Be ruthless in ensuring the adequacy of your water supply.
- **Radon gas.** The granite substrata provides favourable conditions for this cancer hazard. Make precautionary checks with a *geometra* (surveyor) if you are building or renovating.
- **Crime.** The Barbagia and the impenetrable Gennargentu mountains were the traditional haven for outlaws and shepherds, who could hide their kidnap victims for months in the pathless wilderness. Ostentatious displays of wealth can always attract criminal interest.
- **Political demonstrations.** The Sardinian Action Party (*Partito Sardo d'Azione*) strongly resent the extensive NATO presence on the island. Beware of volatile stand-offs, on this and other issues.

Property

The few ruins in desirable locations for conversion are expensive. A stone barn of 82 sq m set in three hectares of *macchia* overlooking the sea at Palau in the northeast will cost €340,000. A double building plot of 1100 sq m in the same situation will cost €80,000. But there are numerous developments, *villaggi turistici,* all round the coast, particularly in the Bosa area in the west, in which several agents offer small bungalows, often semi-detached, or apartments in condominiums with *mozzafiato* sea views, much cheaper and better than their equivalent on the mainland. Local stone and granite, and terracotta tiles are more used now in preference to the cement of yesteryear. The south, around the modern city of Cagliari is the least touristic area. Old apartments are to be found cheap in *centro storico* alleyways. Nuoro, in the middle of the island is the most typically Sardinian and folkloristic, whilst the Costa Smeralda in the northwest is the preserve of the very rich, with villas to match, as well as golf courses and marinas.

Location	Type	Description	Price
Villasimius (Cagliari) 5 minutes from beach.	2-storey villa	3 bedrooms, front garden, backyard barbecue, in condominium parkland.	€124,000
Sassari	New village bungalow	2 bedrooms, large living room, small garden. 5 minutes beach, 25 minutes Alghero airport.	€135,000
Costa Paradiso (north coast)	Semi-detached bungalow	3 double bedrooms, bathroom, living room with kitchenette and terrace. 500 sq.m garden. Sea view.	€220,000
Bosa	First floor flat	Habitable: 1 bedroom. Spacious terrace with sea view. Walk to bar, pizzeria and shops.	€46,000

Agents for this region: www.casealsole.com; www.casatravella.com; www. porto-cervo-realestate.com; www.fpdsavills.co.uk; www.homesinitaly.co.uk; www. brianfrench.com.

THE SOUTH AND SICILY

CAMPANIA

Capital: NAPLES (5 metres above sea level)
Area sq km: 13,595; *Population:* 5,725,098 (density 421 per sq km)
Foreign visitors: 1,775,399; *Italian visitors:* 2,777,419
Regional website: www.regione.campania.it
Climate: Temperatures: Summer 25.4C; Winter 7.9C; mean 18.1C
              Average annual rainfall 790mm.
Airports: Salerno airport and Naples – Capodichino airport.
Unesco world heritage sites: 1995 Historic Centre of Naples, 1997 18ᵗʰ Century
    Royal Palace at Caserta, the aqueduct of Vanvitelli and the San Leucio complex,
    1997 archaeological areas of Pompeii, Herculaneum and Torre Annunziata,
    1997 The Amalfi coast:1998 Cilento and Vallo di Diano National Park, the
    Archaeological sites of Paestum and Velia, the Charterhouse of Padula.
National parks: Vesuvio, Cilento and Valle di Diano

Lying on the Tyrrhenian Sea between the Bay of Gaeta and the Gulf of Policastro, Campania is a mainly maritime region with its capital, Naples, the hub of communication lines between the south and the centre of Italy. It borders Lazio to the northwest, Molise to the north, Puglia to the northeast and Basilicata to the south. It has the highest density of population in Italy.

To the south, the coastal plain of Sele is the most favoured area of the region, with its combination of beaches, climate, and unspoilt hill country. There are concentrations of factories around Naples, Sarno and Salerno, which have a pollution problem, as have the agglomerations of Pomigliano d'Arco, Casoria, Castellamare di Stabia, Pozzuoli, Torre Annunziata, San Giovanni a Taduccio, Nocera Inferiore, Pagani, and Battipaglia.

The islands of Capri and Ischia, and the resorts of Ravello, Amalfi, Positano and Sorrento are associated with many famous names. A rich, aristocratic, cosmopolitan society is very much alive in those idyllic locations – and owners are holding on to their treasured houses. It is easier to rent than to buy.

A huge black economy thrives in this region. Sweatshops of all kinds supply pedlars throughout Italy with their characteristic wares. Naples lives up to its reputation as a riot of illegal building, criminal activity, and noisy street life. *Scugnizzi,* the traditional street urchins, still dart around, and tourists are warned not to leave their cars unguarded for an instant.

Property

Houses with sea views are top of the buyer's list on the Amalfi coast. The market is enthusiastic and prices have nearly doubled in ten years. Apartment blocks along the coast are shoddily built. The coastal areas are overpopulated. This is one of the most spectacular and popular areas of the Mediterranean and it is still easy to find seaside bungalows and villas of great charm.

Agents for this region: www.unicasa-italy.co.uk; www.tecnocasa.it

Location	Type	Description	Price
Paestum – Licinella S. Venere Near seaside	Independent bungalow	3 bedrooms, bathroom, living room, kitchen, verandah. 400 sq m garden	€158,000
Baia Domizia (Bay of Gaeta)	Villa in excellent condition	2 storeys. 3 bedrooms, 2 bathrooms, garden, near the Sea	€158,000
Palinuro (Cilento coast)	Prestigious villa	12 rooms with 7 bathrooms, car park, store rooms, swimming pool and 8000sq m mature garden	€750,000

PUGLIA

Capital: Bari (1 metre above sea level)

Area sq.km: 19,362; *Population:* 4,023,957 (density 208 per sq.km)

Foreign visitors: 313,860 ; *Italian visitors;* 1,940,183

Regional website: www.regione.puglia.it

Climate: Temperatures: Summer 24.8C; Winter 8.2C; mean 19.7C.
           Average annual rainfall 438mm; 122 days of rain per year.

Airports: Bari: (Palese), Brindisi, Foggia.

Unesco world heritage sites: 1996 Castel Del Monte, 1996 The Trulli of Alberobello.

National park: Gargano.

The heel of Italy, Puglia is next to Campania and Basilicata (west) and Molise (northwest), with an Adriatic and an Ionian shoreline. It falls into five geographical regions from north to south:

The Gargano Promontory: very beautiful hills culminating in Monte Calvo (1,055m). Its seaports of Rodi Garganico, Peschici, Vieste, Pugnochiuso, Mattinata and Manfredonia are on the Adriatic.

Coastal lakes: Lesina and Varano.

The Tavoliere plain: (Foggia) between the Candelara and Ofante rivers, backed by the Capitanata Apennines which peak at the Monti della Daunia (1,152m). This is the largest plain in Italy after the Po Valley.

The Murge plateau: which slopes down to Bari and the coast.

The Salento peninsula: south of the seaport of Taranto, hills overlooking the Gulf of Taranto. Brindisi is a seaport on the Adriatic side. Otranto and Gallipoli are coastal towns on either side of Cape Leuca.

A characteristic of the Puglia countryside is its emptiness – the farm workers live in towns. Agriculture is very important despite a shortage of water, partly solved by government irrigation systems. A coastal *autostrada* motorway, from Rimini, ends at Taranto. Lecce, in the middle of the Salento peninsula is at the end of a railway line from Milan. Tourism is a major industry and there are cathedrals, churches galore and Lecce is a gem of exuberant baroque architecture.

The centre of old Bari, previously a no-go area of *microcriminalità* (petty crime), has been cleaned up and transformed into a chic nocturnal paradise, with sea-front bars and restaurants. The Tremiti islands north of the Gargano are considered the pearls of the Adriatic. In the summer packed with Italians, they are best visited in the off-season from Termoli in Molise (see *Molise*).

In 2006 you can still find a ruin to restore in the intensely romantic promontory conjured up by the title of Horace Walpole's gothick novel (*The Castle of Otranto*). In 2010 it will be too late.

Property

Best known are the *trulli*, in villages between Bari and Brindisi: conical stone huts with whitewashed walls. Each cone forms a living space of about 10 to 12 square metres. Clusters of three to five cones with about 5000 square metres of land are most in demand but these are not everyone's idea of a retirement dwelling. At Cisternino prices range from 100,000 euros, unrestored, to as much as 400,000 euros for fully restored property of this kind with a swimming pool. Seven out of ten customers renting – and wanting to buy – trulli are British, who love them so much that the area has been dubbed *Trullishire* by an Italian newspaper (not to mention *Salentoshire*). On a grander scale, the *masseria*, or typical fortified farmhouse of the region, is a very attractive purchase, but you are advised that it is three times cheaper to buy the land and build a fake masseria from scratch than to restore an old one. 18th and 19th century town houses with walled gardens, and apartments in the *Salento Baroque* style have a fascination, whilst the *centro storico* of Bari itself has become a cult area, where properties registered the highest price increase of all Italy in the second half of 2004, of 11.2 per cent. Carole Means and her husband moved to the comune of Ostuni, Puglia in 2000 just before it became the next big thing after Tuscany, Umbria and Le Marche:

> *When we moved here, I think we were the only ones. Then there were a couple of newspaper articles on the Trulli dwellings unique to Apulia, and the expat boom here took off in 2004. Then in 2005 there was the SIPPS fiasco when people thought they were going to be able to put foreign property into their pension pot; lots of people had already bought properties here before the government changed their mind. Someone suggested a figure of 1,000 expats living here. It's not quite like the Dordogne though, you can walk down the street without hearing any English spoken.*

There is a good range of restorable property available. But hurry while stocks last. Locals are still moving out of the towns to the suburbs, leaving the historic centres to northern romantics, epitomized by Dr Michael Cahn, whose excellent website www.pietreantiche.de enthusiastically promotes the philosophy of 'old stones' and offers some fascinating Salento properties (examples below). A reliable supply of water is the main priority.

Location	Type	Description	Price
Soleto	Town house in need of renovation	200 sq m. Magnificent 3-bedroom house with garden and a small ruin	€50,000
Lecce	19th century rustico (country house)	In need of renovation. Garage and 4 hectares of land	€375,000
Melandugno (Lecce) 5km from coast.	Masseria (fortified farmhouse)	250 sq m. Ruin with 50 hectares and planning consent for guest house	€540,000

Agents for this region: www.apuliabella.com; www.apulia.co.uk; www. italianproperty.tv; www.buyahouse-italy.com; www.casealsole.com; www. casaclick.it; www.oikos-immobiliare.it; www.trullinet.com; www.trullilerose. com; www.tecnocasa.it.

BASILICATA

Capital: Potenza (819 metres above sea level)

Area sq.km: 9,992; *Population:* 596,821 (density 60 per sq.km)

Foreign visitors: 48,526; *Italian visitors:* 342,603

Regional website: www.regione.basilicata.it

Average Climate: Temperatures: Summer 20.5C; Winter 0.8C.
                              Average annual rainfall 588.7mm.

Airport: Naples Capodichino

Unesco world heritage site: 1993 I Sassi di Matera.

National parks: Cilento and Vallo di Diano: Pollino.

Basilicata is situated between Calabria and Puglia (Apulia) at the foot of the Italian peninsula. It is 47% mountain, 45% hilly, and 8% plain. There are altitudes between 1,000m and 2,000m in the Vulture mountain range in the west, often topped by picturesque hill towns. Streams

Waterside houses, Burano Island, Venice

Trulli houses, Alberobello, Puglia

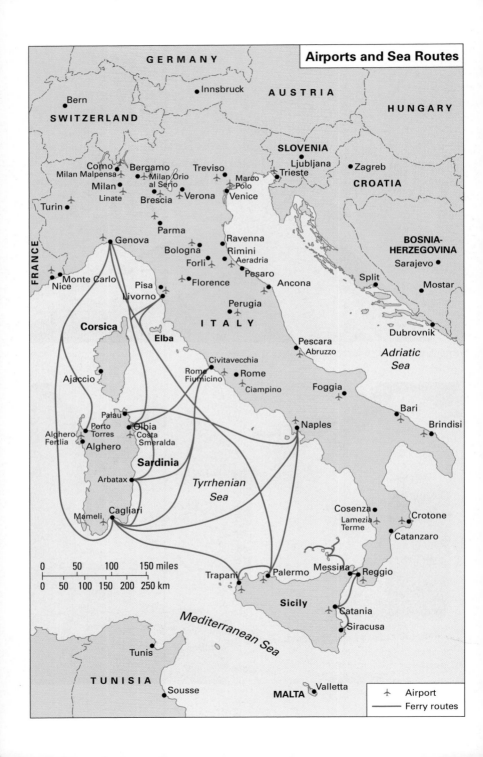

and rivers have worn deep gorges into the soft terrain, especially in the Matera district. The rivers are torrential in winter and dry in summer. The Murge landscape in the northeast of Matera is calcareous with dramatic canyons. In the southeast is a silted plain where rivers drain into the Ionian Sea with sandy beaches at Mataponto and Policoro (ancient Heraclea). In the west the mountains sweep steeply down to the gulf of Policastro and the narrow sandy beaches of Maratea.

The Pollino mountain range is in the southwest. In the Sirino mountains to the west, near Lagonegro, bothies, farmhouses, chapels and schools are to be found among forests at up to 1,000m. Ski resorts with brand new lifts and facilities and superlative views 15 km from the sea are icing on the cake. There are other ski resorts at Viggieno and Monte Volturino towards Potenza.

Earthquakes affect this region. Potenza was devastated in 1980. There is a NW-SW fault line in the Vulture Mountains, and a history of destruction and rebuilding over the centuries. Basilicata is one of the poorest regions in Italy. After massive emigration there are many more Lucanians living abroad than in Basilicata itself.

Mountains and hills predominate in Basilicata, but it also boasts two superb stretches of seaside. You have the choice between the flat and fertile plain of Metaponto on the Ionian, or the Romantic craggy beaches of Maratea on the Tyrrhenian coast.

Property

Rustici ruins and small building plots can be acquired on the coast near Maratea or Policastro for less than €50,000. Brand-new semidetached houses with garden near the beach are offered for €500,000 or less, older properties for half that amount. The magnificent rock dwellings, *I Sassi*, at Matera are enjoying a huge vogue, thanks largely to Mel Gibson's film about Christ, which was filmed there. Government grants of up to 50% are available for their restoration (Ufficio Sassi, Matera), and architects are plentiful. Prices start from about €1,700 per sq m. There is a choice of 14 estate agents in Matera.

Agents for this region: www.casaenotria.com; www.tuttocasamatera. com; www.casa.it

Location	Type	Description	Price
Policoro (Ionian Coast)	Semi detached house.	New semi detached 2- storey, 3 bedrooms (125 sq.m) with 225 sq m garden, 45 sq.m terrace, 25 sq m roof terrace.	€220,000.
Marina di Maratea , Tyrrhenian Coast	Semi-detached house	Brand-new, 130 sq m. 2 bedrooms, spacious terrace. 400 sq m garden .	€480,000 negotiable
Laurenzana at 1000m altitude. 30 minutes from Pollino National Park	Farmhouse 240 sq.m	Needs renovation. Is set in an orchard with an artesian well.	€80,000

CALABRIA

Capital: Catanzaro (15 metres above sea level)

Area sq.km: 15,080; *Population:* 2,007,392 (density 133 per sq.km)

Foreign visitors: 152,853; *Italian visitors:* 1,044,500

Regional website: www.regione.calabria.it

Average Climate: Temperatures: Summer 30C; Winter 6C.

Average annual rainfall 628mm.

Airports: Calabria: Reggio di Calabria and Lamezia Terme.

National parks: Pollino: Aspromonte.

Calabria is the toe of the Italian peninsula bordering Basilicata to the north and stretching between the Tyrrhenian Sea to the west and the Ionian Sea to the east in the direction of Sicily, from which it is divided by the Straits of Messina. It is 41.8% mountainous 49.2% hilly and 9% plain.

On the Tyrrhenian side is Lamezia Terme (Bay of St Eufemia) . A mountain range called Le Serre goes down to the toe, which is crowned by the mountains of Aspromonte (1,955m) in the lee of which Reggio di Calabria faces east over the Straits of Messina, and Locri faces the Ionian Sea to the east.

Flowing eastwards from the Sila range is the river Neto which drains into the Ionian Sea north of Crotone. This estuary is a valuable, luxuriant wetlands area. The Parco Nazionale della Calabria was set up in 1968 for the protection of this magnificent environment.

The whole area is now accessible thanks to the opening up of Lamezia Terme airport to cheap flights and the improvements in the Salerno-Reggio di Calabria autostrada. Above all, there are signs that a new generation of environmentally conscious youthful entrepreneurs is gradually replacing the traditionally corrupt and insensitive developer class of the past. But you have to get away from the big cities and the miles of hideous illegal semi-finished concrete structures which are typical of much of the *Mezzogiorno*.

The other side of the coin in Calabria is the crime. You will notice it in certain areas such as Reggio, where the *Mafia* meets the *'Ndrangheta*. Gioiatauro up the coast is a horrendous place shocking and sinister; no place for a good-natured, indolent individual who does not count his change.

Property

The whole of Calabria is an area of high seismic risk but buildings are constructed to strict anti-seismic norms. The stone built farm if it exists, is seen as an earthquake risk. The property on offer is in new developments, specifically geared to tourism. In the resort town of Tropea prices rose 50% between 2002 and 2005 to as much as €3,500 per square metre in the *centro storico*. The ideal investment is on the seaside, within striking distance of a big town, a modern apartment of two bedrooms with a shaded terrace. Ciro'Martina – at Torre Melisa in Crotone – came top of all Italy in a survey of profitability. A flat there can pay for itself in less than ten years, through July and August rentals alone. Summer bungalows and chalets in the mountains can still be found for less than €40,000. Few would consider this an all year round retirement spot as it gets too hot in summer and public facilities such as hospitals are not as good as in the north of Italy.

When Mel and Kate Holmes moved to Calabria in 2000, they seemed to be the only British neighbours the Calabrians had ever seen. Now Mel says there are 'half a dozen'. Mel explains what to expect:

> *You can get ruins for €10,000 to €15,000 but you spend as much again on renovations. For €22,000 to €30,000 you can get a studio apartment. Other property may not be as cheap. For instance you can't buy farmhouses here like you can in other parts of Italy because they still have farmers living in them. You can occasionally find country*

houses for sale, but these are expensive. We have a garden at our house in Villapiani but it is quite small, 250 sq m with fig, citrus fruit and olive trees. Apartments and houses in old towns are a possibility. You could buy one house to live in and buy a seaside apartment as an investment or for holiday rentals. As I hobby, I quite like helping people who are interested in buying in this area; I have a website: www.calabrianholidays.co.uk.

Location	Type	Description	Price
Tropea Centre	Restored apartment in 18th century building	140 sq m. 3 bedrooms, terrace with view	€650,000
Crotone	New chalet (Villette)	190 sq m. 2 bedrooms, 25sq m verandah, terrace and 140 sq m garden.	€82,500
Amantea (Cosenza). Outskirts	New furnished villa overlooking sea	3 floors, 5 bedrooms. 3 bathrooms. Balconies on the top floor.	€330,000

Agents for this region: www.bingocasa.it; www.tecnocasa.it; www.casa.it; www.homesinitaly.co.uk.

SICILY

Capital: Palermo (5 metres above sea level)

Area sq.km: 25,708; *Population:* 4,972,124 (density 193 per sq.km)

Foreign visitors: 1,533,6186; *Italian visitors:* 2,494,892

Regional Website: www.regione.sicilia.it

Climate: Temperatures: Summer 25.2C; Winter 11.8C; mean 22C.
          Average annual rainfall 433mm; 120 days of rain per year.

Airports: Palermo (Falcone Borsellino) and Catania (Fontanarossa)

Unesco world heritage sites: archaeological area of Agrigento, Villa Romana dei Casale, Isole Eolie (Aeolian Islands) and the eight Baroque towns of the Val di Noto (in south-eastern Sicily, brilliantly rebuilt after the earthquake of 1693).

Geographically, Sicily is a series of broken hilly country in the middle with bare peaks and forested slopes; a chain of mountains along the north and a volcano, Etna, south of Messina in the east in the Catanian plain. Etna is the highest point of the island at 3,650 metres and is still active. The coastal areas can be divided into three, each coast with a different character and climate:

The Northern Shore, from Messina west to Palermo and Trapani, is steep and rocky with deep waters, good harbours and excellent fishing. There is a small fertile plan called Conca d'Oro near Palermo and much forestland on the mountain slopes with dry riverbeds. The weather tends to be harsh, sometimes windy, but it is a healthy climate.

The Eastern Shore, from Messina, south to Syracuse and Cape Passero. The Catanian plain, the best agricultural land in Sicily, is sheltered by mountains to the north and southwest. The climate is agreeable and there are excellent harbours and a good beach.

The Southern Shore, the south coast, has shallow waters, shifting sands, lakes, lagoons and marshes with a sultry climate. There are good orchards, olive groves and some pastures on an inland plateau 100 metres up. The southern shore suffers the scirocco wind.

The interior is thinly populated and mountainous, deforested and eroded over the centuries with sulphur mines. Caltanissetta (538m) and Enna (931m) are the cities in the middle.

Taormina was always popular with the English, especially bachelors, and it is still very beautiful. Noto is pleasant and Syracuse is recommended. The Conca d'Oro near Palermo has stunning scenery. Sicily has 36 parks or nature reserves, including the Aeolian islands (Lipari, Vulcano, Salina, Panarea, Filicudi, Alicudi and Stromboli), which are very chic and highly sought after for romantic hideaways.

It is agreeable to live there from October until the end of May, but the summer months are hot and dry, when air-conditioning is called for.

Property

The island is architecturally rich: Roman, Byzantine, Islamic, Baroque, all these styles are to be found in the buildings of the island. Much of the coastline of Sicily has been defaced by rogue building, the destruction of beautiful areas like Bagheria (Palermo) and Selinunte (Agrigento) is a scandal. Most new houses have flat roofs and are badly constructed. Foreigners are wary of buying property because of the organised crime and links to the mafia. If you own an apartment or house, it is very likely that a man will ask you if you have fire insurance. You pay: you don't argue. Once you have understood this salient fact about Sicily, you can revel in her glorious folklore, climate, wildlife, food, history and people with equanimity; but make absolutely sure there is a water supply before you buy.

Be very careful to establish full, unencumbered title if you buy: properties in Sicily have often passed through generations without being reregistered. And do not expect any work to be done in a hurry. **Agent for this region:** www.brianfrench.com.

Location	Type	Description	Price
Syracuse	Suburban villa	180 sq.m in good condition. 2 storeys, 2 bedrooms, verandah, terrace, garage.	€230,000
Marina di Noto (Beach 500mt)	New villa	100 sq.m, 3 bedrooms, spacious verandahs, garages, private water and electricity, 6000 sq.m of olive and citrus groves.	€265,000
Noto Centre	Ground floor garden flat	3 bedrooms, in good condition, private entrance and garage.	€160,000

Your New Home in Italy

CHAPTER SUMMARY

○ Property purchase fees are usually around 10% of the purchase price but can be as much as 17%.

○ Land and property are considerably cheaper in most areas than in the UK.

○ Mortgages do not have an upper age limit but if you are over 65 you will have to take out life insurance cover. Mortgages run for five to twenty years and may be for up to 85% of the purchase price.

○ Italian property purchase is highly regulated and dealt with by a *notaio*, a legal official qualified in conveyancing.

○ Sometimes buyers are asked for a refundable, 'irrevocable proposal to buy' deposit, (usually a very small amount), but note that: the only deposit with legal validity is the *caparra*, which is normally 10%-30% of the final purchase price.

○ Under-declaration of the property purchase price is normal practice in property transactions in Italy as you pay less tax that way.

○ A *geometra* (the Italian equivalent of a surveyor) is essential to pilot house planning applications through the planning office of the local *comune*. For property purchase they are not essential but definitely advisable for older properties.

○ Before you find a place to buy in Italy, you should consider renting a home first as it reduces the possibility of a wrong choice of region or property type.

○ Many areas of southern Italy including Sicily and Sardinia have water shortages.

○ If possible have the contract checked for you by your own lawyer, especially if it is in Italian.

BUYING A PROPERTY

Overview Of The Property Market

Italy has long been a place for the discerning foreigner, where life contains a large dollop of culture as well as sunshine and café life. Luckily for foreign property buyers, Italians are cutting edge when it comes to taste and style and so they tend to prefer new homes, apartments and villas. Italians might restore a rustic property for holidays, but generally they do not compete with foreign buyers for old, derelict farm properties. Instead, Italians are buying for investment amongst the rental properties in tourist complexes in the mountains, the lakes and popular seaside places including Sardinia. Property investment of this type by Italians has tripled during the last couple of years. Despite this boom, property values overall in Italy are unlikely to rise meteorically, as they have in the UK. However the property market in most areas is showing increases in double figures year-on-year. The continuing availability of rustic properties of charm with land and outbuildings at reasonable prices in a stable Western European country, is a selling point for retirees, while location possibilities have been opened up via cheap flights from the UK, to include the length and breadth of Italy.

Estate Agents and Other Property Advisors

The Federation of Overseas Property Developers and Consultants – FOPDAC (3rd Floor, 95 Aldwych, London WC2B 4JF; ☎020-8941 5588; fax 020-8941 0202; www.fopdac.com; info@fopdac.com) is an association of English speaking estate agents, lawyers and other specialists in the property field who work with people looking to buy European property in a country other than their own – companies must meet very strict criteria for membership.It is a legal requirement that all estate agents, whether Italian or foreign, register with their local chamber of commerce.

Mark Slaviero from Homes in Italy says that the three main considerations are budget, location and the property itself. A well-organised visit with plenty of time for viewings will give positive results. Using an accredited estate agent is essential and UK based agents will be able to provide additional support in terms of translation and handholding. Prices are negotiable but don't make unrealistic offers, carry out some sort of survey before signing any official documentation and the more preparation that goes in at the outset, combined with the right support throughout the purchase will help you to locate and secure your property relatively easily.

The Italian association of real estate consultants is the *Associazione Italiana Consulenti e Gestori Immobiliari* (Via Nerino 5, 20123 Milan; ☎02-720 10974; fax 02-86452597; www.aici-italia.it) while the Federazione Italiana Agenti Immobiliari Professionali (FIAIP) represents over 20,000 estate agents and 7000 estate agencies and has dozens of regional branches. Respected agencies in Italy include *Gabetti* (www.gabetti.it), *Tecnocasa* (www.tecnocasa.it), www.casa.it and *Grimaldi* (www.grimaldi.net). These have regional affiliates throughout Italy, but most agencies are strictly local. Others can be found in property magazines such as. *Italy Magazine* (www.italymag.co.uk).

Estate Agents in the UK and Italy

Brian A. French and Associates: UK ☎0870-7301910; fax 0870-7301911; e-mail louise.talbot@brianfrench.com; www.brianfrench.com: Italian office: sales@brianfrench.com; ☎075-8299630, Mr. Steve Emmett). Areas include Tuscany, Umbria, Le Marche, Liguria, Abruzzo, Rome and Venice.

Casa Travella; ☎01322-660988; fax 01322-667206; www.casatravella.com; e-mail casatravella.com. Various areas in Italy including Sardinia and can help in relocation, restoration, etc.

Elma Homes: ☎01923-893764; e-mail flavio@caseasole.com; www.caseasole.com. Tuscany, Sardinia and Puglia. Comprehensive advice and assistance in buying, renovating, furnishing, translating etc.

Homes in Italy: ☎0845 2297057; fax 01332 204202; e-mail info@ homesinitaly.co.uk; www.homesinitaly.co.uk. Tuscany, Umbria, Le Marche, Abruzzo, Calabria, Piemonte, Liguria, Veneto, Italian Lakes and Sardinia.

Knight Frank: ☎020-7629 8171; info@knightfrank.com; www.knightfrank. com an international agency with associates in Tuscany and North America. Mainly Tuscany.

La Porta Verde: Villa Rosa, Madonna delle Grazie 77, Castello delle Forme, Perugia 06055; ☎+39 075 878 4296; e-mail Linda@laportaverde.com; www.laportaverde.com. La Porta Verde works in collaboration with over 70 estate agents throughout the region of Umbria, providing a huge choice of properties.

Piedmont Properties: Gerald Smith; ☎01344-624096; www.piedmont.co.uk; villas and vineyards in the Monteferrato and Langhe regions of Piedmont (around Asti and Alba).

Undiscovered Tuscany: Linda Travella, ☎01483-284011; fax 01483-285264. Started in 1987. Mainly Lake Como area and the lakes region and Liguria and Tuscany. Complete property purchasing service and long and short-term rentals.

Welcomeservice in Umbria: Via S. Maria 62, 06059 Todi (PG); ☎+39 339 6531677; e-mail info@welcomeservice.it; www.welcomeservice.it and www. italyrealestates.net. Specialise in the sale of villas, historic apartments and houses, farmhouses and investment properties, the rental of villas and historic homes and property management.

Useful Publications & Miscellaneous Contacts

Italy Assist: 26-28 Addison Road, Bromley, Kent BR2 9RR; e-mail italyassist@ email.com; www.italyassist.com. Can help with building renovation in Tuscany, Emilia Romagna, Marche and Umbria and will consider other areas of Italy. Contact Matthew Church.

Porta Portese: comes out in Rome on Tuesdays and Fridays and contains a useful accommodation section.

Ville & Casali: Edizioni Living International (ELI) SpA, Via Anton Giulio Bragaglia, 33-00123 Rome; ☎06-30884122; fax 06-30889944. Ville & Casali is a national property and decoration magazine in Italian, the classified property advertisements are listed in both Italian and English.

La Dolce Vita: important Italian property and lifestyle exhibition at Earls Court Exhibition Centre. Held annually in spring. Contact www.ladolcevitaevent.co.uk or contact the organizers Beat Ltd. ☎0207-307 0020; info@beatcapital.com, for details of dates and London venue.

WHAT TYPE OF PROPERTY?

About 78% of Italian families are owner-occupiers, one of the highest rates in Europe. However, rich Italians looking for a second or holiday home in their own country rarely go for the type of falling down property favoured by foreigners; on the whole they prefer new villas and well appointed apartments.

A high proportion of averagely well-off Italian families live in apartment blocks, many of which were built in the 1960s and 70s. Even when children move out of the parental apartment, usually to get married, they will voluntarily take a flat in the same block as their parents and continue to live as part of an extended family. Italian apartments are not very large and usually there are three bedrooms at most. However, this is not the case in Naples where there is a great deal of overcrowding resulting from poverty and an acute housing shortage. Many poorer families in Naples live in large, single-room apartments in the notorious slums (*i bassi*) of that city.

Unlike the old city centres in other European countries, Italy's town centres, usually the old part (*centro storico*), are still thriving residential districts with the residents living and working in the centre. The houses have been upgraded and improved and are popular with all ages of the community. Many buildings such as cinemas and inner city factories have been converted into luxury living accommodation as opposed to offices.

In Italy, the areas outside the centre are known as *il semicentro*, where most of the purpose-built apartment blocks are located. The suburbs (*la periferia*) are where the least well off generally live, although new housing estates with detached homes and gardens are appearing – Silvio Berlusconi made a fortune in some of the first such property developments in Italy (*Milano Due*).

TYPES OF PROPERTY – GLOSSARY

Appartamento	apartment
Agriturismo	bed and breakfast on a working farm
Annesso	outbuilding
Attico	attic
Baita	mountain refuge, bothy
Baracca	shack
Basso	hut, hovel
Bilocale	apartment with 2 rooms
Borgo, pl. *borghi*	hamlet, village
Box	garage
Casa	house or home, general term
Casa canonica	priest's house, usually next to a church
Casa bifamiliare	semi-detached house
Casa padronale	landlord's mansion
Casale	farmhouse or small hamlet

Casetta	small house
Castello	castle
Civile	standard building
Capanna	barn
Cascina	farmhouse
Casa Colonica	farmhouse
Casolare	house in the country
Dependance	outhouse (granny flat)
Fienile	hay barn
Fattoria	working farm
Fondo chiuso	fenced off holding
Monolocale	studio apartment (one room)
Masseria	huge farming estate in the south, fortified farmhouse
Mansarda	loft, loft conversion
Maso	farm in Alto-Adige region (ancient Celtic word for home)
Palazzina	small townhouse
Palazzo	used to refer to any large building including blocks of flats.
Porcilaia/porcile	pigsty
Podere	farm (small holding)
Rustico	rustic property, usually in need of modernisation
Rudere	ruin
Signorile	high standard, gentleman's residence
Stalla	stable, byre
Terratetto	semi-detached or terraced house
Torre	tower
Trilocale	three-room
Trullo	stone house with conical roof (regional, Puglia)
Villetta, Villino	small villa
Vilette a schiera	terraced house
Vigneto/Vigna	vineyard

The busy old towns and cities are the complete contrast to Italy's rural towns and villages. It is well over a century since the steady departure of families from the countryside towards the cities, or abroad, to escape rural poverty and hardship, depleted the rural population. The migrants left behind landscapes that became desolate in a picturesque way, dotted with farms succumbing to a crumbly fate. Until that is, the arrival of foreign enthusiasts following their own vision of a better life, transformed them into a more comfortable version of their former glory. The arrival of foreigners to buy and restore derelict properties for holidays or retirement, may be helping regenerate the countryside and preserve its buildings, but not rejuvenate it. In 2005, 72% of Italian communities had fewer than 5,000 inhabitants. Many of them have closed their schools as young people move to the cities taking the new life blood of the villages with them. In some areas, dying villages are being resuscitated by local authorities offering incentives for people to relocate back to them from the towns and cities. Technology is being brought to some of these places so that people can work from home using computers, while more facilities such as post offices and petrol garages are being installed to make life there more convenient.

Apartments

Modern Apartments. Most modern *appartamenti* are constructed using a reinforced concrete or steel frame, which is filled in with blocks. The majority of newer apartments were built in three decades from the 1950s. Buying apartments in city centres or by the coast is popular with foreigners. Internally, the walls are plastered and floors are tiled, often with marble. Some apartments come with fitted wardrobes in the bedrooms and there will be bathroom porcelain plus the kitchen sink. All other furnishings and appliances have to be bought by the new owner.

Old Apartments. Nineteenth century and older apartments tend to have high ceilings, which are beamed, and often the walls and ceilings are elaborately decorated. The flooring can be a range of materials including terracotta tiling and wood. Sometimes the tiles have been covered with marble. The stairs, sills and window frames are made of stone, marble or travertine (a light-coloured stone). Externally, the buildings are made of brick, often with peeling stucco. The problem with older buildings is that the fixtures, fittings, plumbing etc. may be old fashioned. However, this appeals to some buyers.

Rural Properties

Farmhouses (Casali). Farmhouses in rural settings are the most popular buy with foreigners. The typical rural farmhouse of 60 years ago or more had the living quarters on the first floor and the animals were stabled on the ground floor. It was usual to climb outside stone steps to the first floor and enter into a very large kitchen with a hooded fireplace where the cooking would be done. The hearth and fireplace were a very important focal point for the family as it provided heat, meals, and a place for them to gather and sit. The bedrooms would be off this main living room. One of the advantages of having the cattle stabled below was that the rising heat from their bodies kept the chill off the bedrooms above. A typical farmhouse also has very thick stone walls to keep cool in summer and the cold out in winter. In the north of Italy where temperatures drop much lower, double-glazing is essential these days. Typically, rural farmhouses had an outside bread/pizza oven (*forno a legna*).

Property buyers should note that such farmhouses are classified as rural buildings and need to be registered for change of use to 'urban' otherwise renovation is illegal. It is as well to consider the implications of this when deciding what type of property to buy.

Of course you can have a well thought out plan and determination to be immune to the tumbledown charms of impractical properties, and still end up with what Carole Oram and her partner describe as 'a compromise':

We started a wish list and then looked to see which items on it we could tick. We then thought about the pros and cons and tried to be practical and objective and not get swept away with the romance of it all. Realistically, this resulted in a compromise. We bought the only renovated part of a very old (500 years) farmhouse. The piles of stones around us are the remains of other buildings. It had been a rental house and was habitable with power, bottled gas, central-heating (which we can't afford to use) and we are still waiting for a telephone line after 10 months. I think it could best be described as a place that had previously been fixed quickly to make a fast buck. We have a raised meadow opposite where the swimming pool is and we have negotiated use of a patch of land for a vegetable garden. We loved the location, although most local visitors and our family and friends think we are totally mad. We don't regret anything so far and love our little casa with all its warts.

Writer Harris Freedman seems to have had a love at first sight experience when he first spotted the place he bought in Umbria:

I went into a realtor's and ended up seeing 50 properties in 30 days. On the penultimate day the realtor said to me 'There's this house I've got, it's not quite what you say you want, but the location is unbelievable.' I went to see it. The track was overgrown, the place was completely unkempt, it needed masses of work but as soon as I stepped out of the car I knew this was it. It was a farmhouse with a 360° view including two lakes, rolling hills and seven or eight towns in the distance. It was March 2001 when I went back to the UK to sell up there. When I came back to Italy in November 2001, I rented an apartment in Perugia (the capital of Umbria), for ten months while the house was being made habitable.

In planning matters the difference between a rural and an urban house is important:

A Rural Building. Farmhouses, pigsties, outbuildings and the land have no value separate from the land. The property will be registered with a plan showing the land and buildings available, but there will be no interior details.

An Urban Building. An urban house (or apartment) is registered with a plan of the interior that has all the internal measurements.

Change of Use. Any request for a change of use from agricultural to urban (i.e. to a dwelling for people), is made through a *geometra* (surveyor) who will provide detailed drawings of any proposed improvements e.g. to convert former stables into a kitchen or the *capanna* (outbuilding) into a flat for renting out. The *geometra* will obtain the permission from the *comune* and then register with *il nuovo castasto* (land registry) which will ratify the permission to change from rural to urban use. Renovations can only start after permission is obtained.

Village Houses. Buying an old house in the historic centre (*centro storico*) of a small town or village can mean acquiring an architecturally and historically interesting (and possibly listed) building. The downside of living in an ancient dwelling is that it will probably need major renovation work. A modern property needs far less attention and will only need basic redecorating. Modern floors of marble or travertine, or sometimes parquet are very easy to care for.

What you will get in an old village house is probably a built-in bread oven (*il forno*) or a fireplace (or both) and probably a storehouse as well. These attractive features are not usually part of modern houses. Note that in villages any new housing is likely to be social housing (*case popolari*) under law 167.

Living in a village house has more advantages than living in a remote one:

- It is connected to a mains sewer.
- It is connected to mains gas and electricity.
- It has a reliable water supply.
- It is close to public transport (buses and trains).
- The shops are close by.
- There is proximity to health care and schools.
- Access to staff for cleaning and gardening.

The disadvantages are relatively few. Some people might find a village noisy or object to the regular ringing of church bells. There could also be a large influx of tourists depending on where you are.

There is definitely a trend of buying houses in villages, especially amongst Americans who enjoy the social life and convenience of an Italian neighbourhood.

Estates and Vineyards (*Ville e Vigneti*). Very large estates created by the nobility are found in the country usually within 50km of a city. Villas of this type can date from the late Renaissance or the highly ornate and extravagant baroque period of the 17th and 18th centuries. A great many estates have vineyards and olive groves attached and still in production which could be useful as a way of helping to fund the costs of running such an estate. Estates are however likely to be a minority requirement for prospective retirees.

Ghost Towns (*Borghi Abbandonati*). Ghost towns, abandoned by the *contadini* (country people) seeking a better or less harsh life, are found mostly in the southern regions, or in the north at high altitude and a long way from a city. Comprising a cluster of buildings they can be an interesting proposition for a buyer who likes a challenge. Abandoned villages are the ultimate restoration project and can be turned into hotels or other living accommodation. In Liguria, a former ghost village, Colletta di Castellano, has been turned into Italy's first cyber village. It was purchased by a consortium that also arranged for Telecom Italia to sponsor a fibre optic link so that Colletta is a working village. The buildings have been transformed into modern apartments and the internet access for all means that those moving there can run a business from home if they wish. At the time of press an entire hilltop village on the edge of Peccioli (pop. 5,000) in Tuscany is for sale at auction (asking price 40 million pounds).

Castles and Monasteries (*Castelli e Conventi*). Castles and monasteries can be converted and restored into living accommodation for private individuals buying as a consortium. A group of 12 Canadians did just this, buying an abbey in Umbria. They arranged a restoration done to the highest standards and when not staying there, the members rent it out very successfully, thus recovering some part of the vast cost of the restoration. Some monasteries on the market come complete with frescos, cloisters and inevitably, a church or chapel within the main buildings. These properties are part of Italy's enormous architectural heritage and it can be very satisfying to bring them back to life. However, it might not be the ideal project for a retiree as it could take much effort and years to complete. Most retired people want to be free to do lots of different things with their time. Buying into a completed conversion might be a better option.

Golfing Estates. Historically, golf is not prevalent in Italy because Mussolini banned the game in the 1920s and 30s for ideological reasons, as an effete English pastime. However, it has gone from being effete to élite, and real estate colonies based on golf courses have begun to flourish, particularly in the North. Houses near golf courses are justifiably 50% dearer than other houses in the area, because of the high quality of the finish, the green-ness of the environment, the degree of security, and the compatibility of the residents. A list of the main Italian golf courses with developments:

Piedmont
Golf Club Villa Carolina (Alessandria)
Golf Feudo di Settime (Asti)
Golf Club Castelconturbia (Novara)
Circolo Gold Bogogno (Novara)

Lombardy
Croaro Country Club (Piacenza)
Golf Club Franciacorta (Brescia)
Golf Club Monticello (Como)

Veneto
Golf Club Jesolo (Venice)

Liguria
Golf Club Garlenda (Savona)
St Anna Golf Club (Genoa)
La Filanda Golf Club (Savona)

Emilia-Romagna
Golf Club Matilde di Canossa (Reggio Emilia)

Sardinia
Circolo Golf Is Molas (Cagliari)

New Houses And Villas

New houses may not have the charm or magic of older properties (or their crumbling walls and ancient plumbing), but they do have several advantages. Modern building standards ensure that new houses are very comfortable and built to a high specification. New houses are well insulated and double-glazed; central heating and air-conditioning are fitted as standard. New property is also covered by a ten-year guarantee (*responsibilità della ditta*), against any defects in the structure. Most services, such as the central heating system, are also guaranteed for a limited period. The types of new houses available are either part of a development, usually coastal or on the outskirts of cities or towns. Such properties are typically built and sold by property developers. There is normally a show house on site so you can get a good idea of what you are buying. The fittings are usually luxurious, especially bathrooms, and kitchens can be built to your specifications. Floors can be marble, ceramic of a high quality timber such as iroko (a pale hardwood from Africa). When completed they are ready to move into (*chiavi in mano*).

New need not mean brand new; Freddi and Vince Ferrigno settled for quite new and slightly neglected as Freddi explains:

We bought a modern villa with four bedrooms and a separate guesthouse. The villa is a few minutes from Brindisi, right on the coast between Casale and Apani. It cost about twice as much as we had planned to pay for a house, but as soon as we saw it, we knew it was the right one. The problem was that it had been empty and neglected for two years so we had to have quite a lot of refurbishing work done. There is a garden which goes all round the house with terraces on either side. Originally we had hoped for more land, but now we are happy with what we havet as we realise it is quite large enough to manage at our age.

Buying a Plot of Land for Building. Before you buy land you should make sure that there is planning permission for building, and check that the size of your intended building and the proposed design is legal. This is a job for a *geometra* (surveyor) who will check at the local town hall (*comune*). You may be thwarted by regulations governing scenic regions, which prohibit building. Plots are usually located in a zoned development area (*terreno edificabile*) on the outskirts of a town.

It is normally easier to look for a large parcel of land with a small stone building or ruin on it and apply for planning permission to change it into a residence.

Buying a House Under Construction. Buying a house under construction is halfway to building one to your own design as it gives you more choice than buying a brand new finished house. Most houses under construction are built from a template, but the buyer can usually select the interior décor from a range of colour schemes and fixtures.

Advantages of Buying Under Construction:
- You can adapt the house/flat to your own taste and needs.
- New houses are better built technologically, better insulated, more spacious etc. than older properties.
- No rebuilding required for years.
- By law (*la garanzia postuma decennale*) the builders' insurance guarantees to repair any faults for ten years after construction.

Disadvantages of Buying Under Construction:
- No guarantee of date of delivery.
- Advance payments are statistically much more at risk than in a private sale. The builder, for example, risks bankruptcy if he fails to sell a certain number of properties immediately.
- You have to be twice as cautious when you buy a house under construction than when you buy a built one.

Essential Enquiries When Buying Under Construction

Who owns the land? Another check to be made: in the unlikely event of a builder building on land he does not own – the house belongs to the owner of the land.

Who is the developer? Be careful not to confuse two or three different actors on the scene of a development: The first is the developer, or promoter of the scheme, who should own the land. The second is the building contractor. The third could be the agency that looks after the sale of the units. It is the developer who is by far the most important of these. He is the legal counterpart of the buyer. If his is a recently created company, perhaps an S.r.l. with a capital of €5,000 (the minimum is €10,000) it is better to tread carefully.

The contract and payments *(stadi di avanzamento).* Scrutinise the contract with great care. Look out for clauses to do with revising the prices, or that are vague about delivery times. Stage payments (*stadi di avanzamento*) should be as small and frequent as possible and linked with the progress of the work. Always withhold a percentage (at least 10%) for payment on transfer of title (*rogito*); not on hand over of keys.

SHARED OWNERSHIP

Condominiums

Most Italians live in apartment blocks in which each apartment is privately owned but certain facilities and structures are shared – such as the foundations, the roof, the bearing walls, the stairs, the entrance, drains, sewers, wells, corridors, terraces, courtyards, porter's lodge, boiler room, heating, car park etc. This is called a *condominio* (condominium) a social urbanistic phenomenon which spread greatly in the second half of the 20th century and had to be regulated by new sections in the Italian Civil Code (*Codice Civile* articles 1117-1139), and continues to be regulated by new precedents and judgments handed down by law courts throughout Italy.

Condominio is differentiated from *comunione*, which is a simple form of co-ownership whereby each owner has a share of a property in its totality. Comunione, co-ownership, was an established concept in Roman law, which described it as *mater controversiarum* (the mother of controversies). Condominio is a more virulent member of the same family – to judge by the litigation it generates in Italy.

The advantages of a *condominio* or *supercondominio* are:
- The organisation and infrastructure are supplied.
- Instant neighbours are on hand for socialising.
- The sharing of expenses and economies of scale mean proper car parks, tennis courts, swimming pools, fitness rooms, landscaping, staff etc. are available, which *could* be beyond your reach if you were on your own.
- Greater security against burglars – possibly.

The disadvantages are:
- Possible stress of constant negotiation/contact with fellow members.

○ The committee meetings, and the other duties required by condominium rules.

○ The rising expenses, which cannot be controlled if you are in a minority.

○ The difficulty of controlling the nuisance level of your neighbours or their tenants.

○ The future problem of selling on the property; condominiums often develop a culture or an ethos which buyers might find it difficult to buy into: too German, too English, too snobbish, too down market, too fussy, too lax etc.

The standard Italian block of flats, with normally friendly neighbours, is a straightforward proposition, in which you will know what to expect. But a *supercondominio* full of foreigners – or of your own countrymen – could hold surprises beyond your control. In general you will need to be a good committee person, with communication, accountancy and political skills if you want to succeed in a condominium. If you are of an independent spirit or devoid of the requisite skill, a condominium is not the right place for you.

Comunione

Caution is also called for when entering into co-ownership of a property – or *comunione*. If you are married and buying a property the notary registering the deed will want to know whether you are in joint ownership with your spouse (*in regime di comunione dei beni*) or separate (*...di separazione dei beni*). This is a distinction, which English common law does not make, unless you have made a pre-nuptial agreement. Italian law assumes you are *in comunione dei beni* with your spouse unless you state otherwise.

If you are friends sharing, make a written agreement covering yourselves against any conceivable eventuality. The pitfalls to guard against are:

○ Unequal sharing of the use of the property.

○ Unequal sharing of expenses.

○ Unequal recognition of works done.

○ Unequal sharing of rents.
○ The consequences of eventual marriage of a co-owner, bringing a new personality into the equation and a possible hostile take-over.
○ The consequences of an eventual divorce or bankruptcy of one of the co-owners, which might require the sell-out of a share; how do you evaluate this? Answer: You take the average of three independent valuations.

Buying in the Name of an Italian Company

To buy a company or to set up a new one is a complicated business which requires the services of a *commercialista*. To buy a property in the name of a company, the notary will tell you what documents are required.

Timeshare

Timesharing – *multi-proprietà* – whereby property is shared on the basis of the right to occupy it for designated times of the year has not caught on in Italy.

THE PURCHASING AND CONVEYANCING PROCEDURE

The Laws Governing the Sale of Real Estate

The sale of real estate in Italy (*La compravendita di un immobile*) is governed by the Civil Code articles 1754-1765 and also by laws (*leggi*) 39 of 3 February 1989 and 452 of 21 December 1990.It consists of two stages:

1. The *Compromesso*, the preliminary contract or *preliminare di vendita*, whereby the buyer pays a deposit known as a *caparra* on an agreed price on a specified property, the contract to be completed by a specified date. It can be a privately signed deed between the buyer and vendor, but it is recommended that it should be done with a notary, publicly registered, and regarded as seriously as a final contract. If the buyer fails to complete he forfeits his deposit. If the vendor pulls out of the contract he must pay back the buyer double his deposit.

2. *Il rogito* – the final contract and transfer of title, registered in the Land Registry office (*Ufficio del Registro* or *Catasto*) by the *notaio*.

Before signing anything, you should get the help of a lawyer or a notary. If neither your notary or lawyer speak English and you have no Italian, Mel Holmes, one of the first Brits to move to Calabria, explains what to do:

> *Use a legal proxy. This can be any professional person such as a teacher, doctor etc. We used an English teacher who is bilingual. We advise other Brits wanting to buy property in Italy to do this so that you have someone on your side who understands the documents they are signing.*

Who Does What

A *notaio* (public notary) who in Italy acts for both the vendor and the purchaser; deals with property transactions under a similar system to that which operates in other European countries such as France and Spain. There are also some lawyers (*avvocati*) who are not qualified to handle property transactions but who are expert in property legislation and can advise you about legal issues that may arise. Foreigners, who are generally not versed in Italian property buying procedures, may wish to appoint both a *notaio* and an *avvocato*. This way, an expatriate can have a competent professional who works for them directly, and who can explain the process to them fully and completely (unlike the notaio, who is the impartial administrator). Italian lawyers based in the UK can represent expatriates in Italy (see addresses below) when you are buying Italian property. Alternatively, your embassy or regional consular office should be able to supply a list of local lawyers who speak your language. The notaio is responsible for gathering together all the necessary documents, checking that the title deeds are in order, that the property is legally registered and that it has no illegal buildings on it. Having ascertained that this is the case, the next step is for the purchaser and vendor to sign a preliminary contract of sale.

You may also want to call on the services of a surveyor (*geometra*) to check the soundness of the building, point out any structural defects and estimate the cost of putting them right. Unlike in Britain, however, surveys are not compulsory and many Italïans do not bother with them. For foreigners buying older buildings, especially those in need of restoration, a survey is almost certainly essential to prevent post-sale surprises.

A geometra can draw up contracts, carry out land searches and also monitor building work and make orders to suppliers if restoration is needed once the sale is completed.

Fabio Ausenda, an Italian who has bought several properties, explains why he thinks using professionals is necessary when buying property in Italy:

A lawyer can verify that the property you are buying is free from rights by other neighbouring properties, for example, rights of way, right to use the waters etc. If you buy farmland, verify that no one else has acquired the right to use your property because they have already been using it for over 20 or 30 years ...in other words a lawyer can tell you aspects that the sale agent may not know and the vendor may hide, or be unaware of because he has never investigated these rights, or they may be written on the deeds but not that evident. The notaio should inform you when he reads the deeds, but if he does not speak English, or if the student interpreter you have taken along does not understand limitations on property these things may not come to light until later.

Lawyers

It is a matter of choice whether you use a locally based lawyer (as many house purchasers recommend) as they will have the best knowledge of the area where you are buying and the problems likely to arise with a particular property. Using a local lawyer has the advantage that it also helps you to make friends in the area where you will be living. If you use a non-local lawyer it might be inferred that you do not really trust Italian lawyers. You can find a lawyer by going to the largest town near your proposed property. You will probably need an interpreter; your house agent can perform this function, if you trust them.

There are also Italian lawyers based in the UK who can represent expatriates in Italy (see below), and English legal firms with specialist property lawyers for different countries (also see below).

Specialist Lawyers Based in the UK:

Bennett & Co: D144 Knutsford Road, Wilmslow, Cheshire, SK9 6JP; ☎01625-586937; www.bennett-and-co.com; international lawyers@Bennett-and-co.com.

Claudio del Giudice: Avvocato and Solicitor, Rivington House, 82 Great Eastern Street, London EC2A 3JF; ☎020 7613 2788; e-mail delgiudice@clara.co.uk; www.delgiudice.clara.net. Specialises in Italian property work and conveyancing.

Enlex Nigro & Partners: 35 Piccadilly, London W1J ODW; ☎ 0207-7347 282; www.nigrolex.it. Real estate in Italy and legal services.

Giambrone & Law: 9 Gunnery Terrace, Royal Arsenal, London SE18; ☎020-8301 8671; fax 0208-301 8149; www.giambronelaw.co.uk. Italian lawyers with expertise on property law of both the UK and Italy.

The International Property Law Centre: Unit 2, Waterside Park, Livingstone Road, Hessle, HU13 OEG; please contact Luca De Giorgi, Italian Avvocato, on ☎0870-800 4591 (e-mail lucadg@maxgold.com); or Stefano Lucatello, Italian Solicitor on ☎0870-800 4565 (e-mail Stefano@maxgold.com); fax 0870-800 4567; general e-mail internationalproperty@maxgold.com; www.internationalpropertylaw.com. Specialists in the purchase and sale of Italian property and businesses, wills and probate, and litigation.

James Bennett & Co: Nightingale House, Brighton Road, Crawley, West Sussex, RH10 6AE; ☎01293-544044; www.jamesbennett.co.uk; info@jbb-law.co.uk.

John Howell & Co: The Old Glassworks, 22 Endell Street, Covent Garden, London WC2H 9AD; ☎020-7420 0400; fax 020-7836 3626; e-mail info@europelaw.com; www.europelaw.com. Law firm specialising entirely in foreign property purchase.

LOCAL PROFESSIONALS

The key local professionals indispensable to the purchase of a property in Italy are the surveyor *(geometra)* and the notary *(notaio)*. The *geometra* performs the functions, which we associate with an architect, – making drawings and specifications, supervising work etc. Architects *(architetti)* also exist in Italy, and it is worth explaining the difference between an *architetto* and a *geometra*.

Comparison of Geometri and Architetti

A *geometra* does all the work we expect of an architect, up to a certain level. An *architetto* has a more prestigious title and operates on a higher plane both financially and artistically. A geometra qualifies by passing the requisite high school exam, and then, following another exam after two years of apprenticeship, he is fully fledged at twenty-two. But an architetto has to do a five-year university course and is usually 28 before qualifying. The result is that architetti know a lot about the artistic and theoretical but little about the practical side of building; they charge much more, seldom visit sites – and the *geometri* get most of the work. There is a state of mutual hostility between these two branches of the same profession. Architetti often exploit geometri and geometri are resentful of this.

The geometra is now a threatened species; the system is changing in Italy to conform with the rest of Europe: they will all become architetti. As it stands, you would only consult an architetto if you were involved in a large project or on a listed building, or if you were looking for an artistic modern treatment for the interior of an ancient building. Architetti are employed by the Fine Arts Commission (*la sovrintendenza delle Belle Arti*) of the Province, which is a sort of local style-police appointed by the Culture Ministry of Rome (*il Ministero dei Beni Culturali*).

THE GEOMETRA

An alert and vigilant geometra should pick up on any faults in a building, which might be used if possible to negotiate a lower price. But certain considerations which are important in the British Isles, such as rising damp, woodworm or rotten timbers, are taken for granted in unrestored properties in Italy, where the price is dictated by the broader picture – the rarity value or the location or the beauty of the environment.

The geometra is familiar with both the legal and technical aspects of land and buildings, and it is vital to have him check all the points listed below before you arrange for the legal side of your purchase, for which you will require the services of a notary or *notaio*, and more checks.

Checklist for the Geometra

So, at the normal domestic level of house buying you would employ a geometra for the purpose of inspections or surveys. A site visit is called a *sopralluogo*. A technical survey is called a *perizia*. A checklist for an apartment or town house should include the following points:

○ Architectural drawings? (*La planimetria*).
○ Floor space in square metres? (*i metri quadri*).
○ Type and number of rooms? (*tipologia e numero vani*).
○ Year of construction? (*anno di costruzione*).
○ Which floor? (*piano*).
○ Type of condominium (*tipo condominio*).
○ Lift? Elevator? (*ascensore*).
○ Porter/janitor? (*portineria*).
○ Utilities and services ok? (*impianti a norma*).
○ Garage? how big? (*box*).
○ Parking space? (*postauto*).
○ Cellar? how big? (*cantina*).
○ Store room? how big? (*ripostiglio*).
○ Balconies? how big? (*balconi*).
○ Terrace? how big? (*terrazzo*).
○ Doors and windows? in what state? (*infissi*).
○ Floors? in what state? (*pavimenti*).
○ Plumbing and bathrooms? in what state? (*sanitari*).
○ Leaks? (*infiltrazioni*).

A checklist for a country property should add the following points: Access roads? (*strade di accesso*). What are they like in winter? How much to repair and maintain? Whose responsibility? Normally they are *strade vicinali* neighbourhood roads, but don't count on the neighbours making a contribution to any repairs.

○ Electricity (see *ENEL* in *Utilities* section).
○ Water (*acquedotto)* (see *Utilities* section).
○ Gas (*gas metano*) (see *Utilities* section).
○ Cracks? (*crepe*).
○ Subsidence? (*assestamento*).

○ Roof? (*tetto*).
○ Rotten beams? (*travi marce*).
○ Rights of way? (*diritti di passo*).
○ Earthquake risks? (*rischio seismico*) (what architectural reinforcements are required by local building codes?).
○ Radon gas risks? (*rischio gas radon*) (this applies to the Dolomites and other granitic areas, Tufa areas might be at risk. Remedial architecture is available.)
○ Flooding risk? (*rischio allagamento*).
○ Landslide risk? (*rischio frana*).
○ If you are putting in a bore-hole for water (*pozzo artesiano*) or an in-ground swimming pool your *geometra* must obtain a *svincolo idrogeologico* or a hydrogeological clearance from the provincial authority.
○ Sewage (*fognatura*) Is it mains (*comunale*) or a private septic tank? (*fossa biologica*). Does it need repairs or replacement? Periodic emptying?

Buyer Must Do's

Do check appurtenances. In particular check that all appurtenances (*pertinenze*) are specified, such as cellars, attics, garages and sheds. Attach a *geometra's* drawing of the property to the contract, signed by both parties and specify such appurtenances in writing.

Do examine the utilities and services with the help of an expert. Water, gas, electricity, oil, boilers, pumps – (*impianti*). Yearly service contracts and guarantees should be obtained from the vendor. Details such as whether or not the gas pipelines arrive at the building can make a huge difference to the cost of heating bills. Remote areas may not be connected to DSL lines which may be crucial for those wanting to work from their nice Tuscan home, e.g. a web designer.

Do make an inventory (*elenco*) of all the items you and the vendor are agreed on for you to keep. Check that all rubbish and all the items you do not want are removed before the sale. Some unscrupulous owners remove all fittings, door handles, switches, radiators, boilers, etc. To avoid this, include them in the inventory. As an extra precaution, arrange with the owner for a final check-up on the day or the day before the final contract. The same argument applies to plants, shrubs, olive trees, tubs and planters etc., which you might or might not want to keep.

PRELAZIONE – THIRD PARTIES RIGHT TO BUY

Il diritto di prelazione – pre-emptive rights, designed to protect the small working farmer of yesteryear, are still available to people who are officially registered as *coltivatori diretti*, literally direct cultivators, who are *confinanti*, contiguous neighbours, giving them the right of first refusal on any non-urban land adjacent to their own. They are entitled to buy this at the declared price. Sitting tenants and individuals, who are conducting a business in the property also have a right to buy.

The state – or the *comune* or other state bodies also have the right to buy, or requisition in certain cases, for example, in the case of an archaeological find, and in the case of listed buildings in the *beni culturali* category.

To avert this threat you have to obtain a disclaimer (*rinuncia*) from any interested party. For this you need the co-operation of the vendor, or of your own professional, *geometra* or *avvocato*.

Do itemise restrictions and limitations on the property. Itemise all restrictions (*vincoli*) and limitations (*servitù*), rights of way (*diritti di passo*) and other burdens (*oneri*) on the property. Make the vendor responsible for any expenses required for eliminating any declared or undeclared restrictions.

Do check planning regulations. The validity of a property sale contract in Italy requires documents proving that any illegal improvements have been sanctioned. The local council (*comune*) can issue a document specifying all the permissions they have granted to the property, although not many councils are aware of this. The sanctioning of illegal work is called a *condono edilizio*. Building permission is: *concessione edilizia*.

Do check for imminent planning threats. If possible go with your *geometra* or an interpreter to the *Ufficio Tecnico* (planning office) of your local Council (*Comune*), which is normally open to the public two mornings a week.

The *ufficio tecnico* can provide you with copies of its plans, and the status of your target property, whether it is listed (*schedata*) and what the neighbours might be up to. The word *zoning* has entered the Italian language.

These researches are not automatically carried out in Italy, certainly not by lawyers or notaries. The key professional to commission for the task is the local *geometra* who will be familiar with the *comune* involved.

Buyer Beware

Beware of the Vendors. Establish first that the vendor(s) have the right identity, and that they own the property. Is the vendor of sound mind? Is he under age? Is there a spouse lurking in the background with a claim to the property? Is he bankrupt?

If he goes bankrupt within two years of selling the property, the property reverts to his estate, on which you will figure as one of the creditors.

If you buy from a company it is even more imperative to check – in the local chamber of commerce – whether the company is still registered or struck off, or encumbered with debt or insolvent (*fallito*). Bankruptcies (*fallimenti*) are common. You and your professional advisers have to be extremely vigilant.

Fraud (*Truffa*). Beware of con men (*imbroglioni*). A single property was once sold to three different buyers on the same day at different notaries. The first notary to register the property in the *catasto* yielded the only legal owner.

THE NOTARY

The *notaio* is a representative of the state whose duty it is to register all contracts, deeds, and titles in the appropriate registry office, and collect all appropriate taxes and duties on behalf of the state. Fees are negotiable and notaries compete for business. Many prefer to be paid in cash (*contanti*). Normally the agent (*mediatore*) will supply one. Not many notaries speak English – despite the high academic qualifications that are required for the job – so bring an interpreter if you don't speak Italian.

By law, the notary must be sure that you understand Italian, i.e. that you understand what you are signing in the contract. If he thinks you do not understand, a notarised translation of the contract must be supplied. The notary himself will arrange this for you at a cost.

Power of Attorney, Proxy (procura, delega)

If you require a power of attorney yourself, i.e. someone to sign for you, the two main requirements are that he should be (a) trustworthy and (b) understand what he is signing, i.e. an Italian speaker you know and trust.

The drawing up of a proxy document can be done at the *notaio's* office or in an Italian consulate anywhere. You need a valid passport or ID and if possible an Italian *codice fiscale* number. Powers of attorney in English can be translated and authenticated by the Consulate.

Documents you need for the Notary

- Passport or other valid ID.
- Italian civil code number (*codice fiscale*).
- If you have obtained an Italian residence you will also need a residence certificate (*certificato di residenza*) in order to avail yourself of certain tax reductions. Passport or other valid on a prima casa, the house where you are resident you pay only 4% taxes instead of 10% if it is not your primary residence.

THE CODICE FISCALE

Any contract or official transaction in Italy requires, along with your identification details, an Italian tax code number (*codice fiscale*) which is made up according to a formula of letters and numbers taken from your name, date of birth, birthplace and sex. Plastic *codice fiscale* cards are issued by your local comune or tax office (Ufficio delle Imposte Dirette). They can also be obtained through Italian consulates. Numbers can be worked out for you on the internet (www. codicefiscale.com).

Deposits

You may be asked to pay the estate agent a deposit for his so-called 'irrevocable proposal to buy' *proposta irrevocabile d'acquisto* or *prenotazione*. Make sure this deposit is minimal: 100 odd euros. The true deposit in the contract is called a *caparra*, which is governed by the civil code. It is normally 10% – 30% of the final price.

There are two kinds of *caparra*: *caparra confirmatoria* and *caparra penitenziale*. The *caparra penitenziale* allows for either party to withdraw from the deal on their own terms, jointly agreed, and the contract is not enforceable.

It is advisable to pay any deposits by banker's draft or non-transferable cheque (*assegno non trasferibile*) and to keep a photocopy of the cheque(s).

Full Declaration versus Under-declaration

Under-declaration of the price is common practice in Italian conveyancing deeds. The lowest you can get away with (*il minimo consigliabile*) is quantified at 100 times the figure given for the *rendita catastale* in the *certificato catastale* (the rateable value in the land registry document). Declare any less than this and you will attract the attention of the tax assessors, who have three years in which to re-assess your declared valuation.

The advantage of this practice is that you pay less tax on the sale. Before the abolition of Capital Gains Tax (INVIM) in 2002, the tax evaded was much greater. But the practice is still embedded, as part of the Italian way. Indeed you can consult with your notary as to the correct figure to declare as there could be risks, which may not become apparent until a later date.

The Compromesso

The *compromesso* or preliminary sale agreement outlines the conditions of purchase and any get-out clauses for the prospective purchaser, which may be applicable in some circumstances. These may include planning permission not being granted or failure of the purchaser's mortgage application. The compromesso also sets a date by which the transfer of property will be completed. Alternatives to the compromesso, the *Promessa d'Acquisto* (purchase proposal) or the *Promesso di Vendita* (promise of sale) are sometimes used.

Once one of the above documents has been authenticated, the purchaser then pays a *caparra* (see Deposits above), which is forfeit if either party reneges on the terms of the compromesso. The caparra is of course deductible from the purchase when the remainder of the money is paid.

The Rogito Notarile

The *Rogito* – or final contract – is the Big Day for which the compromesso has been a rehearsal. The time and date will have been booked well in advance. All you will need are your identity documents and the money (see *Housing Finance* chapter, *Transferring Money for Purchases*).

All parties have to be present, naturally, to sign the contract. The estate agent or *mediatore* will also probably be there (with his hand out) and it is advisable to have an interpreter to help you check all the details of the contract, which the notaio will read out, (unless you have previously arranged for an official English translation).

Ask the notaio to reassure you that he will file the contract in the Land Registry without delay – it is only then that the title officially changes hands. The Land Registry will then take about two months to furnish a certificate of your title.

TAXES AND FEES

Taxes and duties vary on a property sale but are lowest on a property that is a principal residence.

If the house is to be a principal residence and the vendor is a private individual (prima casa):

- Registry Tax – (*imposta del registro*) 3%
- Fixed mortgage tax – (*imposta ipotecaria fissa*) 129.11 euros
- Fixed Land Registry Tax – (*imposta catastale fissa*) 129.11 euros

If the property is a second house (seconda casa) the total tax is 10%:

○ Registry tax – 7%
○ Mortgage tax – 2%
○ Land Registry tax – 1%

The above taxes are levied on the value declared in the deed of sale. This value cannot be less than the rateable value (*valore catastale*), which is obtained by multiplying the *rendita catastale* by 100.

Typical Notary's Fee (*Onorario*); Depending on Property:	
Value of property	Fee
€50,000	€1,400
€250,000	€2,000
€300,000	€2,200
€500,000	€3,000

The fee increases by €100 for each additional €25,000 of value. This is the fee on the *rogito*. The fee on the compromesso is 50% of the above.

In addition the notary will charge for the following:

• Accessory rights (*diritti accessori*).
• Indemnities (*indennità*).
• Searches (*visure*).
• Authentications (*autenticazioni*).
• Expenses (*rimborso spese*).

It is essential to ask the notaio for an estimate of his charges at the very start. His fees may be fixed, but with all those extras he has plenty of room to negotiate. In a typical transaction the total notarial expenses will be between €1,500 and €,2000 for a *rogito notarile* depending on the cost of the property.

POST-COMPLETION FORMALITIES

It is the duty of the notary to file and register the transfer of title and pay all taxes due, with all possible speed. Within 48 hours the local police – the *carabinieri* in a comune – or the *questura* in a provincial capital – must be informed of the change of ownership. The notary can do this himself or supply you with the relevant form. You will also want to transfer the utilities into your name, (electricity, water, telephone, gas, etc.) and arrange for new contracts (*volturazione delle utenze*), for which a photocopy of your contract will be useful.

LAND REGISTRY (ACCATASTAMENTO)

The *catasto* is an official register, created for taxation purposes, which files details of ownership, boundaries, mortgages and rateable values. This register is divided into two parts:

- *Nuovo Catasto Terreni* (N.C.T.), New Land Registry.
- *Nuovo Catasto Edilizio Urbano* (new urban building registry).

The new system came into force on 1 January 2000 by presidential decree. Each census zone of the national territory is divided into 'microzones', and each property is classified in categories. Valuations are based on current market values, and revaluations are possible after any permanent 'socio-economical, environmental or urbanistic' change. The system, recently digitalised, is still in the throes of computerisation but searches via the internet are becoming the norm for accredited professionals and their associations. (www.visurmet.com).

REAL ESTATE GLOSSARY

Abitabilità	literally 'habitability' certificate issued by the Comune ensuring that ceiling heights, window, safety regulations etc. are complied with.
Agente immobiliare	Estate agent.
Acconto	Refundable deposit.
Bucalossi	A tax on renovation work named after the minister who introduced it in 1977 which is not refundable.
Buona fede	Good faith (ignorance of encroaching on another's right).

Caparra	non-refundable deposit – essential guarantee of a sale contract.
Catasto	Office of the Ministry of Finance which acts as a Land registry for updating land maps and plans of real estate.
Catasto certificato	Certificate giving land registry details, ownership, rateable value.
Catasto categorie	Buildings are classified by letter:- A. Dwellings B. Collective institutions such as barracks or schools C. Commercial buildings such as shops D. Industrial buildings E. Special buildings Under categories:- A1. de luxe, A2 civil, A3 economy, A4 popular, A5 ultrapopular, A6 rural, A7 small house, A8 villa, A9 historical building.
Centro storico	The ancient centre of a town or city. Often used as a reference point.
Clausola penale	Penalty clause specifying amount payable for defaulting party.
Compromesso	Preliminary sale contract.
Comuncazione di cessione di fabbricato	Document which must be presented within 48 hours of purchase or rental of a property, to the Comune or Carabinieri.
Comunione dei beni	Joint ownership in the case of a married couple.
Concessione edilizia	Planning permission from the comune essential for any building work.
Condómino	Owner of property in a condominium.
Condono edilizio	Amnesty, by payment, for legalising past illegal building work, essential for the validity of the sale contract.
Conduttore	Tenant of a rented property .(legal word)
Delega	Power of attorney.
Dichiarazione ici (see ici)	Declaration to the Comune for tax purposes to be made by June 30 of any acquisition of a property.
Diritto di abitazione	Right to live in a house – limited to a person or family. No sub-letting or sale allowed.
Diritto di uso	Right to use a property – mainly in an agricultural context, limited to the needs of a particular farmer or family.
Diritto di usufrutto	Right of usufruct – which does not exceed the life time of the beneficiary – but can be transferred.
Fallimento	Insolvency, bankruptcy.
ICI	Imposta Comunale Sugli Immobili. Council (Comune) tax on property, levied according to the Catasto value of the property.
Imposte	Registration
Ipoteca	Mortgage on a property.
Ipotecarie di registro e catastali	Taxes payable by the buyer at the moment of sale, according to the catasto value of the

	property.
Inquilino	Tenant of a rented property (normal word).
IRPEF	Imposta sui redditi delle persone fisiche; Income tax payable on the catasto value of the property – or on the rent, if rented, even if the rent is not collected.
Libero al rogito	'Free on completion' – meaning the property will be freed of its occupants on completion of the sale.
Locatario	Tenant of a rented property.
Locatore	Landlord contract for a property.
Locazione	Rental contract for a property
Mutuo	Long-term loan or mortgage.
Multiproprietà	Time sharing.
Ônere	Burden, limitation.
Percentuale	Percentage – commission.
Perizia	Technical survey.
Permuta	Exchange – or house-swapping – governed by articles 1552-1555 of the civil code.
Pertinenze	Appurtenances – such as garage, attic, cellar or outhouse – belonging to an apartment or house.
Piano regolatore	Development plan drawn up by the Comune for zoning the district into building, industrial, green etc. areas.
Procura	Power of attorney.
Preliminare di vendita	The same as compromesso or preliminary contract of sale.
Provvigione	Commission.
Rendita	Annual rateable value for a property established by the Ufficio tecnico erariale or Tax office.
Ristrutturazione	Renovation, rebuilding.
Rogito notarile	Notarial deed signifying the final contract.
Separazione dei beni	Separate ownership (of married couples).
Sopralluogo	Site visit.
Supercondominio	Complex of more than one building with shared facilities such as access road, car parking, garden etc.
Tabella millesimale	'Table of thousandths', showing the exact share of the expenses of a condominium for each member.
Trascrizione	The public registration of any real estate contract, governed by article 2643 of the civil code and lodged in the local land registry (Ufficio dei Registri Immobiliari).
Trattative	Negotiations.
Ute	Ufficio Tecnico Erariale – the tax office which gives a rateable value to real estate.
Valore catastale	Catasto value – obtained by multiplying by 100 for dwellings, by 50 for offices and by 34 for shops, the basis for the calculation of the sale and ICI taxes.

RENOVATING A PROPERTY

Hiring The Professionals

The Geometra. Once you have bought your property the key person for the initiation of any major building or renovation work is the *geometra* (surveyor). You need him/her to pilot your planning application (*il progetto*) through the planning office (*l'ufficio tecnico*) of your local borough council (*comune*). You probably already have a *geometra* involved in the purchase of the property who will oblige. With the *geometra* you now make an agreement with regard to their duties and fee. The duties will normally be to submit drawings and obtain planning permission (*la concessione edilizia*) from the *comune*, draw up a specification (*un capitolato*) of the work to be done and supervise its correct execution by site visits (*sopralluoghi*), coinciding with stage payments (*stadi di avanzamento*) every two or three months. For this the fee will be at least 6% of the value of the work done.

Renovation Costs. Between €1,000 and €2,500 per square metre.

Builder's Merchants (*fornitori edili*). The boss of the local establishment will be able to recommend not only a *geometra* but also a building firm (*un'impresa edile* headed by an *impresario*) – or, depending on the size of the project, a builder (*un muratore*). The same builders' merchant will be able to recommend all the other tradesmen you need. Ask him to set up an appointment with the impresario or the muratore, possibly in his own office to discuss the project. It is likely that you will also need a go-between – usually a resident expatriate who speaks your language – who is experienced in this kind of work and who will charge you for his/her time and expenses.

Builders and Craftsmen. Before you take on any building firm or tradesmen, ask to see their work. Each firm develops an individual style. The ideal style is a strict respect for the local vernacular. The more local craftsmen you employ the more likely you will be to achieve this. Make sure that there is at least one master veteran mason working on your project. Having satisfied yourself that you like their way of working, tell them so and convey your enthusiasm. By being on the spot yourself, you can encourage the workmen and your vigilance averts mistakes and corrects omissions.

Making a Plan

Before a brick is placed, you must have a master plan of your project that has been thought through so you *get it right first time*. To chop and change during the course of the work is demoralising and expensive. The best ideas occur as you go along? No they don't. Don't make any knee-jerk changes. Only do things you have thought about and slept on.

To make this master plan the geometra is crucial.

Local Tradesmen

Then come the decisions regarding the plumbing (*l'impianto elettrico*), heating (*il riscaldamento*), wiring (*l'impianto elettrico*) and the doors and windows (*infissi*). With all your ideas clear in your head you should make an appointment with the geometra and the impresario or *muratore* for a *sopralluogo* – a tour of the site. Ask the geometra to make a detailed diagram of these fixtures and fittings as a blueprint for the workers.

The Plumbing

The plumber's main job – connecting the water supply to the bath-rooms and kitchen and fitting the central heating – is different to what you might be used to in other countries as pumps take the place of gravity. The water arrives from the mains or your own well into a water tank in the basement or garage from whence it is pumped on demand by a pump under constant pressure (*l'autoclave*). The kitchen alone must have a direct supply of drinking water from the mains, in order to qualify for the certificate of habitability (*il certificato di abitabilità*). The disadvantage of this system is that it is entirely dependent on the electricity supply – no electricity, no water. The autoclave also breaks down or gets airlocked or clogged up once every three years on aver-age, which requires professional attention. A simpler, more foolproof, water supply system must exist, but this is the way they do it in Italy.

Heating

The standard heating system is gas (rarely oil-fueled) hot water pumped through radiators, placed under windows, or walls, in niches (*nicchie*). Aluminium radiators deliver instant heat, but cast iron ones are still manufactured and sometimes preferred for their heat retention and classic look. For buildings which are going to be used all winter under-floor heating is now found to be spectacularly economical.

Doors and Other Woodwork

In Italy the doors and windows (*infissi*) are tailor-made to fit the open-ings and not vice versa. The carpenter (*falegname)* will need to know the measurements of the empty spaces (*il vuoto*) he has to fill. It is better that he should measure these himself. So the *falegname* is a very impor-tant artisan for the aesthetically inclined renovator and you should count yourself lucky if you find a good one: He might also be able to make shelves, tables and furniture to order, effortlessly conforming to the local style which is so right for your house. The carpenter will deliver the *infissi* but he will prefer to leave it to the *muratore* (builder) to fit them.

Upkeep-free plasticised aluminium shutters – and windows – are increasingly replacing wooden ones.

Rates of Pay

The muratore's other skills will include tiling, paving, plastering and particularly bricklaying and masonry work. To help him he will have a labourer (*un manovale*). Specialists in all these skills are often called in. As a rough indication as to the going rate for these workers, in central Italy (cheaper in the South), a muratore gets €23 per hour and a manovale €21. Plastering (*intonaco civile*) – i.e. rendering and skim-ming with a lime-based plaster, excluding materials, is €14 per square metre, floor tiling is €18 per square metre, and wall tiling is €20.

The plumber and the electrician – normally quick, skilful and efficient – are not paid by the hour but will charge for the job. The standard minimum call out rate is €50.

Il Marmista

Another specialist in Italy who deserves special praise is the marble man (*il marmista*). Marble – travertine, dressed stone – is used extensively in Italian buildings for thresholds, worktops, sills, cladding, columns, paving, for shelves, tables and even sinks. Most large towns will have at least one marmista.

BUILDING WORKERS' OCCUPATIONS	
Costruttore	builder
Decoratore	interior decorator
Elettricista	electrician
Fabbro	locksmith or blacksmith
Falegname	carpenter
Ferramenta	hardwear shop owner
Idraulico	plumber
Imbianchino	painter (whitewasher)
Ingegnere	engineer
Intonachino	plasterer
Muratore	builder or mason
Pavimentista	floor tiler
Piastrellista	tiler

Notice of Building Work and Certificate of Habitability

Finally, before any work is done, and after you have obtained the work permit (*la concessione edilizia*) you are obliged by law to put up a notice – supplied by the *comune* – specifying the type of work and the professionals involved. If you are employing direct labour and working yourself it is called *in economia*, in economy. The type of work is described as renovation (*ristrutturazione*) or ordinary or extraordinary maintenance (*mantenuzione ordinaria* or *straordinaria*). The geometra or the muratore will put you right on this legal obligation.

The work done should always be checked for its conformity with the requirements of the local building regulations, the object being to obtain a *certificato di abitabilità*, 'a certificate of habitability'.

This certificate is the responsibility of the *geometra* in charge, who must certify the *impianti*, the electricity, the plumbing and the sewage, to prove that the house is habitable. Without this certificate you will not get an official licence for bed and breakfast or rental operations.

DIY AND BUILDING TOOLS

If you are keen on DIY it is not a good idea to meddle or interfere with the work of the builders while they are there. However well meaning, your attempts to help will usually hold back the work. But DIY activity can save money. A properly paid mason and his labourer cost over €300 a day so there is a huge saving if you can do the same work yourself. Tools and materials are cheap at your friendly builders' merchant. You will find there all you need: tile cutters, angle grinders, drills, trowels and floats.

It is no longer necessary to order sand and cement and have a cement mixer; dry mortar mixes are supplied by the bag – €7.20 for 40kg – which can be mixed in a bucket effortlessly if you invest in a purpose built electric mixer (*un mescolatore*). Weber & Broutin is the best of the several firms supplying the building trade with mortar mixes, etc. Their mortar (*malta* or *intonaco*) is tinted with ochre to reproduce the colour of traditional lime mortar. They also make an excellent macroporous synthetic mortar SANAMUR, which solves forever the problem of rising damp and damp walls by breathing out the moisture faster than it rises. So effective are these products that they should be specified by name in the geometra's *capitolato*. (www. weber-broutin.it). The amateur DIY person requires rudimentary plastering skills to apply these materials – cellars, outhouses, garages can be improved beyond all recognition, given that traditional Italian building came late to the principle of a damp proof course. Throughout Italy the ancient drama of rising damp and peeling stucco is giving way to pristine *intonaco* in muted limewash colours specially designed to tone in aesthetically with historic centres. This technology is extremely recent.

BUILDING GLOSSARY

Addolcitore	water softener	Intonachino	plasterer
Boiacca	slurry, grout	Isolamento	insulation
Brillante	gloss	Isolato	insulated
Cannella	tap, faucet	Lampada	lamp, bulb
Carta da parati	wallpaper	Lampadario	chandelier
Cavo	cable	Lavabile	washable (of
Cisterna	water tank		emulsion paint)
Coibentazione	insulation	Mazza	sledge hammer
Colla	glue	Mazzetta	club hammer
Colore	paint, colour	Mazzuolo	mallet
Colmo	ridge	Mestola	trowel
Coppo	round, Roman roof tile	Murali	rafters
Corrente	current (electric),	Muretto	low wall
	also rafter	Muro	wall
Depuratore	water purifier	Orcio	large oil jar
Forassite	electric tube/	Orto	vegetable garden
	conduit	Pacciamatura	mulch
Forcone	pitchfork	Pala	shovel
Fossa biologica	septic tank	Pannelli isolanti	insulation panels
Frattazza	plastering trowel/	Pannelli solari	solar heating
	float		panels
Gettata	poured concrete,	Paralume	lampshade
	reinforced concrete	Parapetto	wall
	for floors	Pavimento	floor
Giardino	garden	Pennello	paintbrush
Gomma	hose pipe	Piccone	pick
Gronda	eaves=	Pittura	paint
Grondaia	gutter, downpipe	Plafoniera	ceiling light
Imbianchino	painter	Pozzo	well
Imbiancare	to whitewash	Pozzo artesiano	bore hole
Imbiancatura	painting	Pratino	lawn
Imbrice	flat Roman roof tile	Presa	socket (electric)
Intercapedine	cavity wall, dry wall	Radiatore	radiator
	lining	Riscaldamento	central heating
Interruttore	switch	Rubinetto	tap
Intonacare	to plaster to render	Ruspa	bulldozer
Intonaco	render, plaster	Sabbia	sand

Sabbia fine	fine sand	Tegola	roof tile
Sabbione	coarse sand	Tegola di colmo	ridge tile
Satinato	satin finish	Tempera	wet paint
Scalpello	chisel	Termosifone	central heating
Scavatore	excavator (machine)		radiator
	digger	Tetto	roof
Scavatorino	mini-digger	Tinta	die, shade
Smalto	oil paint	Tinta unita	single colour
Soffitta	attic/loft	Traspirante	breathing,
Soffitto	ceiling		microporous
Solaio	attic floor	Trave	beam
Sottomisure	rough planks	Travicelli	rafters (small
Spina	plug (electric)		beams).
Spugna	sponge	Tubo	pipe
Stuccare	to point or grout	Valvola	valve, stopcock
Stucco	plaster	Vanga	digging spade
Tassello	plug (wall plug)	Velo	final skim coat of
Tavola	board, plank		plaster
Tavolone	big plank	Zappa	mattock, hoe

POOLS

Swimming pools are expensive to build and maintain, and they require constant attention. However if you wish to rent out a country property in Italy in June, July and August, they are indispensable. But planning permission is required, and might be refused. Before buying the property you should therefore check with your surveyor (*geometra*) or directly with the planning office (*ufficio tecnico*) of your local council (*comune*), to ascertain their rulings on the subject. Some councils have strict aesthetic and environmentally conscious restrictions relating to the shape and materials used.

You will choose according to your terrain, your pocket and your instincts but you must not forget to check on the obvious requirement: water. The geometra is required by law to furnish a 'hydro-geological clearance' (*svincolo idrogeologico*) with the local provincial authority before permission for a pool is granted. This safeguards against environmental damage.

As for the building of the pool, there are numerous specialists in this field in Italy, consult the swimming pool magazines such as *La Piscina* (published by di Baio editore) or *Piscine Oggi* for ideas and addresses.

Siting and Building a Swimming Pool

A decent sized pool 50ft x 16ft (15m x 5m) requires a flat area of at least 70ft x 36ft (20m x 10m), The ideal orientation is for a sun terrace or *plage* overlooking the water in the direction of the afternoon sun (south west); the pool, if rectangular, being aligned on a NE.SE axis. The plage should be at least 10ft wide (3m) to allow for sun beds and gangway. The arc from the NE to the NW should be screened off from the north winds (*maestrale* and *tramontana*) by windbreaks or hedges (see gardening). Deciduous trees near pools should be avoided; debris in the pool can be a nuisance. A raised pool surrounded by a low 18in (45cm) wall for sitting on can prevent this, and be advantageous for safety and comfort. A motorised roller cover is also recommended. A waterfall effect, a natural pond with a swimming area, fountain, a paddling pool, a pool-house – all these should be considered, as well as the options of solar heating and ozone filtration. Some permanent residents, especially arthritis sufferers, hanker after a heated indoor pool which can be used throughout the winter, perhaps with a counter current (*controcorrente*) swimming system. If you have a superfluous barn or building on your site consider this option.

Useful Websites

www.culligan.it – for water purifying installations.

www.gruppoazzurro.it – 24 pool and service companies throughout Italy.

www.assopiscine.it – 150 associated pool industry companies.

RENTING A PROPERTY

Why Rent?

If you are thinking of buying a property in Italy, renting reduces the possibility of making a wrong decision, which could mean years with a property you do not like. If you have not decided on a region, you could plan to rent properties over several months in the regions that appeal to you. The value of renting in your chosen region(s) is that you can find out first hand what they are like. It allows you to become familiar with the region, the amenities and most importantly, the local people. You can also check out following:

- Is the climate bearable in summer?
- Is the winter climate pleasant?
- What are the best locations, within the region, during winter?
- Which parts of the region are convenient for connections to roads and airports?
- How easy is it to get telecommunications connections?
- How far away is the coast/skiing area?

Many people who rent first in Italy, progress to wanting to buy an Italian place of their own. However, you might be one of the few who enjoy the renting experience and decide to rent permanently. That way you can retain your capital and if you rent out your own property in your home country, you could find that after paying your rent in Italy, you are still making money. Of course, some foreigners who rent permanently in Italy do so because they are expatriate workers who have their accommodation arranged for them as part of their job package.

Prospective buyers of Italian property usually have to make their own arrangements to find somewhere they can stay for the length of time it takes to explore a region and view the properties for sale there and ultimately choose the one they will buy. In Italy it is possible to rent every kind of property from a studio apartment (*monolocale*) to a large villa.

There are other possibilities for somewhere to stay depending on how long you wish to remain in one locality. For instance, some prospective purchasers might prefer to move around a particular region staying in hotels, hostels, *agriturismos* (working farms that take paying guests), colleges and religious guest houses, etc. or to travel around in their own motorhome.

Long-Term Rentals

A long-term rental is a rental for three months or longer. For this duration, it will be much cheaper to rent than to pay the weekly rates for vacation rentals. Typical prices might be €1,000 (£660) per month for

a furnished flat in Florence. Accommodation in a rural area of Tuscany might be €700 per month. Outside Tuscany and Umbria you should pay even less.

Rentals for longer than a year are usually unfurnished (*nonammobiliato*) and long-term furnished (*ammobiliato*) properties are difficult to find.

Italians sometimes prefer to rent to non-Italians because the strict rental laws in Italy mainly protect tenants rather than landlords. It is very difficult to evict Italian tenants, even if they have defaulted on rental payments. Non-Italians can be easier to deal with. However, this is not always the case as Belinda Scaburri found out when she first tried to rent an apartment with her Italian husband while they went house hunting in Le Marche:

Despite there being an enormous demand for rental properties, the laws are still such that landlords are not protected and are therefore nervous and reluctant to enter into rental agreements which, in many instances, end in the law courts. We imagined that we would appear the ideal tenants; in actual fact, we presented the very worst type of tenant risk. We were not employed, we 'claimed' to be looking for a house to buy and, being foreigners (my husband, being a northern Italian, constituted as much of a foreigner as myself), we could say we had nowhere to go should we decide to stay at the end of the tenancy. A combination of luck, timing and a telephone number spotted on an internet site meant that we did find ourselves a house to rent.

Short-Term Rentals

If you are looking for short-term rentals there is a great deal of choice. There are apartments, cottages, villas, chalets and even castles. However, as mentioned the best prices are out of season and if you want to rent for a couple of months this is the best option, especially if you are good at negotiating and come to an agreement with the owner/agent about the rent. Also, if you are renting in the off season, you should check out the property first to make sure that if you stay there during winter, the heating is adequate (i.e. there is central heating or a wood-burning stove with a local supply of wood).

Agents

Vacation rental agents offer long-term rentals based on a monthly rate that is cheaper in the off-season (i.e. November to March). It is worth contacting agencies to ask about this as a renting possibilty. You can find a list of vacation property agents and the properties they offer for rental on the internet.

Useful Contacts

www.brianfrench.com (Umbria/Le Marche)

www.housearounditaly.com (Abruzzo)

www.initaly.com (all regions)

www.laportaverde.com (Umbria)

www.smithgcb.demon.co.uk (Piedmont)

www.knowital.com (mainly Lucca, Tuscany)

www.casa.it

www.homesinitaly.co.uk

www.tuscanhome.com

www.welcomeservice.it

Dealing With Agents

If you decide to rent a farmhouse or a villa in a rural setting similar to the kind of property you hope to buy, and you arrange it through an agent, you will have to pay the agent a month's rent as a fee for his services, and if it is a long-term rental then you will be asked for 10% or 20% of the first year's rent. It is a good idea when the contract is drawn up to include a clause that will let you terminate the contract if anything unforeseen crops up.

Many tenants are asked to produce proof of income such as a bank statement to show that they are solvent. You will be asked to pay a deposit, which is refundable upon departure if the house is in good condition. You will also have to pay the utilities and other expenses, these include, gas, water, telephone, electricity and maintenance. It is also likely that you will have to pay a rubbish tax as well.

To-Let Adverts

Apart from following up *affittasi* (to let) signs posted outside apartments, the obvious place to look for advertisements in the classified sections headed *appartamenti da affittare* (flats to let), of main local papers. It is possible to contact the private Italian owners of properties to let direct. They advertise in 'local' papers like the daily Roman paper *Il Messaggero* and Milan's paper *Seconda Mano* which is published on Mondays and Thursdays, and supplements that come with property magazines. For other newspapers see the *Media* section of the chapter *Adapting to Your New Life*. Adverts in the city papers above are likely to be mainly for city rentals.

GLOSSARY OF RENTAL TERMS	
Affittasi	to let
Affitto	rental/lease
Canone mensile di locazione	monthly rent
Conduttore	tenant
Contratto	contract
Contratto di locazione	rental contract
Dare la disdetta	to give notice of termination of the contract.
Deposito cauzionale	deposit (against damage)
Inquilino	tenant
Locale	room
Locatario	tenant
Locatore	landlord
Locazione	rental
Mora	in arrears
Pattuizioni	stipulated agreements
Pianterreno	ground floor
Primo/ seconda/terzo/ quarto piano	1st/2nd/3rd/4th floor
Rata	instalment
Risarcimento danni	payment for damage
Riscaldamento	central heating
Servizi	kitchen and bathroom
Sublocare	sub-let
Unità immobiliare	a unit of property
Utenze	utilities, services

You can also consult the local expatriate communities' websites for long-term rental listings. For example The Grapevine (www. netemedia-net/grapevine) is the local network for northern Umbria.

For short-term rentals check out also adverts in the British newspapers including *The Sunday Times, The Sunday Telegraph* and *The Observer*, magazines and on internet sites. The internet has numerous sites covering every Italian region including www.italianbreaks.com, www. italianencounters.com and uliviera@hotmail.com (e-mail for Tuscan rustic apartments). The Italian Tourist Office (www.enit.it) and local tourist offices are other sources well supplied with contacts for short-term renting. Also check out the Italian publication *Casa per Casa* (www.casapercasa.it), a weekly free property magazine published in regional editions. The *English Yellow Pages* (www.englishyellowpages. it) is another useful source of adverts of properties to rent.

Tenancy Laws

Obtaining a tenancy agreement is usually easier if you are a non-resident, since anyone with *residenza* status is protected by state laws from being evicted (*sfrattato*). The length of rental contracts varies. When the landlord or landlady (*padrone/padrona*) wishes to have the property back, the tenant (*inquilino*) will be sent notice to quit.

Tenants' Responsibilities. If you sign a rental contract, make sure that you understand all the conditions. Tenants also have responsibilities, such as obtaining an annual certificate to confirm that the central heating boiler and gas heaters conform to European Union requirements. The tenant is liable for the cost of the certificate. Check with other expatriates as well as the landlord to find out exactly what is expected of you and what the landlord is responsible for as local conditions and rental contracts vary, as does the quality of the landlord.

Holiday Lettings and Furnished Lettings. The rental laws and protection for tenants do not apply to holiday or furnished rental properties. For holiday rentals, the client and the owner's agent agree terms regarding the deposit etc. and although this is normally a written agreement rental contract laws do not apply to it.

Insist that the owner provide an inventory of the contents, and check that all the appliances work, with the owner, before signing any agreement. Rent is usually paid monthly or by direct debit (*bonifico bancario*), cheque or cash. Most contracts require 6 months' notice in writing regarding termination. If the tenancy is less than a year, then three months' notice is adequate.

If you are renting a flat in a condominium (apartment building where all communal charges are paid by the members), you should have an agreement with the owner about who is going to pay the communal charges set out in the building's covenant (*regolamento).*

OTHER ACCOMMODATION

If you do not want to arrange a rental in one spot so that you are free to move around the region on your house hunt, the tourist accommodation options including hotels and guesthouses, agriturismo and religious guesthouses, may be useful. You will find further information on these under *Travelling in Italy* in the *Quality of Life Chapter.*

UTILITIES

It is important for anyone contemplating a move to Italy to ascertain whether or not their property is connected to the main services – water, electricity, gas, sewage and telephone. The further away the property is from the nearest telephone line or mains, the greater the cost of connection. Such costs can add considerably to the price of an Italian property and you should therefore expect to pay a lower price for property without services/utilities than would be asked for a property with them. Carole Oram explains the problems with her remote property in Umbria:

> *We needed a better source of water, so we had a new well sunk. We now have spring and well water. Electricity seems to be reliable. Bottled gas is extortionately priced and getting even more expensive. We have heard that there are grants for solar power and pellet burners. We had a wood-burning stove installed which also vents two additional rooms, which helps as the winter is very cold.*

Most houses and flats in towns are connected to mains services. Another important consideration when purchasing a rural property is

the provision of a well-made access road. Many roads to rural properties are at best a rocky path the majority of which are not suitable for
any vehicles other than four-wheel drive, tractors and diggers. A good
road is essential and if shared with other properties (*strada vicinale*)
it is a good idea to draw up an agreement about the upkeep and the
division of costs with the help of your *geometra* (surveyor) or through
direct consultation with the neighbours involved.

Electricity

The national electricity company *Ente Nazionale per l'Energia* commonly known as ENEL/Enel (www.enel.it) had the monopoly for supplying electricity before privatisation in 1998; even so there is still little
competition. Enel monitors your consumption of electricity every two
months and sends estimated bills (*bollette*): your bill is adjusted twice
a year when meters have been read. Bills show your account number
(*numero utente*), amount payable (*importo euro*) and due date (*scadenza*).
You can pay your bill at the bank, post office or the electricity board's
own offices but the easiest way to pay bills is by direct debit from your
bank. You can read your own meter and dial your meter reading (*gli
scatti*) or report breakdowns on telephone number 800 900 800.

   You can also find more information on services provided on the
website www.prontoenel.it. The cost of electricity in Italy is relatively
high. There is a standing charge (*quota fissa*) of €3,70 for every two
months and the consumption charge is based on the power rating of
the property, the maximum being 6KW. The charge per Kilowatt hour
(*scatto*) is €0.13 on a 6KW power rating. Changing your power rating
from 3KW to 6KW can be costly but probably worth it; otherwise you
can only run one large appliance at a time to prevent a fuse blowing.
Out of 22 million electrical service contracts in Italy 18 million are for
3KW, including most apartments.

Arranging a Contract with ENEL. After purchasing your property
and if the estate agent hasn't arranged for the electricity to be transferred to your name, you will have to sign a new contract (*volturazione delle utenze*) at the local ENEL office. You need to bring
identification with you either your passport or residence permit,

the registration number of the meter and the previous owner's paid electricity bill.

As part of safety regulations new electrical systems in your property are checked every year and a certificate of inspection is issued.

Resident and Non-Resident Tariff

Note: If you are supplied with electricity on a resident basis and the property is your main residence (*prima casa*) you get a reduction; non-residents pay a premium rate.

Remote Properties. The cost of providing electricity to a rural property can be prohibitive especially if the property is over 500 metres or more from an electricity pylon. It is possible to install a generator or solar power but this means weak current and not enough power to work washing machines, dishwashers, televisions etc. The diesel to run the generator can be costly. In the long run and for your own comfort and convenience, mains electricity is a priority.

Plugs. Most Italian plugs have two or three round pins so if you are bringing electrical appliances from another country you need to purchase plug adaptors. The two-pin plug has no earth wire so large appliances using a high wattage must be plugged into earthed sockets.

Fuses. When there is an overload in the electrical system, a circuit breaker is tripped. The fuse box is usually situated by an entrance. For this reason, it can be a good idea to keep a torch on or near the box. Before inspection and reconnecting one must make sure that all high power appliances are switched off.

Bulbs. All electric light bulbs in Italy are screw fitting. You can buy adaptors to change appliances such as lamps from bayonet to screw fittings.

Gas Tanks

Mains gas is widely available in northern Italy for central heating and cooking. Unfortunately the mains gas network does not penetrate the rural areas where many foreign residents buy homes. For inhabitants of these areas who need central heating, the solution is a gas tank known in Italian as a *bombolone*. Gas tanks can be loaned from the larger gas companies for example Agip gas, Shell gas, and Liquigas, and installation is governed by strict regulations. For obvious reasons, the tank should not be immediately adjacent to the house or road; it must be at least 25m away. The tank can be sited underground and pipes laid to connect it to the house. The contract with the gas company supplying liquid gas will stipulate a minimum annual purchase usually in the region of €1,300. The size of your tank depends on your needs.

Bottled Gas. Bottled gas (*bombola gas*) is commonly used in rural areas but can be used in towns and cities. It is mostly used for cooking though it can also be used for portable gas fires. There us a deposit to pay on the first bombola you buy; then you exchange your empty bottle for a full one. The bottles weigh 10 kg and 15 kg and a 10kg bottle costs €17, plus a delivery charge if necessary. A bottle used just for cooking will last an average family six weeks. The bottled gas is sometimes kept outside with a connecting pipe to the cooker. If you choose this method you must buy propane gas and not butane, as propane can withstand changes in temperature – butane is for internal use only. For those who do not wish to go to the bother or expense of arranging connection with mains gas, bottled gas is a useful alternative.

Water

The water supply is under the control of the local commune, eg CIGAF, and there are conditions governing the various uses of this precious commodity. There is usually plenty of water in the North of Italy but in central and southern parts there may be only a meagre supply. For this reason it is essential if you live in a rural area especially in the south to have a storage tank (*cassone*), which can be topped up when the water supply is on, or which can be filled by tanker, though the latter is expensive. For flat-dwellers in the main towns and cities a 500-litre tank may be sufficient. In remote rural areas it may be necessary to store several months' worth of water in huge underground tanks. Water shortages can be made worse whatever the region by the poor infrastructure; much water is lost because of old leaking mains water pipes. If water in your area is metered it may be rationed to a fixed number of litres per house, regardless of the number of occupants.

Recycling Water. Due to the shortage of water in some areas, there are restrictions on watering the garden and a ban on swimming pools. However, if you are clued-up and possess a little ingenuity there are solutions. It is possible to recycle water used for washing and bathing for the garden by draining it into a separate tank (*serbatoio*). You can also install a water purifier (*depuratore*) at great expense (approx €9,500). This is probably essential for a watering a large area such as lawns or orchards.

When is a Swimming Pool not a Swimming Pool? Answer, when it's a *vasca*. The way round the swimming pool ban is to build an artificial water basin (vasca) common in rural areas and ostensibly for domestic use when the mains water is cut off. The idea is that it fills up during the winter when rain is plentiful; it may also be fed by a spring or well. With a proper lining and some kind of filtering system to keep the water clean, a *vasca* could be used as a swimming pool, the less obviously the better.

Wells and Water Diviners. When you buy your house, it might state there is a well (*pozzo*) on your land. You should have confirmation by an expert, that there is plenty of water and that it is not likely to dry up. Also, make sure who owns the well and what your rights to use it are, e.g. that it cannot be stopped or indeed diverted or drained away by your neighbours. Having a well or natural water source can make your life easier. You may even wish to call in the services of a water-diviner (*rabdomante*) to detect where the water is and put markers down for future boreholes. You can take a water sample to be tested by the local water authority to make sure it's safe to drink. In general water is hard in Italy with a high calcium content. The water stains sinks and deposits settle in taps, kettles etc, which require cleaning with *anticalcare*. It is possible to install a water softener – this has many benefits and prevents furring of appliances and pipes.

Telephone Installation

The Italian telephone service (*Telecom Italia*) was privatised in 1997. In 1998 deregulation meant competition was introduced. To get a new telephone line (*nuovo impianto*) installed in your home you must first apply at the local Telecom Italia office; there, you can fill in the application form. You need to bring your passport (and a photocopy) for identification purposes. Note that if you live in a remote rural area the cost of a telephone line, especially if the nearest connection point is miles away is likely to be prohibitive and the waiting time can be a year. The cost of installation will appear on your first bill.

Carole Oram bought a remote property in a forest 7 km from the nearest village in June 2005 and 10 months later, she may be just about to get her landline installed:

We are having to wait ages for a landline telephone installation. This is because of the chaotic Italian systems. Before we completed the deal on the property we investigated the time needed to get a phone here and we were assured it was three months maximum. We had a series of missed dates and excuses and in desperation went to an Italian solicitor who got the Italian telecoms to start work. We know of Italians in nearby villages, who have had to wait a year. We have no idea how much it is going to cost as we have quotes ranging from €1,800 to €3,000.

Bills. Billing payments can be paid by direct debit from your bank. All calls are itemised on your bill.

Directories and Yellow Pages. If you have a private phone – you are given a copy of the local telephone directory (*elenco*) www.paginebianche.it and a copy of the Yellow Pages (*pagine gialle*) www.paginegialle.it annually. There is also an *English Yellow Pages* (EYP) which can be bought.

The EYP contains names, addresses, postcodes, telephone and fax numbers plus e-mail and website addresses. You can contact EYP, www.englishyellowpages.it. There is also the Into Italy information website (www.eypdaily.it).

Mobiles. The Italians have taken to mobiles (*cellulari* or *telefonini*) and the number of providers is growing as is the quality and coverage of the services. For more information *see Keeping in Touch* in the chapter, *Quality of Life*.

currencies **direct**

Foreign Exchange... How to get the most from your money

When you start to plan your retirement to Italy there are lots of things that you need to consider to make sure that your new life is a happy one. Currencies Direct explain how one of the most important things that you need to consider, and often one of the most overlooked, is foreign exchange.

If you're retiring to Italy you will no doubt have to change your hard earned money from sterling into euros. Whether it's to buy a new house or simply to transfer your savings to live off, foreign exchange can't be ignored. Unfortunately, no one can predict the exchange rate as many economic and political factors constantly affect the strength of the pound. Exchange rates are constantly moving and there is no guarantee that they will be in your favour when you need your money, so it is vital that you protect yourself against these movements. A lack of proper forward planning could potentially cost you thousands of pounds and reduce your spending power abroad.

For example, the affect the exchange rate can have on the cost of a new house can be seen if you look at what happened to the euro during 2005. Sterling against the euro was as high as 1.5124 and as low as 1.4086. This means that if you were buying a house worth €200,000 it could have cost you as little as £132,240 or as much as £141,984, a difference of almost £10,000.

However, it is possible to avoid this pitfall by buying and fixing a rate for your currency ahead of time through a **forward contract**. This is the *Buy now, Pay later* option and is ideal if you still have some time to wait before your money is due in Italy or if you are waiting for the proceeds from the sale of your UK property. Usually a small deposit will secure you a rate for anywhere up to 2 years in advance and by doing so you will have the security of having the currency you need at a guaranteed cost and knowing exactly how much money you are taking with you.

Another option available to you if you have time on your side is a **limit** order. This is used when you want to achieve a rate that is currently not available. You set the rate that you want and the market is then monitored. As soon as that rate is achieved the currency is purchased for you. You can also set a 'lower' level or 'stop' to protect yourself should the rate drastically fall. This is ideal for when you don't have to make an immediate payment and you have a specific budget available.

If however you need to act swiftly and your capital is readily available then it is most likely that you will use a **spot transaction**. This is the *Buy now, Pay now* option where you get the most competitive rate on the day.

It is however fair to admit that many of us do not have the time or sufficient knowledge of these options to be in a position to confidently gauge when the foreign currency rates are at their most favourable, and this is where a foreign exchange specialist can help. As an alternative to your bank, foreign exchange specialists are able to offer you extremely competitive exchange rates, no commission charges and lower transfer fees. This can mean considerable savings on your transfer when compared to using a bank.

It is also very easy to use a foreign exchange specialist. The first thing you will need to do is register with them as a client. This is usually very straightforward and requires you to complete a registration form and provide two forms of identification, usually a copy of your passport and a recent utility bill. Once you are registered you are then able to trade. Your dealer will talk you through the different options that are available to you and help you to decide which one is right for you depending on your timing, circumstances and foreign currency needs. Once you have decided which option is best for you and agreed a rate you will then need to send your money. With clearance times at each end some companies can complete the transfer for you in as little as a week.

Even once you have retired to Italy you may find yourself in the position where you need to regularly transfer funds from your UK bank account to Italy. This may be because you are still receiving a pension in the UK or perhaps you have decided to rent out your house until you settle and so are receiving rental income. If this is the case using a reputable foreign exchange specialist to do the transfers for you can make sure that you get more of your money each time, even on small amounts. This is because unlike your bank they will offer you competitive exchange rates on these smaller amounts plus they won't charge you commission and transfers are often free.

Currencies Direct is a leading commercial foreign exchange company; offering superior rates of exchange and a personalised service they meet the needs of thousands of private and corporate clients every year.

With offices in the UK, Spain, Australia, South Africa and India Currencies Direct is always on hand to help you. For more information about their services, please contact one of their dealers who will be happy to discuss your currency requirements with you.

UK Head Office: 0845 389 0906
Email: info@currenciesdirect.com
Web: www.currenciesdirect.com

Housing Finance

CHAPTER SUMMARY

- Mortgages in Italy typically were for 75% or less for a property ready for habitation. With competition between banks now rife, it is perfectly possible to get mortgages for 85% or even 90% and a rate of interest that compares favourably with UK rates.

- Re-mortgaging in the UK to pay for an Italian property is easier in some ways as building societies and banks lend cash more readily and mortgage rates are more stable in the UK than in Italy.

- It is advisable to become an Italian resident before you buy a property in Italy. Residents pay lower property costs on a primary residence and lower utility charges. There is no inheritance tax in Italy but capital gains will still have to be paid if the Italian property is not your primary residence.

- *Imposta Comunale sugli Immobili* (ICI) is the Italian equivalent of the Council Tax and is just as unpopular in Italy as here. It is however often cheaper, averaging about £1000 per year.

- According to an article in the *Sunday Times* of 5 February 2006, Britons lose out because British banks offer such a poor deal on foreign exchange. This can be remedied by using the services of an international currency exchange company such as Currencies Direct, which offers commercial exchange rates.

- Don't forget that if you are making payments to Italian companies you can send a postal order (vaglia postale).

- You can also open a Giro account in the UK and a post office account in Italy and transfer money from the UK to Italy for a fixed fee. Small amounts of cash can be sent in a registered letter.

AFFORDING THE MOVE

Using Your UK Home As Funding

Before departing for Italy, deciding what you are going to do with your UK home is a paramount consideration. The decision will vary depending on individual financial situations. Many people sell their UK home and use the funds to buy a property in Italy and provide enough additional funds to live on for their retirement there. Currently, the UK housing market is slowing down, which is not beneficial for anyone trying to sell up in the UK and retire abroad, as it may take you longer to sell your UK property than you expect. If this is the case, you should not sign any documents committing you to buy a property in Italy, unless you have exchanged contracts in the UK; this is assuming that your UK property is your only source of funding. While you are waiting for a buyer you could consider letting the UK property to fund renting in Italy while you look at Italian properties to buy. Property prices in Italy are rising by an average of 10% a year so it is unlikely that Italian property agents will try to persuade their clients to accept a lower sum for their property.

Below are some of the options for dealing with your UK home. Rather than sell outright, you can progress through some alternatives first before deciding what will suit you best in the long-term.

Deciding What to do With Your UK Home

- Sell it to have funds for purchasing an Italian property outright and fund your retirement in Italy with the excess. (If you sell it you will have nowhere to return to if things do not work out in Italy).
- Not sell it for the time being, but instead remortgage it to pay for an Italian property. (This could put your UK home at risk as it will be used as collateral if things go awry financially with your property in Italy).
- Rent it out to fund rental of an Italian property for your trial period.
- Rent it out to help fund a mortgage on Italian property.

○ Rent it out to cover its upkeep and maintenance costs while you decide whether or not to sell it or while you are trying to sell it.
○ Rent it out as a private landlord to avoid paying management fees.
○ Rent it out through a letting and property management agency. and pay fairly hefty charges for a full management service.
○ Leave it empty and arrange for someone you trust to keep a regular eye on it.
○ Employ a house sitter through an agency.

MORTGAGES

Italian Mortgages

A mortgage (*un mutuo)* is normally required to buy, build or renovate a property. In principle you borrow from a bank against the security of your property; if you default on your agreed repayments the bank repossesses the property. Most financial institutions tailor the mortgage and offer a personalised package including insurance cover. Different banks have different rules and possibilities. The smaller banks offer straightforward loans, and the insurance is up to you. Recent legislation in Italy has allowed any bank to issue mortgages, subject to strict rules against excessive usury to protect the consumer. Non-residents are treated with more caution than Italian residents.

There is an excellent Italian website dedicated to mortgages and loans for instant competitive quotations online: www.mutuionline. it. They have a stable of over 30 Italian banks (including the Banca Woolwich) to compare on their website. Recently, the bank coming up with the most competitive quotes was the *Monte dei Paschi di Siena,* for a ten-year mortgage with monthly repayments. The Dutch bank ING (www.ingdirect.it) have had great success offering services to Italians including online bank account Conto Arancio and their mortgage product Mutuo Arancio, which is very competitive.

Mutuionline offer a service in English, 'Mortgages for non-residents", which explains everything to you in clear English, and offers you a free quote. You will note in the small print that they do not offer mortgages for *rustic* properties. Outside Mutuionline other important lending institutions are: www.unicreditbank.it, www.bancaintesa.it, www.deutschebank.it, and www.gabetti.it. In order to consider your mortgage the bank will require the following documentation, which it will photocopy:

- The preliminary sale documents, the *compromesso* or *preliminare di vendita,* between you and the vendor of the property in question, or a land registry proof of your title.
- Your passport.
- Your Italian fiscal code number, *codice fiscale.*
- Your most recent tax returns (at least three).
- Your most recent bank statements (at least three months).
- Any other documents proving your income.

The bank will also require documentation on the property itself, which only your surveyor, *geometra,* can supply:

- *La provenienza del bene* – the provenance of the property.
- *Il certificato storico ventennale* – a 20-year retrospective certification of the property.

Non-residents may find it difficult to obtain a mortgage to buy a dilapidated or isolated rural property, but easier to buy it first and then obtain a mortgage for renovation.

The bank will normally require at least four weeks to process your application. The next step is to get the mortgage registered officially with a notary (*notaio*) who will require you and the representative of the bank to sign a deed in his presence, which he will then register against the title of the property in the local Land Registry, *L'ufficio del Registro.* You must set up the appointment with the notary well in advance, if necessary giving a power of attorney to a third party to sign on your behalf *una delega* or *procura speciale.* You, not the bank, have to pay the notary's fees, which are at the notary's discretion.

WHAT KIND OF MORTGAGE?

Fixed rate	– if you want to be sure of the exact amounts and the end total, in advance, and if you foresee growing inflation.
Variable rate	– if you foresee a drop in inflation, have a medium to high income and like taking risks.
Mixed rate (renegotiable every 24 months)	– if you are unsure of the present state of the economy and want to have the option of adapting to more advantageous conditions in the future.
Capped rate	– if you want to keep to a flexible rate whilst limiting the risks, and at the same time retain the guarantee of a fixed rate without the extra costs.
Balanced rate	– if you have a feel for market movements and like to manipulate the balance between fixed and variable rates.
Interest only	– if you expect to be able to pay off the capital sporadically and can keep up with the monthly interest payments.

Banks sometimes offer cheap promotional introductory rates for a brief initial period (3-6 months).

Useful Contacts

Casa Travella: ☎01322-660988; www.casatravella.com. A property agent that may be able to give assistance with obtaining mortgages with some banks, for instance *Banca Popolare di Sondrio* in Como, or *Banca di Toscana* depending on the region and the branches.

Conti Financial Services: 204 Church Road, Hove, E Sussex BN3 2DJ; ☎0800-018 2811; fax 01273-321269; www.mortgageoverseas.com. Conti have many years of experience arranging finance for clients (both UK and non-UK nationals) purchasing properties overseas as independent mortgage brokers.

Mortgage Tax

A single tax called an *imposta sostitutiva* of 0.25% is levied by the notary on the delivery of the mortgage. It is so called because it is a substitute for the previous stamp duties and VAT taxes in force.

Tax Concessions on Mortgages

Interest payments on a mortgage for the purchase of a first home are deductible from the IRE tax (see below). The deduction is at the rate of 19% on a maximum sum of 3,615 euros, subject to certain conditions, and only if the property has become your principal residence within one year of purchase. There are also tax concessions on the expenses of renovation.

An Italian Versus a UK Mortgage

There are two possibilities: one is to remortgage your UK property, the other is to take out a mortgage with an Italian bank using an Italian property as security. UK-based banks will not lend money on foreign properties; Italian branches of UK banks operating in this field, as well as one or two specialised UK lenders will. All banks and mortgage providers, even those with a British name, are registered in Italy. They all operate under Italian banking regulations and only offer euro mortgages.

Re-mortgaging in the UK is easier in some ways: banks lend cash more readily than in Italy, but you could end up putting your UK home at risk in order to buy property in Italy. Interest rates are more stable in the UK than in Italy, and likely to remain lower. The Italian mortgage interest rate is generally about 1.4% higher than the European Interbank Rate, which was about 2.2% in 2005. Some mortgage lenders can offer a rate as low as 3.27% on a 70% mortgage. On the other hand, the charges involved with setting up an Italian mortgage (*un mutuo*) are high and have to be paid up-front. Lower interest rates, however, make the Italian mortgage more attractive at the end of the day.

Mortgage Providers & Broker

Banca Woolwich: ☎ 02-58 488309; www.bancawoolwich.it.

Conti Financial Services: ☎ 01273-772811; www.mortgageoverseas.com.

Istituto Monte dei Paschi di Siena: www.mps.it

Micos Banca: www.micosbanca.it. Specialist house mortgage bank

Unicredit Banca per la casa: ☎ 02-8545651; www.bancaperlacasa.it

PROPERTY TAXES

The majority of those buying a house in Italy will have only two taxes to pay: the ICI and the IRE, for which you are well advised to consult a local accountant or *commercialista*. A commercialista is a qualified professional registered in the local *Albo dei Dottori Commercialisti* who will take care of all your taxes, for a fee. It is impossible to navigate the labyrinth of Italian taxes without the help of a *commercialista*.

The ICI is the *Imposta Comunale sugli Immobili*, or property tax, which is levied by the local borough council *comune*, and calculated according to its own criteria within minimum and maximum limits imposed by the state, and in proportion to the *valore catastale* or rateable value of the property. It is payable in two instalments – normally at the post office – in June and December. When you buy your property you or your commercialista must report it to the comune in a *dichiarazione* ICI. It is an unpopular tax which seems cheap to foreigners, averaging about €1,000 per year per property, with a reduced rate for primary residences and a 50% reduction on uninhabitable properties. Unfortunately, if you miss the payment due date, you are automatically fined, as Freddi and Vince Ferrigno, Brindisi residents since 2003, found out the hard way. Freddi explains:

> *We are just beginning to find our way around the council bills and other bureaucracy. To begin with, it was a nightmare. If you don't pay your local property tax on time you get a fine of 60%! The taxes are quite high, about €800 property tax and the* spazzatura *(rubbish tax) is about €600 a year. The rubbish isn't collected from the house; you have to take it to the rubbish collection point.*

The IRE tax is the *Imposta sul Reddito*, literally income tax, levied at between 23% and 43% at the time of writing. Whether you are resident or non-resident, your property is regarded by the state as having a *rendita catastale*, literally a land registry (notional) income, which is taxable, even though it is yielding no actual rent. IRE is also levied on earned income, which may apply to retired people depending on their financial arrangements.

All habitable property must be registered in the urban building register, *catasto edilizio urbano*, which gives it a rateable value. IRE is payable in two instalments, June and November, the form required for it is: *modello di pagamento unificato* F.24. For more see details of IRE see the *Tax* section in the chapter *Personal Finance*. Both ICI and IRE are payable on-line. The IRE is under the control of the Revenue Ministry, *Ministero delle Entrate*, who have as enforcement officers not only the Tax Police, *Guardia di Finanza*, but also the *carabinieri*.

Taxes Due on the Purchase and Registry of Property. Registration Tax *L'imposta del registro* of 3% of the purchase price of the property. Note that it is 7% if the property is a second home or the buyer is not resident in the municipality where the property is located which is often the case with a foreign purchaser.

For registering the preliminary contract of sale (optional) i.e. the *compromesso* or *contratto preliminare di compravendita*: €129,11; which is deductible from 0.5% levied on the deposit money or *caparra confirmatoria* – subject to minor variations.

For registering the property on completion of the sale: principal residence €129,11 otherwise 1% of the declared value.

VAT on Property Bought from a Builder or Cooperative. If you buy a property from a builder or a Cooperative Housing Association you have to pay:

1. 4% VAT if the property is going to be the buyer's main residence and he/she is resident in the same municipality where the property is located; or if the buyer is going to obtain residence in that municipality within 18 months of the date of purchase.
2. 10% VAT in all other cases (e.g. second home; if the buyer is not resident in the municipality where the property is located as is often the case with foreign purchasers).

Removal of Inheritance and Capital Gains Taxes

What you lose on the swings you gain on the roundabouts: the Berlusconi government 'suppressed' the capital gains tax, (the old INVIM), abolished the inheritance and gift tax, and there is no such thing as a wealth tax. One object of these cuts was to attract capital back to Italy, but there is no cause for rejoicing. Residents of Italy will still pay tax on their worldwide income (including investment income). IRE tax will still regard the profit on the property as income, and tax (*plusvalenza*) will have to be paid on the profit if it is not the primary residence.

MONEY TRANSFERS

There will be situations where you need to send money to someone in Italy or vice versa; or you might need to transfer money within Italy. Telegraphic Transfer, via Western Union or American Express is the most expensive way, but may be unavoidable if you want to send money to the USA. The most usual system between banks is SWIFT, which takes a day or two, and costs from €25 upwards. A more cost-effective method is to open a post office account in Italy (www.poste. it/en/bancoposta/tr) and a Girobank account in the UK. Transfers between post offices take three to 10 days, and there is only a fixed charge to pay however much money you transfer. The least effective way of transferring money is to send a cheque drawn on a foreign bank account; it could take a month to clear and the charges will be very high. For small amounts it would be simpler to send cash with an International Registered Letter.

There is another possibility for making payments to Italian companies, which is to use a postal order (*vaglia postale*), obtainable in a post office. You pay a small charge in addition to the actual amount and up to 120 written words is allowed. There is also the online postal order (*vaglia online*) and an international money order (*vaglia internazionale*). To transfer large sums, i.e. for your house purchase, the best method is to use a specialised company see *Importing Currency For House Purchase* below.

Importing Currency for House Purchase

When buying property in Italy, you will, under normal circumstances have to pay in euros. Thanks to the Single Market, you can take as much cash as you like with you, but there is no advantage in doing so, and it is certainly risky. If you take more than €8,000 in cash with you into Italy you are required to declare it. Taking a large amount of cash is not only risky; you could be suspected of being a drug dealer, or a terrorist by the Italian Customs if they find out.

Currency is nowadays normally sent using electronic transfer; the SWIFT system is the best known. There are charges involved at both ends so you need to know who is paying for them, and how much the receiving bank in Italy is likely to charge. The receiving bank should charge very little. The use of bank drafts is not recommended as they are far too slow, and there is the risk of losing the draft. If you are transferring to an Italian bank, it is useful to know the IBAN (International Banking Number). The IBAN system, is gradually becoming standard all over the EU.

Since the UK is not part of Euroland, anyone buying property abroad is confronted with the painful possibility that a percentage of their money is going to disappear into the pockets of a high street bank. Fortunately, this need not be the case, since a number of specialist foreign exchange companies have now started up to lessen the pain of the transaction.

A specialised foreign exchange company such as Currencies Direct (www.currenciesdirect.com; tel 0845-389 0906) and others that advertise in magazines about foreign property, can help by offering better exchange rates than banks, not charging commission, and giving you the possibility of utilising a number of specialist buying tools including: 'forward buying' – fixing the rate that you will pay up to two years in advance – and 'limit orders' – waiting until the rate you want is reached. For those who prefer to know exactly how much money they have available for their property purchase, forward buying is the best solution, since you no longer have to worry about the movement of the pound against the euro working to your detriment. Payments can be made in one lump sum or on a regular basis. It is usual when building new property to pay in instalments.

INSURANCE

Italy has a bad reputation for petty crime – burglary, pick-pocketing and theft. However, this is much worse in the cities than in country areas and villagers often leave their homes unlocked. However, isolated farmhouses etc. are particularly vulnerable. The rates of crime detection are appalling – less than 10% of burglaries are solved. As a result, insurance premiums are high and because it is expensive to insure house contents, most Italians do not bother. Foreign residents from Britain will find that insurance quotes from Italian firms are at least double what they would expect to pay in the UK. Italian insurance companies are also notoriously slow about settling claims.

Some English owners and permanent residents find it easier to insure their properties in Britain, particularly for the provision against loss of rent and for properties left unoccupied. SAGA provides cover for owners over 50 www.saga.uk. Schofields (www.schofields.ltd.uk) are specialised holiday home insurers with Lloyds' connections.

To protect their houses from burglary it is normal and advisable in Italy for ground floor windows to be protected by grilles, and shutters reinforced by iron bars and latches etc.

Most mortgages include a house insurance policy, and estate agents sometimes offer house and contents insurance at competitive rates to their clients and it is worth asking them about this. For owners of second homes, an alternative to an Italian insurer is to use a British company such as those listed below, who will insure rural properties in Italy. Annual rates vary depending on the extent of the cover but are roughly £4 per £1,000 of the house value and £9 per £1,000 of the contents value.

Roy Thomas of Copeland's says that it is essential to cover earthquake damage if you live in a high-risk earthquake zone. You can find an outline map of these at http: www.smithgcb.de. As winter weather can be extremely harsh your policy should cover full perils, including flood, storm and burst pipes. Finally beware of onerous clauses that specify that the property must be inspected weekly for cover to be effective.

Useful Addresses – UK based Insurers

Andrew Copeland Insurance Consultants Ltd: 230 Portland Road, London SE25 4SL; ☎020-8656 8435; fax 020-8655 1271; info@andrewcopeland. co.uk; www.andrewcopeland.co.uk. Provide insurance for both holiday homes and permanent residents.

John Wason (Insurance Brokers) Ltd: 72 South Street, Reading, Berkshire,

RG1 4RA; ☎0118-9568800; fax 0118-9568094; email:overseas@jwason-insurance.co.uk: www.johnwason.co.uk. An independent insurance broker able to offer a wide range of products from a selected panel of major insurers.
Property Insurance Abroad: PO Box 150, Rugby CV22 5BR, England; ☎01788-550294; fax 01788-562579. Will provide a free quote.
Schofields: ☎01204-365080; www.schofields.ltd.uk. Insures holiday homes in Italy, let or unlet.
Woodham Group Ltd.: 17 Fircroft Close, Woking GU22 7LZ, England; ☎01483-770787; www.woodhamgroup.com.

Italian Insurance Companies

Italian insurance companies generally cover the following risks:

- Public liability (*responsabilità civile*).
- Fire and material damage.
- Water damage.
- Broken glass.
- 'Atmospheric events'.
- Investigation of the damage.

Agencies vary considerably in the guarantees they offer and in their interpretation of them.

Be careful to note whether your valuation of the property is index-linked in the contract (*indicizzata*). The contract is based on the information you give which is generally as follows:

- Year of construction of the building.
- Use of the rooms: living, working, storing, etc.
- State of upkeep of the building.

The value of the house is based on the cost of rebuilding it from scratch including plumbing, wiring and heating, but excluding the value of the site. The local college of builders usually provides their updated formulae to calculate this figure. In the event of an accident you must inform the insurer in writing within the terms of the contract – usually three days. The contents and furniture are included in a comprehensive policy if you are permanently resident in a house at a reasonable rate, but if the house is a holiday home, or left empty for long periods, the Italian premiums asked on furniture are prohibitively high – as much as 7% of the value. This reflects the fear of burglary.

Reale Mutua (www.realemutua.it), founded in 1827, is the largest mutual insurance society in Italy with 356 branches. Annual insurance premiums for holiday houses in rural Tuscany are between €300 and €600. A separate policy on a swimming pool might be €170.

Part three

A New Life
in Italy

Adapting to Your New life
Quality of Life
Personal Finance
Healthcare
Crime, Security & the Police
Returning Home

Adapting to Your New Life

CHAPTER SUMMARY

- Open-air markets held in streets and village squares throughout Italy are still very much part of Italian life and are often the best place to buy the freshest, most desirable local produce in season.
- Expect to find delicious food in the plainest-looking restaurants; especially if you dine where the locals are dining.
- Italy's ancient city centres have a dazzling array of small shops selling handmade products from leathergoods to sausages.
- Italy is holding out against the Americanisation of its eating habits, and McDonalds is in retreat from the Slow Food organisation, which promotes locally-sourced ingredients and regional cooking.
- It makes for safer overtaking to have a left-hand drive car in Italy, but buying a used car is expensive. It may be preferable, to look round for a promotional deal (e.g. free insurance and 0% finance) on a new car from a dealership.
- Italian car insurance is notoriously expensive and basic policies are third party. Fully comprehensive insurance is so expensive that most Italians do not bother with it.
- Dipped headlights on motor vehicles are required at all times on motorways and dual-carriageways.
- There are three levels of local government: twenty *regioni*, 106 *province* and over 8,000 *comuni*. Of the *regioni* five, including the islands of Sardinia and Sicily, have semi-autonomous government. The chief executive officer of the commune is the *sindaco* (mayor), and he or she should be cultivated at all costs.

SHOPPING

Italy excels in design and manufacturing. It produces exquisite objects of desire for discerning consumers, and Milan is the style capital of the world. No wonder that Americans, from the home of the shopping mall, flock to Italy for a very superior fix of retail therapy. Whether it is shoes in Vigevano, handbags in Naples, painted crockery at Deruta, glass at Murano, jewellery in Arezzo or Ferrari cars in Maranello, Italy tempts the consumer with the best quality products that the globe can offer. Every large town has at least one shopping centre (*centro commerciale*), which is up to the best European or American standards of quality and design. The *Ipercoop* Co-op chain now dominates the scene. It is a mutual co-operative society, which sells everything from white goods (made in Pordenone), to bread baked fresh on the spot in wood-fired ovens. Preference is given to local products and goods sourced in Italy under strict ecological control. *Superal, Conad, Esselunga, Upim, Standa, Despar* are names of other chains, and *Auchan* from France has partnered *La Rinascente* of Milan to carve a large niche in the north.

At a daily level, shops for basic needs, *negozi di prima necessità* – are to be found in every village or town quarter *rione*. At the lower end of the social scale weekly or permanent street markets under awnings supply the needs of locals and tourists alike in towns and cities throughout Italy.

Indoor Shopping

The Small Shops. Back in the ancient city centres the local townsfolk (*borghesia*) maintain a tradition of dazzling small shops and boutiques which are more alluring than anything in Bond Street or Fifth Avenue: *Fendi, Furla, Valentino, Gucci, Versace*, big names or no names – Via Montenapoleone in Milan, Via Condotti in Rome, Via Tornabuoni in Florence, the Rialto in Venice, the covered arcades of Bologna – all cities have shopping streets (*corsi*) which attract discreet hordes of opulent shoppers and gourmets.

o **Food shops** (*alimentari*) are an area in which Italians excel throughout the world. A slicing machine will dominate the counter for salamis, hams and cold cuts. Most produce will be seasonal, and

rolls, *panini* or sandwiches can be ordered expressly, put on the
scales, and paid for by weight.

o **Papershop** (*edicola*) sells papers, magazines, stationery.

o **Tobacconist** (*il tabacchaio*, or *la tabaccheria*) is marked with a big
T sign, which stands for *tabacchi*. As a state monopoly outlet the
tabacchaiol tabaccherialtabacchi is also the place for postage stamps,
official forms and bus tickets.

o **Chemist** (*farmacia*) dispenses medical advice as well as medicines,
but does not handle photographic products.

o **Houseware shop** (*casalinghi*) sells anything for the house from
electric blankets to dustpans.

o **Gift shop** (*articoli da regalo*) sells souvenirs, crockery, cutlery etc,
beautifully packaged.

Most shops are open from 8.30am to 7.30pm and close for three hours
or more at 1pm for lunch. They are closed by law for one day in the
week. American Sarah Rasmer, found that the shopping hours took
some getting used to:

*Small, family run businesses close for funerals and vacations; they will
leave a note on their door to notify their customers. Most businesses
close for at least a couple of weeks in August. Many shops are opening
on Sunday afternoons; and some do not close for lunch. All tabacchi
shops, which sell various items like stamps and prepaid phone cards in
addition to cigarettes, remain open for lunch.*

Most villages have a weekly vegetable stall (*fruttivendolo*) and fish van
(*pescivendolo*).

Bargain Shopping

One way to have designer clothes but not pay their usual outrageous
prices is to buy from factory outlets. Expat groups and websites are
good places to find out about the best places to shop, as is the website,
www.made-in-italy.com, which is a prime source of information about
shopping in general as well as factory outlets. Also worth a look is
www.italydaily.it/Italian_life/Shopping/luglio/outlets.shtml and www.

dolcevita.com/outlets/outlets.html. The following publications are guides to bargain shopping in Italy and worth looking at: the best-selling bargain finder which details over 1,200 outlets *Lo Scoprioccasioni,* (5th edition in English 2004; ISBN 88-86132-13-1) at €16,50 (www. scoprioccasioni.it/eng_chi_siamo.html by Editoriale Shopping Italia S.r.l. They also arrange day shopping trips in Milan, Venice, Florence etc. (info@scoprioccasion.it; tel/fax 0344 86176). In addition, the annual outlet guide *La Guida Agli Spacci* by Marina Martorana lists over 2000 outlets 2004/05 edition €12 from Italy's online bookstore www.unilibro.com; also try www.guidaspacci.it.

Outdoor Shopping

Street shopping and outdoor markets are still very much a part of Italian life and are not likely to decline in popularity. There are food and produce markets, flea markets, mixed markets, antique markets and so on. Many of the mixed weekly markets in small towns are fairly dull and similar in content. They tend to sell lots of cheap household goods and some foodstuffs. Those in large cities are bigger and more interesting with produce, cooked food, clothes, shoes, hats, handbags and more. The tourist office will be able to provide a list of markets locally and locals will tell you which are the best ones. If collectibles are among your retirement interests, or you are just looking for objects for your home, there are also monthly antique markets. A list of collectors' markets in central Italy can be found at www.italyfarmhousesrental.com/antiquemarkets.htm.

One of the pleasures of retirement in Italy is to visit the open-air produce markets held in streets and squares across Italy where you can watch the variety of fruit and vegetables displayed on the stalls rotate with the seasons, and where you can buy and eat them in a perfect state of ripeness. Organic food is trendy in Italy and much of the produce on sale is grown with far fewer chemicals than you are probably used to, or may be organic but not officially certified. Much of the foodstuff sold in markets is therefore wholesome as well as at its freshest. Olive oil, eggs and wine are best bought direct from a local producer or farm. They may not always have a sign up so just ask around about where to go. The website www.initaly.com/regions/ has a list of food markets in Italy and their day of operation.

SHOPPING GLOSSARY

abbligliamenti	clothes
agenzia di viaggi	travel agency
barbiere	barber
calzoleria/calzatura	shoe shop/footwear
calzolaio	cobbler/shoe repairer
cartoleria	stationery/bookshop
confezione	clothes
drogheria	grocer
ferramenta	hardware
fioraio	florist
fotocopisteria/typografia	photocopying/printing
frutta e verdura/fruttivendolo/	fruit and vegetables/greengrocer
giocattoli	toys
gioielleria	jeweller
ipermercato	hypermarket
latteria	dairy
lavaggio a secco	dry cleaning
lavanderia	laundry
libreria	bookshop
macelleria	butcher
orologiaio/orologeria	watchmaker/repairer
ottico	optician
panificio/panetteria/panettiere	breadshop/bakery/baker
parruchiera	hairdresser
pasticceria	cake/pastry shop
pastificio	fresh pasta
pelleteria	leather goods
pescheria	fishmonger
salumeria	delicatessen
sarto/sarta	tailor/dress-maker
surgelati	frozen food

Expat Cravings

To satisfy expatriate cravings for the comfort of 'traditional' British food products including Ambrosia Creamed Rice, Cadbury's Creme Eggs and Chocolate Fingers, Jaffa Cakes, English Mustard, Monster

Munch, Marmite, Marks and Spencer foodstuffs, Heinz Beans, Christmas puddings and many more it is possible to order them on the internet from the following sites amongst others.

FOOD AND DRINK

Many myths have grown up around the Italians, and their eating habits are no less liable to exaggeration or misconception than other aspects of their lives. Admittedly, whether the pasta is cooked *al dente* (just right) or *una colla* (sticky and overcooked) is a subject treated with an almost religious reverence. However, despite the world-famous ice creams, pizzas and pasta dishes, the Italians boast one of the lowest incidences of heart disease in Europe (and consume less ice cream than most of their European neighbours). The basis of Italian eating tends towards quality, not quantity, and as with all matters of Italian life, is subject to the rigorous demands of *la bella figura* (cutting a fine figure). Just as the majority of Italians looks upon drunkenness as a disgusting and unnecessary foreign fetish, obesity is similarly unacceptable, unless accompanied by a corresponding amount of Pavarotti-like charisma. Even so, it is noticeable these days that the problem of childhood obesity widespread across Western Europe embraces Italy too. An article in *Corriera della Sera* claimed that one in three Italian children is now overweight.

Although every Italian region proclaims the excellence of its own cooking, the region of Emilia-Romagna is considered by some to exemplify the finest and richest of Italian cuisine. However, every region has specialities: Tuscany is renowned for its high-quality meat and Genoa for its herb-based dishes while the food of the south is the spiciest. Writer Harris Freedman who has lived in New York and London and now lives in Umbria finds the cuisine of Italy a varying delight:

I love the way the food is simple, always freshly made and delicious wherever you are in Italy. You never have the same food in another region; each has its own cuisine. All the sauces are different.

The three main meals of the Italian day are treated with varying degrees of importance. Breakfast, *(colazione)* is usually a frugal offering of croissant *(cornetto)* or biscuits *(biscotti)*; although cereals are gaining popularity in the Italian market. Lunch *(pranzo)* is treated as the main meal of the day in the southern regions, although home-cooked food is increasingly being superseded by convenience food. Finally, dinner *(cena)*, as in the majority of Mediterranean countries, is eaten late in the evening, usually between 8pm and 10pm, especially during the summer months.

Eating Out. Traditional Italian restaurants are signalled by the *ristorante trattoria* or *pizzeria* signs. Sparse or unpretentious decor is common and does not reflect on the quality of the food or service. When eating out with Italians you should offer to split the bill *alla romana* – dividing it by the number of those present. However, if you have been invited out to dinner, your host or hostess will probably insist on paying the entire bill. As far as giving tips is concerned, service was traditionally added at the customer's discretion, usually at around 10%-15%. These days though, a 10% charge is generally included in the total bill, as is a cover charge per person. The easiest way to tell if service is included is by looking at the bill *(il conto)*, it will have *servizio* and *coperto* for service and cover charges respectively.

Slow Food. Italy, unlike France, which has surrendered to Disney and Macdonalds, is still holding out as a counter culture to the Americanisation of Everything. Americans are attracted in Italy by what they miss out on in America, such as fresh produce that has a taste, culinary artisans at work, life in the piazza, and slow food. Slow Food began in Italy and has grown into an international movement (whose symbol is a snail), which now includes Slow Travel. Slow Food is lobbying against genetically modified organisms, and is pro organic food. Also, through its publishing company *(Slow Food Editore)* it produces a range of books, which deal, in encyclopaedic fashion, with all the food traditions of Italy, historical and regional. If you want to join the Slow Food Association, buy their publications, or find out where you can eat and drink slow food in your area contact the Slow Food International Office (Via Mendicità 8, 12042 Bra (CN) Italy; ☎(0)172 419611; fax (0)1792 414498; e-mail info@slowfood.it, www.slowfood.com).

Italian eating habits are far more discerning and infinitely healthier than you could ever imagine. Italians are still providing a role model for every aspiring *buongustaio* (food and drink connoisseur) the national gastronomic motto seems to be, enjoy, but not to excess. In Italy, McDonalds, whose penetration into Italy in 2000 sparked demonstrations in 20 Italian cities, has not managed yet to be a serious threat to real food and drink in Italy.

Drinking. As mentioned above, the Italians are not great drinkers and being drunk (*ubriaco*) carries a special disapproval amongst the majority of Italians, which would be thought curious amongst the beer-swilling section of the British pub population. However, drinking wine from a young age is an accepted part of the culture, unlike in the UK and USA. Alcohol sales have flagged in Italy, as mineral water (*acqua minerale*) sales escalate nationwide. Italy is now second only to France in annual consumption of mineral water.

Another beverage that has taken off in Italy is beer; however sales have now slowed because the price of beer has nearly doubled in the last two years thanks to sharply hiked taxes on production and sales, so while Italians like beer, they cannot afford to drink as much as they would like to. According to a recent poll carried out by Assobirra (the Italian beer producers' federation), two out of three Italians drink beer. This applies mainly to the twenty-something party crowd of cosmopolitan Europeans that can be found in most major commercial cities of Europe. Along with the drop in beer sales, the annual consumption of wine is dropping to such a low level that the wine marketing board now regularly advertises it in order to encourage sales. If you prefer wine-bars then look for the signs *cantina* or *enoteca* above the door.

Wine. Most of Italy is wine country and there is no time to do justice to the many varieties here. Suffice it to say that some areas have gone in for professional production and export while others have kept their traditions and best wines a secret from the outside world. The north-

west (Piemonte) is famous for its vermouths and spumantes and pur-
plish wines and barolo and barbera grapes. The northeast, particularly
the part under Austrian influence, has gone in for mass production.
Probably the best-known wines abroad are those from central Italy,
especially the Chianti wines from the Tuscan hills between Florence
and Siena. Southern Italy has the Neapolitan wines of Ischia, Capri
and red and white wines from the area around Mount Vesuvius. Sicily's
best-known wine is probably the sweet and treacly Marsala.

WINE LABEL GLOSSARY

DOCG – *Denominazione di Origine Controllata Guarantita*: the highest quality,
similar to France's *appellation contrôleé*.

DOC – *Denominazione di Origine Controllata*: the second highest quality.

DS – *Denominazione Semplice* – the equivalent of the French vin de table.

Messo in bottiglia del produttore all'origine: estate-bottled.

Classico: from the central, i.e. best area of the region.

Imbottigliato nello stabilimento della ditta: bottled on the premises of the firm.

Riserva: wine that has been aged for a statutory period.

Wine Colours: Bianco (white), *Rosso* (red), *Rosato* (pink), *Chiaretto* (very light red),
Nero (very dark red).

Secco: dry.

Amaro: bitter or very dry.

Amabile/Abboccato: medium sweet.

Dolce: very sweet.

Spumante: bubbly.

Frizzante: slightly fizzy.

Vin/Vino santo: sweet dessert wine made from dried grapes.

Stravecchio: very old, mellow.

Vino liquoroso: fortified wine.

MEDIA

Newspapers

Italy, along with many Western nations is experiencing falling newspaper cir-
culations, though recently, offers of free and low priced classic books and
other collection gimmicks have caused some newspaper figures to rise temporarily. Many newspapers are available to read for free on the internet; the

website www.Italian.about.com/od/newsstand lists quite a few of them along with links to their websites. There is no real equivalent of the well-established British tabloids and US supermarket newspapers and only the down market papers, such as *Il Messaggero,* carry horoscopes, cartoons or fun features.

REGIONAL ITALIAN PAPERS

Newspaper	City	Political leaning
La Nazione	Florence	Socialist
Il Mattino	Naples	Christian Democrat
Il Messagero	Rome	Communist
Il Resto del Carlino	Bologna.	
L'Ora	Palermo	at the forefront of anti-Mafia movement in the media environs of Sicily.
Il Tempo	(Rome)	
La Gazzetta del Mezzogiorno	(Bari)	
La Nuova Sardegna	(Cagliari)	
Paese Sera	(Rome)	
Il Piccolo	(Trieste)	
La Nuova	Venezia (Venice)	

Of about 80 daily Italian newspapers only a handful are distributed throughout the country. The most popular Italian dailies are *Il Corriere della Sera* (Milan) and *La Repubblica* (Rome) – both of which boast a daily circulation of between five and six hundred thousand.

Il Corriere della Sera and *La Repubblica,* are constantly vying for circulation supremacy, mostly using *allegati* (enclosures) of books or DVDs, which are offered free with the paper, or artistically packaged and offered to readers at special prices. *La Repubblica,* tends to create the most controversy and excitement, with its strengths for political insight and cultural reporting. There are no separate Sunday papers as such in Italy; instead all of the national dailies print on Sunday and then have a day off on Monday.

The website www.italydaily.com is a useful link to the sites of the most important daily Italian newspapers both national and local and the academic website www.tcd.ie./CLCS/Italian/Italianmedia.html

gives a very useful rundown and description of Italy's newspapers and magazines and tells you where to access local newspapers online.

Magazines

The Italian magazine market is swamped with publications that churn out the same themes, features and cover-spreads week after week. The main three publishing houses, Mondadori, RCS Mediagroup and Hachette Rusconi are in constant competition to control a saturated market. The better-quality magazines include *Panorama* (which supports the rightist government) *and L'Espresso*, both of which contain a good deal of serious and well-written news and arts coverage. At the other end of the spectrum are *La Gente, Oggi, Novella 2000, Eva Express* and the incredibly lurid *Stop,* which are pure gossip and scandal reading.

A list of Italian Magazines and their websites can be found at www.ciaoitaly.com/categories/magazine.htm

Expatriate Websites & Magazines

The Informer (www.informer.it), was formerly a monthly newspaper but is now totally online in a format that contains a variety of both useful and interesting articles ranging from tax and money matters to general interest, and is a mine of information highly recommended for expatriates in Italy. *The Informer* also has electronic newsletters and extensive archives of information available online to its subscribers (www.informer.it). There is a fortnightly English-language paper published in Rome: *Wanted in Rome* (www.wantedinrome.com) sold on news-stands and in some bookshops, and the Metropolitan. English language magazines *Italy* (www.italymag.co.uk) and *Italia!* (www.Italia-magazine.com) are two lifestyle and property magazines There is also *The International Spectator* published by the *Istituto Affari Internazionali* (www.iai.it/) which is a way of keeping up with international affairs online. Other expat websites that are not magazines as well include www.expatsinitaly.com and www.escapeartist.com/italy/italy.html and www.romebuddy.com (mostly Rome but also the rest of Italy).

The English Yellow Pages (via Belisario 4/B, 00187 Rome; ☎06-4740861; fax 06-4744516; www.intoitaly.it) updated annually, will be invaluable to any new arrival in Italy. The directory contains listings for English-speaking professionals, businesses, organisations and services in Rome, Florence, Bologna, Naples, Genoa and Milan and is available at international bookstores and from news-stands. The online version also has listings for Palermo and Catania. For a free listing, contact the above address. Free classified ads can also be posted on the website.

English Books

Expats usually have wide-ranging tastes, which include a large component of Anglophone literature, which was once catered for by the independent and often quirky, English-language bookshops of Italy's cosmopolitan cities. Such shops have been largely superseded by Amazon and other online purveyors of cut-price books worldwide.

> **English Language Bookshops**
> **Anglo American Bookshop:** (Rome) ☎ 06 6783890; www.aab.it.
> **Almost Corner Bookshop:** (Rome) ☎ 06 5836942.
> **American Milan Bookshop:** (Milan) ☎ 02-878920.
> **Lion Bookshop:** (Rome) ☎ 06 32650437; fax 06 32651382.
> **Paperback Exchange Bookshop:** (Florence) ☎ 055 293460; fax 055 265
> 8395; www.papex.it.

Television

The Italians are telly-addicts and Italy has more terrestrial channels than any other country in the world with an output of programmes that tend to be of a uniform awfulness. This saturation of television space was the unsurprising response to the deregulation of the television board in 1976; before this time, there had only ever been one, black and white, state-run channel, heavily influenced and censored by church authorities. The great majority of these relatively new channels are crammed with rubbishy quiz shows and low quality sitcoms and soaps, while the three state-run channels, RAI 1, 2 and 3 manage to provide a higher quality programming and command higher viewing levels. However, the standard is evidently not high enough and viewing figures are falling for the state-run channels. The state channels (RAI 1, RAI 2, RAI 3) are now no longer as subject to political patronage as they once were. RAI 3 tends to show more cultural programmes than the others.

The important independent television channels are Italia 1, Canale 5 and Rete 4 that collectively account for about 45% of Italian viewing and are owned by Prime Minister Berlusconi's Mediaset empire.

Satellite packagers include RAI Sat and Sky Italia. A full list of TV channels in Italy can be found at www.obs.coe.int/db/persky/it.html. Information in English on the Italian licence fee and how to pay it is at www.abbonamenti.rai.it/Ordinari/canone_eng.asp.The company Solsat (www.solsat.com; info@solsat.com; ☎+34 616 314 068) can provide its clients anywhere in Europe with a Sky digibox and a fully activated Sky Digital Viewing Card at the same time. Insat International (http:sky-cards.no-ip.com/sky/sky-tv-italy.html) supplies Sky Viewing Cards and digiboxes for expats living in Italy.

Thanks to satellite technology it is now possible to receive a huge variety of international channels via satellite, including BBC World (free to air), BBC Prime (subscription only), CCNI (free to air), CNBC, The Disney Channel and other good quality English language channels throughout Europe.

Video and DVD

For those unable to find enough substantial fare, at the right time of day, on Italian television and the available satellite and digital channels, there is always recourse to DVDs (or videos if you are behind with your technology). Italian TV and videos operate on the PAL-BG system. The UK operates PAL-I, the USA and Canada operates NTSC and France operates MESECAM. TVs of one system do not correctly work with another (you can get black and white instead of colour, or have no sound). Having a multi-system TV and video (i.e. that play all system types) is the solution. Most of the ones sold in Europe are multi-system. Expats are well recommended to buy a multi-system video player so they can watch videos they have collected around the world during their travels.

DVD players, however, offer the advantage that each DVD gives the viewer the chance to choose the language they hear – i.e. original language or a number of dubbed languages. With this capability, expats may no longer have to search out the obscure shops that sell imported videos in their original language, or order them from outside Italy, and can buy them locally or from Amazon Italy (www.amazon.it). A larger selection of DVDs in English is available from Amazon.co.uk and www.bbcshop.com while www.choicesdirect.co.uk and Amazon UK both still have a wide selection of videos as well as DVDs.

Blockbuster now operates rental stores in the larger cities and as they now hire out mostly DVDs, buying a DVD player can give you a much wider choice of films to rent.

Online Bookshops and DVD/Video Suppliers

www.amazon.com.

www.amazon.co.uk: cheaper postage than Amazon.com for books sent to Italy.

www.bn.com: US company Barnes and Noble.

www2.uk.bol.com: UK store of Bol.

www.choicesdirect.co.uk: supplies UK PAL video by mail order.

www.internetbookshop/it: one of Italy's largest online sources of books, DVDs and videos (in Italian).

www.unilibro.com Italy: claims to be Italy's largest online bookstore with English versions (also supplies CDs and DVDs).

Radio

The airwaves in Italy are crammed with a diverse range of obscure stations; over two and a half thousand of them. However, the three main radio channels are Radio 1, 2, and 3. The first two feature light music and entertainment while Radio 3 is similar to the UK equivalent, broadcasting serious discussion programmes and classical music. The total audience for radio nation-wide is estimated at 35 million. However, there are so many stations that this audience is hopelessly fragmented and some local stations are estimated to have no more than a few dozen listeners.

As with television, the main radio channels are all under the wing of a powerful sponsor who consequently has a substantial influence over the station's output.

BBC World Service. For details of schedules, advice and information about BBC World Service radio (www.worldservice@bbc.co.uk) and BBC Prime (bbcprime@bbc.co.uk) and BBC World Television (bbc-world@bbc.co.uk) you have to go to the BBC World Service website. You can also sign up for a monthly e-mail update of the BBC World Service Network, highlighting BBC World Service radio programmes.

CARS & MOTORING

Buying and Selling a Car

Buying. Expats moving permanently to Italy have the choice of importing their own cars to Italy, or buying a new one after arrival. It generally makes sense to buy a car in Italy, not least because it is safer to have a left-hand drive vehicle for overtaking. There are other good reasons for not importing your British vehicle as Vince Ferrigno (English despite Italian origins) explains:

> *I am happy driving a right-hand drive on the right hand side of the road. I also like my automatic gears. It is very difficult to get automatics here; Italians are all boy racers who would be lost without their gear sticks. In retrospect though it was probably not a good idea to reregister a British car in Italy as it was a nightmare. Midway through the process we couldn't get any insurance as a British company wouldn't insure a car in Italy and the Italians wouldn't insure it because it didn't have an Italian registration. I probably should have just bought a car here; they are much cheaper in Italy.*

All of the main European makes, and their spare parts, are available in Italy. To buy a car with Italian registration plates, you must be an Italian resident. If you buy a used car in Italy then you will be liable to pay ownership transfer fees (*passaggio di proprietà*), which cost about €440 (£300, US$533). When considering buying a car, it is worth bearing in mind that hiring a car in Italy is very expensive compared to the UK. It currently costs £200 a week to rent a medium-sized car with unlimited mileage. However, there are an increasing number of budget rental agencies that are offering more competitive rates, especially for long-term rentals.

There are second-hand car deals at most car dealers. Most of the cars have been part-exchanged for newer models and come with a year's guarantee (a legal requirement). There is considerable bureaucracy and expense involved in buying a second-hand car. Firstly, you have to pay the ownership fees *(passagio di proprietà)*, you then have to wait a minimum of two weeks for the arrival of the car log-book *(libretto di circolazione)*. As it is an offence to drive without having the log-book (commonly called the *libretto*) to hand, you must obtain interim documents *(foglio sostitutivo)*, which expire after three months though you should have received your log-book long before that time. Additional irritations used to include reminders to pay fines incurred by the previous owner – though this happens far less frequently as a result of the computerisation of records.

There is also the problem of persuading dealers to give expatriates hire purchase agreements. One American expat couple had the following experience:

The dealer seemed reluctant to sell us a car at first, even though we took someone, who knew both my husband and the owner, with us. They told us that there is more paperwork for them to fill out because we are foreigners. The whole process took several weeks, but we did manage to buy the car we wanted in the end. We were advised to buy either German or Italian made cars because they are the easiest to sell on. Diesels are also popular.

Selling. When selling a car, the popular motor magazine, *Porta Portese* is invaluable if you are living in Rome. Otherwise you can buy and sell cars online at www.secondamano.it or through the classified adverts of free newspapers. You can check all the models on the market and the current used prices in the magazine *Al Volante,* which costs one euro and includes pictures of all makes and models sold in Italy. Alternatively, simply stick a 'for sale' sign *(vendesi)* in the car window. Or you may prefer to sell your car to a garage in part-exchange for a new one. The buyer then pays ownership transfer fees (see above). At least in this version of second-hand car dealing, the legwork generally has to be done by the garage.

Car Tax. A tax stamp (*bollo*) must be purchased for your car and is obtainable from the ACI and renewable at the post office. The tax is dependent on the power rating and size of the engine. The tax is paid on a regional basis and cost depends on region though variations are not huge.

Driving Licences

EU driving licences are a standard pink and holders of these may drive their home registered car in Italy with no alteration to their licence at all. However, holders of the old UK green-coloured driving licences must first obtain a translation, available free of charge from the Italian State Tourist Office (1 Princes Street, London W1R 8AY; 020-7408 1254), or update them for the new style (using form D1 available from most UK Post Offices). Owners of Italian-registered cars should theoretically have an Italian-registered licence, this involves converting your EU driving licence to an Italian one. To do this a certificate confirming that you have never been convicted for a driving offence in the country of issue is required – such certificates are available from the nearest Embassy or Consulate. In practice, however, many expatriates avoid doing this and carry an international driving licence instead.

Non-EU driving licence holders are in a slightly different situation and the usefulness of their drivers licence depends on where it was issued. Some countries have reciprocal agreements with Italy to recognise each other's driving licences. Further information can be obtained from your embassy. If your country does have a reciprocal agreement with Italy (America does not) you can apply to exchange your current licence for an Italian one. The Italian licence replaces your previous one – it is not in addition to it.

If your country does not have a reciprocal agreement with Italy you will need to take a two-part driving test, in Italian. The first part is a written test and the second part (after passing the written test) is the road test. The written test is a multiple choice, which is difficult for non-Italian speakers. Foreigners usually opt for an oral test, which is in Italian, but examiners are a bit more lenient to foreigners with broken Italian. Taking driving lessons for the oral test is a great way to learn the necessary vocabulary for the exam. Exams must be taken at a driving school (*scuola guida*), who will also apply for the licence for you after you have passed the tests.

It is possible to drive in Italy for a year, on an International Driver's Licence, though you must always carry your national licence to show at the same time. International licences can be obtained from your national drivers' association (e.g. the AA in the UK, or your state organisation in the US). However, international licences can also be obtained via the internet from sites such as: IDL International (www.idl-international.com) who can supply five-year licences.

All Nationalities. It is a legal requirement to carry your driving licence (*patente*) and all of your car documents (*libretto*) and passport with you while you are driving. You may be required to present any or all of the papers if you are stopped by the police and can be fined for failing to do so.

Insurance

The usual Italian car insurance covers the car and passengers, not the driver, and is nearly always third party. Full, comprehensive cover (*kasko*) is available, at a price, upon consultation with the insurance company. Note that insurance is rather more expensive than in other EU countries, which is why most Italians do not bother to be comprehensively insured. Medical cover for the driver is not usually included, but is an extra. The expense and the fact that Italian insurance companies are notoriously slow and mean regarding claims mean that most Italians go for the minimum insurance. Often drivers do not report minor accidents because it puts up the cost of insurance. Instead, they just come to an agreement, particularly if they both live in the same town to have the person at fault pay the damage costs directly to the repair shop. For less serious accidents where the person at fault admits liability and signs a friendly agreement form (*costatazione amichevole*), which is carried in all Italian cars. With this, you can attempt to speed up matters, as it is a straightforward procedure for your insurance company to ask the other party's insurance company to repay them.

Copeland Insurance (230 Portland Road, London SE25 4SL;

☎020-8656 8435; fax 020-8655 1271; www.andrewcopeland.co.uk) can also provide insurance in Italy in certain circumstances and AXA insurance (www.axa-italia.it) is widespread throughout Italy and a list of regional insurers there can be found on their website under 'Carlink'. You may get a better deal from Direct Line which operates in Italy (www.directline.it) and offers cheaper rates on Italian insurance and Aurora Assicurazioni (wwww.auroraassicurazioni.it) has been recommended as offering a good deal.

Roads

Driving in Italy can be a costly if you use motorways. The tolls (*pedaggi*) on Italian motorways (*autostrade*) are expensive at about €0.50-€0.60 per ten kilometres. As you drive on to an autostrada you collect a toll ticket, which you pay on exit. Alternatively buy a 'Viacard' from tollbooths (must be paid for in cash) and usable at both manned and automatic tollbooths. You can also use your credit card in automatic toll booths. The Italian Highways Association has a very useful website (www.autostrade.it) with routes, toll charges and a toll calculator. *Strade Statali* (SS) are the equivalent of British A roads. *Autostrade* and *strade statali* are main roads and are numbered, while smaller roads such as *strade provinciali* and *secondarie* are not. It takes courage and an ability to learn to drive like an Italian to survive on Italian roads.

In Europe it is normal to give way to cars entering traffic from the right – even if it is a small side road they are coming from. Not all drivers approaching you from the right will slow down to make sure you will give way. Unless the road joining the one you are on has a solid white line across it where the two roads meet, you do not have right of way. One of the biggest changes in Europe has been who has right of way at roundabouts. Though it is supposedly the person on the roundabout, this was not the case until recently in Italy and some other European countries. More information about driving in Italy can be found on the Slow Travel website (www.slowtrav.com/italy/driving/introduction.htm.

Italian petrol (*Benzina*) is cheaper than that in the UK, but more expensive than US residents are used to. Petrol is unleaded comes in two octane ratings, 95 and 98, and cars are set-up to take only one of these. *Gasolio* (diesel) is popular in Europe because it is much cheaper than unleaded petrol and is as widely available as unleaded petrol. LPG (Liquified Petroleum Gas), known as GPL in Italy, is becoming increasingly popular because of its lower price and environmental cleanliness. Only those petrol stations displaying the GPL symbol sell GPL. Petrol stations along the *autostrade* are open 24 hours while those on secondary roads usually open between 7am and 12.30pm and then from 2.30 to 7pm or 7.30pm and close on Sundays. Petrol brands include Agip, Api, Erg, Esso, Q8, Shell and Tamoil.

Accidents

Italy has one of the highest road accident rates in the whole of the EU. This, despite traffic law enforcement by the *Vigili Urbani* (traffic police), battling the ingrained dangerous driving techniques for which Italians are known. The accident rate is astronomical (approximately 250,000 injured each year) of which around 5,000 a year are fatalities. Italian driving licences operate on a points system. You lose your licence if you get 20 penalty points on it, and have to take your driving test again. This also means much higher motor insurance premiums. Italy has one of the highest densities of cars in the world; higher than both the UK and the USA, which may also be a factor in the high accident figures.

Part of the insurance documentation that is required to be carried in every car is an insurance claim form *(costatazione amichevole)* that has space for the parties involved to sketch the accident scene as well as other questions that need to be answered. Never admit liability or your insurance company has good grounds not to pay up, which leaves you financially liable. Both parties are required to sign the accident claim forms.

If you have an accident it is mandatory to stop. After an accident you are expected to take the names and addresses of witnesses and their car details if applicable. Always inform your insurance company of any accident you have whether or not you file a claim – the small print of most European insurance policies requires you to do so (unless the accident is a fender bender) and failure to do so can invalidate your insurance. If you see an accident happen, even though you are not involved, you are required to stop and help.

The red triangle in the boot of your car should be placed 50 metres from the accident to warn approaching drivers and you are obliged to wear a fluorescent tabard or jacket whenever you get out of the car. You can be fined by the police on the spot, for non-compliance with any driving regulations.

Breakdowns

- The Italian Automobile Club, *Automobile Club d'Italia*, is the Italian equivalent of the RAC and the AA. The head office of the ACI is at Via Marsala 8, 00185 Rome (☎06-49981; fax 06-4457748; General Secretariat ☎06-49982426; Presidency ☎06-49982469; Tourism Department www.acit.it).
- The emergency 24-hour phone number is Rome 06-4477 with multilingual staff providing round the clock assistance.
- If your car comes to an unprompted and definitive halt, then dial 116 (ACI breakdown Service) from anywhere in Italy, from either a telephone box or a mobile phone.
- On motorways, you can also use SOS phones that are placed every 2km along the road and connected with the motorways radio centres: road assistance can be provided either by the ACI 116 or by a local operator. The service is permanently available on all roads throughout Italy.
- In all emergencies (personal injury and all kinds of accidents or mishaps) dial 113 (police), 112 (Carabinieri) or 115 (Fire Brigade).
- Note that it is the law that you have to wear a reflective safety vest to walk to an emergency telephone to summon assistance for a breakdown or accident.
- Breakdown service comprises transportation of the car from the place of breakdown to the nearest ACI garage or, in major cities, the roadside repair of the vehicle if possible.
- Road Assistance provided by the ACI is free of charge only for tourists with an AIT or FIA Assistance booklet, otherwise the service for all motor vehicles up to 2.5 tons is chargeable.
- An annual subscription can be purchased from the ACI that covers breakdown service either within Italy only, or throughout Europe, depending on the fee paid.

INSTRUCTIONS/INFORMATION ROAD SIGNS

Accendere i fari in galleria	Switch on headlights in tunnel
Attenzione	caution
Caduta massi	fallen rocks
Casello a ....metri	toll in ....metres
Curve	bends
Dare precedenza	give way
Deviazione	detour
Divieto di accesso	no entry
Divieto di sorpasso	no overtaking
Divieto di sosta	no stopping
Divieto di transito	no right of way
Lavori in corso	roadworks
Passaggio a livello	level crossing
Pedoni	pedestrians
Rallentare	slow
Senso unico	one way
Sosta autorizzata	parking permitted
Strada chiusa	road closed
Strada ghiacciata	icy road
Tenere la destra	keep to the right
Transito Interrotto	no through road
Uscita camion	truck exit
Veicoli al passo	dead slow

Main Points – Driving Laws

O Italian speed limits are as follows: 130 kph (80 mph) on the *auto-strade, 90 kph (55 mph) on highroads (le strade statali)* and 50 kph (30 mph) in all built-up areas. Some three-lane autostradas have been given a higher speed limit of 150 kph (93mph).

O Be warned that if you are caught committing a minor motoring offence hefty fines (in the region of €150 to €250) are usually made on the spot.

O It is still legal to ride a moped from the age of 14. Helmets are compulsory but the law is often flouted.

O Italian regulations stipulate a limit of no more than 0.04% milligrams of alcohol per litre of blood (which is about 50% less than the UK limit).

o The police can breath-test drivers randomly, without having to have due cause.

o Dipped headlights are compulsory at all times on the autostradas and dual carriageways (*superstrade*) and all out of town roads e.g. ringroads (*tangenziale*) and slip roads (*raccordo*). Motorcycles have to drive on dipped headlights during the day at all times, on all roads.

o Circular signs announce restrictions (or the end of them), rectangular green ones are used on the *autostradas* and rectangular blue ones on the secondary roads.

LOCAL GOVERNMENT

Running parallel to central government in Italy are three tiers of local government listed in order of ascending importance: il comune (the town council), la provincia (province which is equivalent to a French département) and the twenty regioni (regions); the latter comprising the country's largest administrative units. Of the twenty regions, only five have evolved any kind of semi-autonomous powers; Sicily, Sardinia, Trentino-Alto Adige, Friuli-Venezia-Giulia and Valle d'Aosta. The devolution of power in these regions was necessitated by both geographical factors and ethnic history. There are 106 province and 8,100 comuni.

For example, Trentino-Alto Adige was only annexed to Italy after World War I and has a strong German-speaking contingent with pro-Austrian sympathies. It remains an uncomfortable Italian annex with a strong move towards political and administrative independence, which has included violence in the past. The five regions are known as *regioni a statuo speciale* and they differ from the other fifteen regions in that their assemblies resemble mini-parliaments, which enjoy varying economic and administrative powers – similar to the Scottish Parliament and Welsh Assembly in the UK and Federal Parliaments in Germany and Switzerland.

All five autonomous regions have total control over their education systems, although legislation passed in 1970 provides, theoretically, for limited powers of autonomy in the assemblies of the remaining fifteen regions. All regions are governed by an elected council (*giunta regionale*) and president and the next division, the *provincia* also has an elected council and president under proportional respresentation. In practice, however, central government remains a major interfering force in these areas. Additionally, 14 cities have a special constitutional status as *città metropolitane* (metropolitan city areas) including Milan, Naples, Rome, Genoa and Turin which gives them a great deal of power over local spending and allows them to charge small additional taxes.

Each of Italy's 106 provinces has a two-letter sign, which forms part of the post-code and is also evident on official documents like driving licences and identity cards. The bureaucratic function of the *provincia* (provinces) is to represent the national government at local level, but this is merely one of the two tiers of local government. A good deal of the provincial budget goes into sponsoring usually costly cultural and other prestige projects, which are deemed to increase international awareness of their existence and tourist potential, as well as spending on schools and roads. Finally, the comunes, elected once every five years (as are all other tiers of government), deal with all matters of local administration – local taxes, administration of social security services, housing, roads and transport etc. The comunes are headed by the *sindaco* (mayor) who is assisted by *gli assessori* (the councillors). An excellent website www.perjol.net/Italia/italkom.html gives you not only a list of all the regions, provinces and the provinces' capital towns and links to all their official websites representing a mine of information about local matters in Italy (in Italian).

RETAINING YOUR RIGHT TO VOTE IN UK NATIONAL AND EUROPEAN ELECTIONS

Electoral Registration from Abroad

If you are a British citizen living abroad you can apply to be an overseas voter in UK Parliamentary and European elections. You must have appeared on the electoral register in the UK within the previous 15 years.

You can register as soon as you move abroad by completing an Overseas

Elector's Declaration form from your nearest British consular or diplomatic mission. For more information contact www.aboutmyvote. co.uk or for Northern Ireland www.electoralofficeni.gov.uk.

RELIGION

As the home of the historic administrative centre (the Vatican), as well as the focal point of world Catholicism, Italy has a unique religious heritage that has permeated almost every aspect of Italian culture. Although the Vatican ceased to be a political power in the eighteenth century, its spiritual influence, backed up by the Papal road show, is still capable of producing profound awe amongst the Catholic populations of underdeveloped countries worldwide. The Vatican is also a member of the United Nations, which belies its claim to have no interest in politics. In Italy itself, however, there exist extreme attitudes of both devotion and profanity to Cattolicesimo (Catholicism). The traditional areas of fervour are the poor regions of the south and the area around Venice, while the area from Emilia Romagna to Umbria has a reputation for sacerdotal antipathy.

The Vatican has often caused controversy in Italy by not limiting itself to religious pronouncements, which has not done its reputation much good. For instance it had a long-running feud with the Italian government on the basis that it regarded parliament as ideologically unsound and all its members were therefore ineligible for Communion. This state of affairs was finally remedied by the Lateran pact of 1929 that secularised the Italian state. The Vatican showed equal implacability towards members of the former Italian Communist Party and anyone of that persuasion was excommunicated, despite the fact that many of them were fervent Catholics.

In contemporary times, Pope John Paul II who died in 2005, was one of the few non-Italian popes. He caused outrage in many quarters for his ultra-conservative dictats on current issues of concern, and many people believe this conservatism has led directly to devastating effects on some countries. For instance, the Papal commendation of large families while on visits to the faithful in Africa shows his blinkered disregard for what is the main problem facing that continent along with AIDS, namely an ecological crisis exacerbated by poverty often caused by overpopulation. Meanwhile, back on home ground, the majority of Italian Catholics have reacted to papal dictums with common sense. Despite a religious ban on 'non-natural' birth control and abortion on demand, Italy has one of the lowest birth-rates in the world, whilst also having one of the most prosperous condom industries. Coincidentally, Italy also has one of the lowest teenage pregnancy rates and abortion has been legal since 1981.

Away from the developed areas of Italy, religion moves in mysterious ways. Although generally more devout than their metropolitan countrymen, the country people mingle Catholicism with the old religions of folklore and magic, inherited from pagan times. Even amongst the highly educated, occult consulting is very popular, fortune-telling, witchcraft, and sooth-saying are services apparently indispensable to the estimated 10 million plus Italians a year, who are willing to pay for them.

English Speaking Churches and Services

All Saints' Church: Via Solferino 17, 20121 Milan; ☎02-655 2258; e-mail frnigel@boxingkangaroo.org.uk; www.allsaints.it. Rev. Nigel Gibson.

American Church of the Anglican Communion in Florence: fax 055-294417.

Anglican Church of All Saints: Via del Babuino 153, 00187 Rome; ☎06-3600 1881; e-maio j.boardman@allsaintsrome.org. Reverend Jonathan Boardman.

Bologna: ☎05 198 2891.

Christ Church: Via S. Pasquala a Chaiai 15b, 80121 Naples; ☎081-411842; vicar@Christchurch.it. Also serves Bari, Capri and Sorrento.

Church of the Holy Cross: Via Mariano Stabile 118b, 90139 Palermo; ☎091-334 831; e-mail holycrosspalermo@libero.it. Rev. Ronald Rogers.

Church of the Holy Ghost: Piazza Marsala 3, 16122 Genoa; ☎010-889 268.

Città della Pieve: near Perugia,: Anglican worship. St John the Baptist, Via Beato Giacomo Villa, in the Umbrian hills. For details contact Peter Hurd (☎057 829 9260).

Methodist Church (Evangelica Metodista): Via Porro Lambertenghi 38, Milan; ☎02-6072631. English-speaking service.

Methodist Church: Via Banco di San Spirito 3, 00186 Rome; ☎06-686 8314.

Roman Catholic Church: San Silvestro in Capite, Piazza San Silvestro, 00187 Rome; ☎06-6785609. Father Larry Gould.

St Andrews Church of Scotland: Via XX Settembre 7, 00187 Rome; ☎06-4827627. Reverend John Ross.

St George: Campo San Vio, 253 Dorsoduro, 30123 Venice; ☎041 520 0571. Rev John-Henry Bowden.

St Mark's Church: Via Maggio 18, 50125 Florence; ☎05 5294 4764 (also fax); www.stmarks.it; e-mail Lawrence.maclean@virgilio.it). Founded in 1877 and considered a minor masterpiece of the Pre-Raphaelite movement. Located on the ground floor of the 15th century Palazzo Machiavelli at the above address on the south bank of the Arno. Sunday sung Eucharist followed by drinks in the ballroom of the Palazzo Machiavelli is a good way to meet people. The notice-board in the church foyer is 'full of job and house offers for anglophones'. Rev. Lawrence MacLean.

St Peter's Siena: Anglican in Via Garibaldi, Siena. Same chaplain as St Marks, Florence.

University Church: Perugia; occasional services ☎057 829 9260. Peter Hurd.

US Air Force Base Chapel: Aviano: ☎04 1520 0571.

www.Europe.Anglican.org/directory/webdir2.html: a webpage that provides a comprehensive list of Anglican places and times of worship in Italy.

Quality of Life

CHAPTER SUMMARY

○ Concessions for pensioners vary widely on a regional basis and are often most generous as regards free/cheap travel on public transport within any large city.

○ Concessions on intercity train travel for the over 60s have just got less generous (down from a maximum 40% concession to a maximum of 15%). The good news is that train travel in Italy is cheap anyway and there are regular special offers which pensioners can take advantage of.

○ Amateur astronomy is a very popular leisure interest for all ages in Italy. One of the best places to see the starriest skies is in the crystal clear air of the mountains.

○ The 19th century French writer Stendhal found that the sheer quantity and quality of masterpieces that he confronted on his Italian travels, made him dizzy and disoriented. Stendhal's Syndrome later became a recognised psychological condition.

○ Agriturismo is a government initiative to promote tourism in the countryside by providing inexpensive accommodation on local farms, with meals prepared from local and home-produced food.

○ The Italian Popular Sports Federation has a list of sports that can be done at any age including cross-country skiing, guided trail walking and canoeing.

○ Italy has 10 national public holidays. At local level there are thousands of festivals celebrating all kinds of things from truffles to pine nuts and from saints to snakes.

○ Cheap airfares are provided by several low cost airlines operating in and out of Italy. There are always special offers for flights around and to and from Italy and it pays to keep an eye on the special bargain websites, especially if you are able to travel at short notice.

WHERE TO GET INFORMATION

The Italian State Tourist Board

The Italian State Tourist Board (ENIT) has an extremely detailed website (www.enit.it) with all kinds of information on the regions, provinces and municipalities of Italy. You can find a list of villages in a region and information about schools, bus services, the name (and photo) of the head of the local municipal council and much more, as well as regular tourist information on where to stay and what to see and do. The 20 regions of Italy also each have an official website:

Official Regional Websites – North to South

Piedmont: www.regione.piemonte.it   **Tuscany:** www.regione.toscana.it

Lombardy: www.regione.lombardia.it   **Umbria:** www.regione.umbria.it

Liguria: www.regione.liguria.it   **Le Marche:** www.regione.marche.it

Val d'Aosta: **Lazio:** www.regione.lazio.it

   www.regione.valdaosta.it   **Abruzzo:** www.regione.abruzzo.it

Trentino Alto Adige: **Molise:** www.regione.molise.it

   www.regione.taa.it   **Sardinia:** www.regione.sardegna.it

Veneto: www.regione.veneto.it   **Campania:** www.regione.campania.it

Friuli-Venezia-Giulia: **Puglia:** www.regione.puglia.it

   www.regione.fvg.it   **Basilicata:** www.regione.basilicata. it

Emilia-Romagna: **Calabria:** www.regione.calabria.it

   www.regione.emilia-romagna.it   **Sicily:** www.regione.sicila.it

---

Provincial Websites

Each region of Italy is made up of two or more provinces and each province has a website where you can get all kinds of information from local clubs, libraries and societies to information on hunting and fishing (*caccia e pesca*). Most sites will have an URP (*Ufficio Relazioni con il Pubblico*) where you can ask for information of almost any kind, relevant to the locality. Most of the websites names conform to a pattern: for example the province of Chieti in the Abruzzo region would be www.provincia.chieti.it, or you can just type the name of any province, e.g. *provincia di* …., into your search engine.

PENSIONER CONCESSIONS

There is an array of pensioner concessions in Italy but they vary from region to region. This is because Italian regional governments have considerable control over local budgets and some regions can afford to be more generous than others. The majority of concessions are available to those living within cities or their purlieus, as they involve free, or concessionary travel on public transport including buses and local trains. Pensioners on the lowest incomes, i.e. minimum pensions, are likely to get the most concessions. For instance the Regione Lazio, which includes the capital Rome, has a *Carta Senior* (www.cartasenior. regione.lazio.it) valid for free travel for all pensioners on all the bus lines within the Rome area, all local trains and the Rome metro. In addition the card entitles pensioners to a 5%-10% discount on edibles and basic necessities in supermarkets and hypermarkets. Additionally, the least well off, and the very old, get shopping vouchers up to the value of €900 which can be exchanged for goods in any participating business. In 2005, 10,000 pensioners received the maximum €900. The Lombardy metropolitan district of Milano provides free local transport (trams, metro, local railway and ferries on Lake Iseo) to the disabled, and pensioners on the lowest incomes, but better off pensioners have to pay a small charge.

The other area where pensioners can expect concessions are on tickets for cultural events (*cultura/spettacoli*) and places of interest such as national parks and tourist sites. Many of these concesssions are budgeted for on a regional or provincial basis so the level of reduction varies widely. Often the *ridotto* (reduction), *rid.* for short, is the same for the under 25s as for the over 65s, reflecting the fact that many of Italy's younger adults are still students at the age of 25, or if they are working, 89% of them are earning less than 1000 euros a month.

Train Travel

Train travel cards for the national rail system FS (Ferrovie dello Stato) have just got less generous for the over 60s; the new *Cartaviaggio Relax* replaced the *Carta Argento* in 2006. Whereas the Carta Argento allowed 40% and 30% discounts on first and second-class train travel respectively, *Cartaviaggio Relax* allows discounts of 15% on the price of both first and second-class, and 10% on long distance trains and sleeping berths. The good news is that train travel in Italy is very cheap anyway, and mostly efficient (apart from the frequent strikes). More information at www.trenitalia.it.

MAKING NEW FRIENDS

Of course most people know how to make new friends and do it instinctively or subconsciously, but moving to another place, in another country with another culture and language can be hard on even the most honed social skills and you can suddenly feel like a mute idiot, or as one foreigner implanted into the UK and having mastered some colloquialisms put it 'a complete plonker'. Undoubtedly, language skills are pretty essential and once you have made headway in that area, you can branch out into Italian *terza età* (third age) with enthusiasm. A good starting point can be the numerous clubs and associations for seniors or getting involved with local activities and voluntary work. The Italians are normally warm and welcoming and if you reciprocate and learn Italian, you should have no difficulty forging local friendships. Most Italians know that the British have a reputation for being reserved, so they will make allowances should you indicate a preference to shake hands, rather than perform the social cheek pecking that gatherings in Italy engender.

If you are in one of the regions popular with expats, your friends will inevitably include expats, which is no bad thing, as Carole Oram, who moved to Umbria with her partner in June 2005, explains:

We are lucky enough to have met many people and the rules are quite simply different here. It seems that everyone in the expat community is more open to make new friends. You are all in the same boat with a very large thing in common and we have a great social life. We socialize with expats including Dutch and Americans as well as the locals. The Italians are crazy, warm and for the most part helpful; and they have a different perspective on life, which is after all why we came here in the first place.

SPORTS & LEISURE PURSUITS

Italians are very keen on leisure pursuits and amateur sporting activities: cycling, skiing, walking, football, tennis and watersports to name but a few. Golf, which was once banned by Mussolini, is considered elite. Lady golfer Freddi Ferrigno who had to give up her favourite recreation in the UK because of ill health was delighted when she found she could play again with her husband, thanks to the micro-climate of Brindisi: she explains:

> *In the UK my arthritis and asthma were both very bad, but after moving to Italy, the marvellous climate and mild winters have done wonders for my health. We are keen golfers and there are two courses both within 40 minutes drive, which is exactly the same as we had to drive in the UK to get to a golf course. Golf is our main recreation, but if you are into ballroom dancing, it is a big thing here.*

Among the land-based sports listed on the website of the *Federazione Italiana Amatori Sport per Tutti* (Italian Popular Sports Federation) are cycling (*ciclismo*), canoeing, mountain biking, night walking (*marcia notturna*), trail walking, long distance walking over several days (*marcia di più giorni*), guided walking (*marcia guidata*) and trekking and cross-country skiing/snow walking (*sci da fondo/ciaspole*). All of these can be done by any able-bodied, fit person with no special skills or previous training. ENIT (Ente Nazionale per il Turismo) which is the Italian State Tourist Board, has a very useful site (www.enit.it) for all kinds of information on leisure activities and excursions in Italy.

Alpinismo

The *Club Alpino Italiano* (Italian Alpine Club) founded in 1863, has a membership of 304,000 organised into 480 sections located all over the country, not just in the Alps (CAI HQ, via Petrella 19, 20124 Milano; ☎ 02 2057231; www.cai.it). Main regional branches: Torino, Aosta, Varallo, Agordo, Firenze, Domodossola, Napoli, Susa, Chieti, Sondrio, Biella, Bergamo, Roma, Milano, Auronzo, L'Aquila, Cuneo, Tolmezzo, Intra and Lecco). The CAI exists to promote all forms of *alpinismo* (alpine pursuits). As well as being responsible for encouraging climbing, hiking, trekking, bivouacking, caving and staying in mountain refuges, the CAI also runs courses in mountaineering, climbing etc. and trains and provides mountain guides, mountain and cave rescue services, mountain medical services and much more.

The CAI is also behind the ambitious plan for a 6000km *Sentiero Italia* (Italian Way) mountain walking path which will run from Reggio Calabria in the South to Trieste in the northeast and which will include Sardinia and Corsica.

Amateur Astronomy (Astrofili)

Amateur astronomy is an extremely popular pursuit in Italy, probably because there are large swathes of the country, especially the crystal-aired, mountain regions, where you get a vision of the night skies in their full, star-saturated glory. This is something that is virtually impossible to do in the UK's light-polluted southern regions where only the brightest stars are easily visible. All a beginner needs is keen eyesight, and powers of observation. For a deeper appreciation it would be advisable to swot up the structure and history of the universe (not necessarily Stephen Hawking's *A Brief History of Time;* a science text book will be just as useful). There are plentiful local Italian clubs of *astrofili*; you should be able to find one in your area; you can start with the website www.astrofili.org and also the website of the *Unione Astrofili Italiani* (www.uai.it) which lists all the local associations around Italy and their contact details.

Arte e Cultura

Where to begin? Over 50 years ago the expression '*beni culturali*' was coined as a blanket term that applied to everything that represented the cultural aesthetic, history, anthropology, archaeology and so on in Italy, which has a richness of these things that surpasses anything in Europe: Etruscan Art, Legacy of Imperial Rome, Byzantine Art, Marine Republics, Renaissance Art, Baroque Art, Arts of the 18th Century, Arts of the Reunification of Italy etc. It is impossible, to try to do them justice here. Suffice it to say, that Italian arts and culture must be one of the reasons for retiring to Italy in the first place. It is easy to be overwhelmed by the quantity and quality of *arte e cultura* and it is advisable to appreciate it in small intensive doses, if you do not wish to experience Stendhal's Syndrome. This is a psychological state first described by the nineteenth century French writer who became dizzy and disorientated after encountering a plethora of Renaissance masterpieces.

Useful Sources of Information on Arts and Culture

Ministero per i Beni e le Attività Culturali: via del Collegio Romano, 27, 00186 Rome; www.beniculturali.it; Responsible for all areas of culture, arts, spettacoli and for the guardianship/protection of the Italian landscape.

Arte in Rete: www.arteinrete.it/Musei/In_Italia/ Information on over 3000 museums in Italy; organised regionally.

ArtDream Guide: www.artdreamguide.com/adg/adg_ITA/home.htim. Is a guide to museums and exhibition centres specialising in modern and contemporary art.

Associazione Dimore Storiche Italiane (ADSI): www.dimorestoriche.com The illustrated website of the Italian Historic Houses Association allows you to search for historic houses and their opening times according to region, gives directions, details of events such as concerts held at the houses and tells you what are the main things to see.

Cinema Italiano: www.cinemaitaliano.net. Site dedicated to the history of Italian cinema, classic films, classic directors, scripts and images.

Italianrus: www.italianrus.com. Guide to Italy and Italian culture (art, architecture etc.).

Lo Spettacolo: www.lospettacolo.it What's on nationally: cinema, theatre, music and tv.

Ornithology (Ornitologia)

Most birdwatchers are aware that Italy has vast areas of untamed countryside that provide many different kinds of habitats for a wide range of European birds, many of which will be familiar, but many more will be interestingly unfamiliar or exotic. For instance, the vast salt pans around Cagliari, Sardinia are home to thousands of pink flamingos. A website which carries stunning photographs of individual Italian species and their Latin and Italian names, is www.scricciolo.

com. If you are new to birdwatching, moving to Italy would be a great excuse to start a new interest. The national bird protection society is the *Lega Italiana Protezione Uccelli* or LIPU (www.lipu.it). Not only is birdwatching a great way to learn more about birdlife, but it should also take you to places in Italy that you might otherwise never get around to exploring: coastal habitats, mountain forests and wetlands etc. LIPU organises birdwatching holidays that can include camping and trekking. Such events can last a day, a weekend, a week or longer. The birdwatching group nearest to you can be tracked down through the LIPU website. *Ucelli* (birds) need all the protection they can get in Italy as many smaller species such as finches are shot for sport, or the table, or in the name of crop protection.

Canoeing and Rafting

Much of Italy's canoeing and rafting takes place on the River Noce in the Val di Sole, Trentino, which is an international kayaking competition venue. The river has sections suitable for both experienced and novice canoeists and rafters. The other popular river sport that is suitable for most people is hydrospeeding (whizzing down channels in a specially padded diving suit and helmet using a water-bob which you lie on to keep afloat) All equipment for these sports is provided by the canoeing and rafting centre and a qualified guide always accompanies a novice. The season lasts from May to October. Further information can be obtained from the national canoeing and rafting organisation: *Centro Canoa Rafting,* Val di Sole (Via Gole 105, Dimaro; ☎0463 973278; www.raftingcenter.it; info@raftingcenter.it; www.valdisole.net).

Cycling

Competitive cycling is something that Italians have long been passionate about, but you don't have to be a lycra lunatic with the killer instinct of Lance Armstrong to enjoy cycling in Italy. Alongside the official sport cycling organisations is the more laid back bicycle tourism organisation *Federazione Italiana Amici della Bicicletta* (www.fiabonlus.it) which is linked to the European Cyclists' Federation and organises rides and reunions as an alternative way of tourism. However, its primary aim is to promote cycling in Italy as an environmentally friendly means of transport that reduces pollution and congestion in towns and cities. It has associations in every region of Italy and organises local events, runs cycle excursions and works to promote bicycle friendly reception on trains. You can load your bike as accompanying item on Regional, Direct and Interregional trains that carry the bicycle sign, and you pay a charge. However, if your bike is partially dismantled and stored in a bicycle bag it can be carried free of charge but will probably need to be insured against theft, especially on night trains. Some international trains have a dedicated bicycle carriage or special bicycle spaces in passenger carriages.

FIAB is also behind the Italian National Cycle Network (Bicitalia) which proposes a network of 12,000km cycle routes consisting of a series of north south routes, criss-crossed by east-west routes. This is an ambitious project as it will have to cover every region and find safe routes for cyclists into the centres of historic towns and cities including Milan, Rome and Naples. You can find details of the proposed national routes at www.fiab-onlus.it/English/bicitale.htm.

There are already projects in progress to create cycle networks within regions and provinces, which are not part of the national network; they include those around Turin, Trento, Bolzano, Modena, Lodi, Brescia, Franciacorta and Mantova.

National Federazione Ciclistica Italiana (www.federciclismo.it) The other Italian national cycling organisation has local branches throughout the regions which you can find on the website www.federciclismo.it/regioni/index.asp.

Fishing (Pesca)

Fishing is popular with all age groups and all levels of society in Italy. As you would expect, you cannot fish in any river, lake or other stretch of water within Italy unless you have a licence (*Licenza di Pesca nelle Acque Interne*), which you obtain from the administration offices, usually the hunting and fishing department (*Dipartimento Caccia e Pesca*) of your local comune. Each comune has a slightly different system and the charges also vary slightly between regions. There are several different permits; *Licenza di Tipo A* is for professional anglers, while *Licenza di Tipo B* is for local residents. Some communes issue the Licenza di Tipo B for up to ten years at a time. Italians whose second homes are in the comune pay slightly higher charges than permanent residents of the comune, while foreign non-residents can only get a 3-months permit (*Licenza di Tipo D*) which cannot be renewed in the same year in which it was bought.

To obtain a licence, you will need to fill in an application form (*domanda*) which you get from the post office where it must be given a tax stamp (*marca da bollo*) which costs about €15. The application form, complete with *marca da bollo* is known as a (*domanda in bollo*). You then present this at the municipal offices with a variety of documents which vary from region to region but will include a couple of mugshot photographs (which may have to be certified) and an identity document.

Even armed with a municipal licence you still cannot fish anywhere you want, for instance private lakes and waterways (*Centri Privati di Pesca*). Privately owned fishing spots issue their own permits which you will need *in addition* to your muncipal licence. Day or annual permits for private fishing are obtainable from local fishing shops (*negozi per la pesca*). Charges are usually modest. Flyfishing in the Dolomites is said to be excellent.

Fishing in the ocean from a beach or a boat does not require a licence. There may be other regulations such as a closed period for some species for the spawning season and a minimum permitted size for fish caught. Bass fishing is very popular and there is a National Federation of Bass Clubs. BASS also stands, somewhat ungrammatically, for Bass Anglers Sportman Society. The website www.bassmania.net which is also an online magazine, is where you can learn more. Off Sardinia things get a little wilder, and you can charter fishing boats to go after Bluefin, Bonito, Dorado, Barracuda, and Amberjack as well as the ubiquitous bass.

National Parks

Italy has 21 national parks (and three more in the pipeline) all overseen by the *Ministero dell'Ambiente*. Some national parks stretch over more than one region like the *Parco Nazionale dello Stelvio*, which incorporates parts of Lombardy and Trento-Alto Adige in the north west of Italy. Details of all the parks can be found at www.parks.it/indice/ NatParks.html. They include land-locked parks such as Gran Paradiso in Piemonte and Val Grande in Val d'Aosta, protected marine areas (*Aree Marine Protette*) such as Asinara promontory and the surrounding sea area in northeast Sardinia and the Arcipelago Toscano (The Tuscan Archipelago), and coastal strips such as the Cinque Terre of Liguria (a UNESCO World Heritage Site). In addition the provinces have their own conservation designated areas (*riserve statali*) which include woods, mountain summits, aboretums, hot springs etc. The national parks designation also includes areas dominated by ponds and wetlands (*zone umide*).

Activities available in state parks vary according to the natural features and facilities of the park: archery, skiing, birdwatching, diving and fishing are just some of the dozen or so available. However, by far the most widespread activity carried out in parks is hiking. On the National Parks website www.parks.it you can search for your favourite sport or activity, or find out what activities are on offer at your nearest one. National Parks are a great resource in the outdoors and fantastic areas of exploration for all ages. To find out more about them, go to their website, or key in to your search engine *Parchi e Aree Protette* (Parks and Conservation Areas) followed by the name of the *provincia* in which you are interested.

Snow Walking

Snow walking using special shoes known as *ciaspole* or *rachette da neve,* has only recently been taken up as a recreational activity in Italy. The original snow walking was done by hunters and peasants, who attached circles of wood, criss-crossed with strips of leather beneath their shoes, so that they could move about the mountains in winter, in pursuit of their livelihoods. Army training in the mountains, developed a modern, efficient snowshoe, which has spilled over into civilian life making this a recreation accessible to all ages. Unlike downhill skiing no particular preparation is required and if you can walk, you can snow walk. It is particularly popular amongst retired people and those who have never learned to ski. Slopes navigated this way are not usually very steep and snowshoes are now made of durable, light materials including titanium alloys, which mean that it is not as strenuous as cross-country skiing (*sci da fondo*). Walking boots or trekking shoes are worn with the snowshoes attached. Snow walking is done among the ski areas of the Dolomites and itineraries include Val Gardena – Alpe di Siusi, Alta Pusteria, San Martino – Passo Rolle, Alta Badia, Plan de Corones, Madonna di Campiglio and Val d'Isarco. Further information can be obtained from the websites of the mountain provinces of Italy e.g. www.dolomiti.it/ita/sport/ciaspole/htm or by doing an internet search for 'ciaspole'.

Walking and Rambling

Walking is a popular family activity in Italy. Italians are just as keen on it as tourists and foreign residents; and what native wouldn't want to savour the amazing landscapes of Italy at this time-honoured pace? The Italian long distance paths are in the north of the country: they are the *Sentiero Italia* (*Percorso Camminaitalia '99* or SI); the *Alta Via dei Monti Liguri* (*Ligurian Alta Via* or AV) which is a section of the E1 and E7 European Long Distance Paths; the *Grande Escursione Appenninica* (GEA) which is a stretch of the E1; and the *Grande Traversata delle Alpi* (The Italian Alps Grand Traverse or GTA) which is a segment of the E10 European Long Distance Path. However, you can walk almost anywhere in Italy and the national parks (see above) are also popular with hikers.

Many local and regional paths are unmarked so you will need large scale maps such as the IGM Military Series (the equivalent of the UK's OS), but not all areas are available. For the Alpine regions there is also the IGC series. Large scale maps for the Dolomites are published by Kompass and Berndt and Freytag. Edizioni Multigraphic are producing maps for each province but they are not all available yet (though Tuscany and Central Italy are). If you are buying maps before you go to Italy, try specialists The Map Shop in Upton on Severn (www.themapshop.co.uk/italy.htm; ☎01684-593146).

Dolomites Trekking (£11.99) from Trailblazer is an excellent guide to Alta Via 1 and 2 and many other walks in the Dolomites. You can find a list of books in English on walking in Italy at www.walkingonthe

web.co.uk/countries/italy.htm and useful walking information on the Italian National Parks (see also above) website www.parks.it including information for 'Accessible Trails' which have been designed specifically with disabled people's access and enjoyment in mind, though they are open to all.

> **Useful Contacts**
>
> **Associazione Sentiero Italia (Italian Trail Association):** via San Gervasio 12, 50131 Firenze FI. Develops waymarked trails in the northern Alpine region of Italy.
>
> **Federazione Italiana Escursionismo (Italian Walking Federation):** Via La Spezia 58r, 16149 Genova; www.fienazit.freeweb.org and www.fietalia.it. Federation of walking and mountain clubs all over Italy. FIE also coordinates the development of the European long distance paths in Italy.

Winter Sports (Sport Invernali)

Italians indulge in a variety of snowsports but skiing and boarding are the most popular. The 2006 Winter Olympics were held in Turin showcasing the range of competitive snowsports including, bob (bobsleighing) curling, ice-hockey, ice dancing as well as the boarding and skiing events. Italy has a dozen Alpine resorts including Sauze d'Oulx, Bardonecchia and Sestriere, which are close to the French border, while further north in the Val d'Aosta you will find Courmayeur (Italy's most glamorous resort) and Breuil-Cervinia, while in the north-east, in the Dolomiti range are Madonna di Campiglio and Cortina d'Ampezzo. The best skiing is undoubtedly in the northern Alpine region – but if you live further south in Italy, you might want to try the Gran Sasso, east of Rome and home of the purpose-built Campo Felice resort. Even in the toe of Italy, Calabria, you will find a few cross-country skiing trails in the Sila Massif. Italy is skiing mad, and produced Europe's most charismatic competition skier of the 1980s and 1990s, the unstoppable Alberto Tomba ('Tomba la Bomba').

You can get further information from the *Federazione Italiana Sport Invernali* (via Piranesi 44/B, 20137 Milano; www.fisi.org).

ITALIAN SPORTS FEDERATIONS

Archery: *Federazione Italiana Tiro con l'Arco; www.fitarco_Italia.org.*
Athletics (Track & Field): *Fed. Italiana Athletica Leggera (FIDAL); www.fidal.it.*
Aviation: *Aero Club d'Italia (AECI); www.aeci.it.*
Fencing: *Federazione Italiana Scherma;* www.scherma-fis.it.
Fishing & Sub-Aqua: *Fed. Italiana Pesca Sportiva e Atività Subacque;* www. fipsas.it.
Gliding: *Federazione Italiana Volo a Vela;* www.fivv.it.
Hang Gliding/Paragliding: *Federazione Italiania Volo Libero;* www.fivl.it
Horse Racing: *Fed. Italiana Sport Equestri* (FISE); www.fise.it.
Hunting: *Federazione Italiana Caccia (FIDC); www.fidc.it.*
Golf: *Federazione Italiana Golf (FIG); www.fig.it.*
Martial Arts (Judo etc): *Federazione Italiana Atletica Pesante (FILPJ).*
Motorcycling: *Fed. Motociclistica Italiana; www.fmi.it.*
Motor Sports: *Automobile Club d'Italia (A.C.I.); www.aci.it.*
Parachuting: *Fed. Italiania di Paracadutismo Sportivo;* www.fipas.it/inglese.
Tennis: *Federazione Italiana Tennis* (FIT); www.federtennis.it.
Waterskiing: *Fed. Italiana Sci Nautico;* www.scinautico.com.

TAKING COURSES

University of The Third Age

As good a place to start for as any could be the University of the Third Age or U3A as it is known internationally. This is a char- ity registered voluntary organisation with bases in different coun- tries for informal (i.e. no diplomas or degrees), continual learning, which is aimed at seniors. It was founded in Toulouse in 1972, and other chapters have followed in several European countries including Britain, Spain and France. You can follow courses online or in person. The Italian U3A is extremely active. There are 500 branches of the *Università della Terza Età* (University of the Third Age) in Italy; 74 of them in Piemonte. They are often linked to the local university or cultural association. For a taster, you could start before you leave the UK at the English chapter of U3A (www.u3a. org.uk/courses/online/list.htm) whose online courses range from

Astronomy to The Romans. You register by filing an application form. Fees vary according to course and whether it is online (with or without tutor) or in person.

In Italy you can apply to the Italian *Università della Terza Età*. Their website www.unitre.net/it enables you to enter the name of your *comune* and find the nearest centre to you, where you can go for courses. Courses can include anything from painting on glass, to Italian for Foreigners, and from the History of Religion to the Mythology of the Stars, and from Choral singing to Yoga. The *Università della Terza Età*, depending on which branch you belong to, also organises cultural visits to monuments, galleries and museums which are a great way to socialize with Italians. The annual registration fee in Italy is about 35 euros and the cost of courses varies up to 100 euros. Fees may be waived for those on very low incomes.

Italian Universities for Foreigners

The well-known university for foreigners in Italy is the international *Università Italiana per Stranieri di Perugia* (the Italian University for Foreigners in Perugia) in the region of Umbria, which offers language and cultural courses for all levels of ability. It claims to be able to teach anyone Italian from scratch to survival language in four to eight weeks and accepts students aged 8 to 80. It has a four-week summer programme in Italian language and culture, that attracts students from all over the world and costs about €2000 plus board and lodging costs. Italy's only other university for foreigners is in Siena, but it is on a smaller scale; about a quarter the size of Perugia. Siena offers four intensive, ten-week language and culture courses for foreigners a year, starting in January, April, July and October. It is slightly more expensive than Perugia. It also offers a three-year degree course in Italian language and culture.

The John Cabot American University in Rome (www.johncabot. edu/summersession/summer_intro.htm) offers summer sessions in art history and Italian studies as well as other non-Italian subjects such as natural sciences and business administration.

Useful Contacts

Italian University for Foreigners in Perugia *(Università Italiana per Stranieri di Perugia):* Palazzo Gallenga, Piazza Fortebraccio 4, 06122 Perugia; ☎ 075 57461; www.unistrapg.it..

Università per Stranieri di Siena (Siena University for Foreigners): Via Pantaneto 45, 53100 Siena; www.unistrasi.it

UK Open University – Study in English

You can also study Italian art and architecture, and the Renaissance (as well as many other courses) in English, with the UK's Open University; see www.open.ac.uk/courses/ for what is offered. The course materials can be posted to your Italian address, which could work out quite expensive. You will also be allocated a tutor. Contact with the tutor is by telephone and email and the student will be given a study calendar, which informs him/her when assignments are due. There are also tutorials to attend (usually one per month) but these are not compulsory and may not be practical for students resident in Italy. It is however a chance for students to meet the tutor in person. For most courses a computer is essential. Students can register via the OU website or by telephoning 0044 870 333 4340 from Italy. More general information about becoming an OU student can be found at www.open.ac.uk/learners-guide/course-choice/eventline/index.htm.

Italian Language Courses

Foreigners come to Italy, keen to learn Italian on courses that take place in the glorious cities and smaller towns of Italy, mostly during the summer. You can find courses on offer in all the most popular cities: Bologna, Florence, Rome, Siena, Milan etc. Many courses come with different types of accommodation and a full cultural programme, or are combined with Italian cookery classes and there are even classes for anyone wanting to learn Italian for singing opera. Most schools can arrange one-to-one courses in the teacher's home if requested.

The *Dante Alighieri Society* (www.dantealighieri.com) is the International Italian cultural organisation charged with disseminating Italian language and culture worldwide, and it offers courses (Italian

Language, Italian for Opera singers, Italian Cookery) in Siena. However, as Stephanie Martin of the *Siena Scuola Dante Alighieri* explains, they have tailored some courses towards foreigners who have come to live in Italy:

> *We have been inspired to design a specific course* 'Siena Magnifica' *to cater for the increasing number of people moving here who want an understanding of the town near where they are living, or who are thinking of moving here. A number of our past students have moved to Italy from the USA and Britain to live their dream in Tuscany. About 22% of our students are aged 61+.*

Other organisations offering courses for all ages include Italian Language Schools (www.ilsonline.it) and *Istituto Linguistico* (www.ilm. it): both are chains with schools in several cities. ILS has a school in Otranto, a beautiful small town in Puglia. Www.bolognalingua.com is a small association of experienced teachers offering one-to-one tuition in their houses in Bologna. The *Torre di Babele Scuola di Italiano* (www. torredibabele.com) in Rome has two-week Senior Class courses (four a year) for students aged 50+. You can find others by doing a web search (e.g. learning+language+italy) for Italian courses in Italy and you will be spoilt for choice or check the website www.it-schools.com which lists Italian language and culture schools all round Italy. Alternatively, if you want to study locally, check the website of the provincia where you are living for a language school (*scuola di lingua*).

Art Courses

Most budding artists could feel intimidated learning to paint in Italy through being constantly confronted by the masterpieces of some of the best artists ever to put paint and brush to canvas, wood and plaster. These are a potent reminder of how little chance there is of arriving on the same artistic planet as Giotto, Raphael, Titian et al. Such feelings of inadequacy not withstanding, many artists, or those who dabble, but would like to improve, feel inspired to paint by the glorious landscapes, and almost everything else around them in Italy.

There is a wide choice of painting holidays in Italy, usually fronted by a British or American artist/instructor but these are usually for people who want a relaxing holiday rather than an intensive schooling from a taskmaster. The website www.art-courses-italy.com/ which is part of the *Scuola Leonardo da Vinci* language school, offers drawing and painting courses in Florence, including one for watercolour painting; while Tuscany Painting (www.Tuscany-painting.com) offers painting and art workshops in Tuscany, Florence and the Cinque Terre. Courses on offer include a half-day painting workshop *en plein air* and a full day in Chianti and a rather more demanding workshop week in the Cinque Terre.

Italian Cookery Courses

One of the most exciting things about retiring to Italy is the chance to enjoy Italian cooking in all its mouthwatering splendour of seasonal and regional specialities, while knowing that you are eating one of the healthiest diets in Europe. Most people, when confronted with piles of fresh ingredients from toadstools to tentacled and pincered sea beasts, not to mention bouquet-sized bunches of herbs unrecognisable in their natural state, are flummoxed as to how to prepare them in their own kitchen. A cookery course could be just the way to learn. Italian cooking has such a great reputation that quite an industry has grown up around showing people how do it. A couple of useful websites that list courses available around Italy are www.cookitaly. com, www.italiancookerycourse.com and www.it-schools.com. The *Dante Alighieri School* in Siena has Language Courses combined with cookery as well as dedicated Cookery Programmes. Stephanie Martin of the School explains:

The best way to learn the art of Italian cooking is to come here and experience it hands-on. Our school has a large, fully-equipped kitchen and our cookery course attracts foreign families already living in Italy and is popular with older people from late forties upwards. The oldest is a lady aged 85 who has been twice.

GARDENING

A garden – or at least a terrace or courtyard – is a priority for most retired people, especially in Italy, where life outdoors is encouraged by the climate: a place to grow your own herbs and to enjoy the sun in winter and the shade in summer. If you have pets or grand-children or give parties, or want to practise the healthy and creative hobby of gardening, a garden is indispensable.

There are varying hardiness zones and soil qualities in Italy that the keen gardener should be aware of. The climate ranges from the frost-free Southern coastal and island regions where the lemon tree grows, to the permafrost of the Alps. In between are the continental climate of the Po valley with extremes of heat and cold and the milder climate of the central regions where the olive tree grows.

The soil: most of the country is mountainous or hilly, and calcareous; heavy clay soil predominates. There are fertile volcanic plains in Campania, Lazio and Sicily. Puglia has a deep productive soil, and the Po valley yields a rich alluvial tilth, especially in the Lugo area where the peach orchards flourish. Acid microhabitats by the lakes in the north promote the growth of massive camellias, azaleas and rhododendrons, while much of the southern uplands is sheer and barren rock, and scrub (*macchia*), as is Sardinia.

The problem of water is another decisive factor. If there is a shortage of water – and the equivalent of a hosepipe ban on public water is universal throughout Italy, you should radically reconsider your project. Why retire to a desert? It is no fun living through the heat of the summer without an abundance of water. Gardens in hot climates depend on rills, pools and fountains and lush shady greenery for their charm. Tropical jasmines, mandevilleas, bougainvillea, Chinese hibiscus, lemons, gardenias and plumbagos, only luxuriate with abundant irrigation. They depend on constant attention and labour.

But if you find yourself stuck with a shortage of water and labour – which is the normal situation for the house owner in Italy – do not despair. The recent science of *xeriscaping*, pioneered in the droughts of Arizona, makes a virtue of indigenous – and exotic – plants, which thrive in arid conditions and only need watering to establish themselves in the first year. These plants are: rosemary, oleander, cypress, santolina, lemon verbena, rue, curry plant, artemisia (listed below for their insect repellent qualities) and:

- Lavender planted in rows, or clumps of three.
- Teucrium fruticans, planting as lavender.
- Saltbush (atriplex halimus) – *(porcellana del mare)*.
- Crape myrtle or Pride of India *(lagerstroemia indica)*. Go for the white and red varieties.
- Pomegranate *(melograno)*. Go for the dwarf variety *(nana)*.
- Jerusalem sage *(phlomis fruticosa)*.
- Cistus *(cisto)*.
- Kitchen sage *(salvia officinalis)*. Go for the common thin-leafed variety for the best flavour.

For climbers:

- The potato vine *(solanum jasminoides)* flowers profusely until the winter and comes back even when cut down by the frost, like a scentless jasmine, blue tinged.
- The Banksian rose – *(rosa Banksiae)* the only rose that requires no attention, used for pergolas, thornless, flowers in spring, shady insect free foliage.
- The strawberry grape – *(uva fragola)* known as the Concord grape – the only grapevine that requires no insecticide, large leaves, high vitamin C.

For trees:

- The Carob *(carruba)* in the south.
- The Fremontodendron, a fragrant evergreen, from California and Mexico, with showy yellow flowers in Spring.
- The Olive *(ulivo)*

Olives. If you have land and are at a loss what to plant, plant an olive grove. For this you need holes a cubic metre in volume, dug with an excavator, refilled and heavily manured, at five metre intervals in a regular *quincunx* (chequerboard) formation. Plant three-year-old potted plants from a nursery in the spring, with the final earth level at least a hand's breadth above the rootstock. Choose the *Taggiasco* in Liguria, the *Correggiola* in central Italy or the favourite type of your region (and a pollinator). The olive tree is attractive even when neglected and superbly rewarding: when tended to it will yield oil for centuries. For more information there is an excellent English-speaking website at www.olivematters.com. Carole Means found that her garden in Puglia was not only a pleasure, but also a source of income:

> We had to buy a house, which was already renovated as we did not have the resources to do up another house. Our house is in the country and has an acre of land with olive and fruit trees, which we harvest ourselves. We sometimes sell the olives.

Ilex. You may also consider either a *lecceto* or ilex grove – mop-head ilexes planted regularly as above, with a three-metre spacing; will form a dense shaded area screening against sight and sound – or a walnut grove, an investment yielding valuable timber in 25 years time.

Grass. For grass sow a mixture of rye grasses, (*loietto* and/or *lolium perenne Manhattan*) and Bermuda crab grass (*gramigna* and/or *cynodon dactylon Uganda*), thickly in autumn. The crabgrass is green in summer and brown in winter. The rye grass is green in winter but dies back in the drought of summer. For large areas such as olive groves, invest in a ride-on mower.

Planning Your Garden

If gardening is one of your chief pleasures it would be wise to make your garden a priority and not an afterthought. The factors listed above should stimulate you to decide what possibilities are viable. Seek out the local nurseries and garden centres as soon as possible; ask them to make a plan and an estimate for supplying and planting what you want. At least aim to get the windbreaks, screening, shade and orchard plants into the ground in the first year. It is surprising how soon they will work their magic and give you no cause to regret years later that you didn't plant things when you first came.

For terraces – *tufo blocks* are best (soft porous sandstone), set on a screed of sand or grit; sweep a mixture of dry sand and cement into the cracks and water in with a hosepipe.

The aesthetic side of gardening depends on taste and fashion; one man's yew is another man's *Leylandii*. But certain design rules are immutable, and the enemies of the garden are the same for everyone. These should be borne in mind from the very start when sizing up a potential property.

The design rules are governed by the dimensions of the land and the quantity of the humans, animals and machines using the garden, and by the orientation of the sun and the direction of the winds.

- Paths must be wide enough for a wheelbarrow or a wheelchair – 3ft/90cm.
- Ramps for wheelchairs should not exceed an 8% gradient.
- Lintels or arches should be at least 6ft 6in/2m.
- The headroom for pergolas at least 8ft 6in/2.5m.
- A terrace for 12 people dining, with barbecue and side tables, needs an area of at least 20ft x 12ft/6m x 4m.
- The terrace should have a fall of 1inch in 6ft/3cm per 3m to carry off the rain.
- Risers and treads of all steps must be even and regular conforming to pre-ordained proportions (Wren's 15 inch tread to a 5 inch riser is the ideal).
- A wall to sit on should be 16in-24in/40cm – 60cm high.
- A safety railing or wall should be 3ft/90cm high.
- A tennis court needs an area of 120ft x 60ft/36m x 18m.
- A car park for six cars needs an area of 50ft x 33ft/15m x 10m, and shade.
- A 40ft/12m swimming pool and its surround needs at least 66ft x 33ft/20m x 10m.
- Hedges and windbreaks should be on the north side to protect against the tramontana wind.
- Shade trees should be on the south of the house.
- Large trees (*piante di alto fusto*) must be planted no less than 10ft/3m and hedges (siepi) no less than 20inches/50cm inside the boundary (by law).

○ Boundary hedges and fences must not exceed 6ft 6in/2m in height (by law).

○ The natural flow of human pathways should be respected and retained.

○ Dead-end and shaded areas, which are not in a corridor, should be provided, for privacy.

○ Water and electricity should be laid on for irrigation, garden machinery and lighting.

○ Terrace, pathway and step lighting are desirable.

○ An easy access tool shed big enough for a lawnmower.

○ A covered wood store.

○ A compost emplacement.

All these should be visualised in the first survey of a potential garden.

Recommended Nurseries	
Name and Location	**Website and Speciality**
Montivivai (Lucca)	www.montivivai.com
	Specialises in indigenous and old-fashioned fruit trees. Full landscaping service and garden centre.
Rose Barni (Pistoia)	www.rosebarni.com
	Online shopping for bare root roses, Rugosa, Chinensis etc. Worth visiting for container - grown roses in winter. An eclectic selection of plants, inspired by monastic herbs, grown by Don Leevers and Lindsay Megarritty
Vivaio Venzano,Mazzolla, (Volterra) Walter Branchi Roses Baschi (TN), Umbria	A superb selection of old roses for Italy www,rosebranchi.com
N. Sgaravatti e C. Sementi Valdarno (Arezzo)	Excellent seeds, grass seed mixes, bulbs etc. branches at Ancona, Mestre and Rome garden centres. www.Sgaravatti.net/uk
Mediterranean in Puglia	www.exposalento.it
sardinia.com	Four nurseries in Sardinia. Commercial landscaping. Specialises in Mediterranean plants for xeriscaping.

Otherwise consult the yellow pages – *pagine gialle* – for *vivaio* (nursery) or 'garden center'. An excellent website for all gardening matters is www.giardinaggio.it.

Enemies of the Garden

Enemies of the garden in Italy are: neglect, drought, frost, wind, fire, water, insects, animals, prying eyes, thieves and vandals, slippery and dangerous surfaces, and noise.

Neglect. To combat neglect you should foresee yourself or someone else tending to the garden, closing it down for the winter, mowing, weeding, cleaning, sweeping, for at least one hour a week, especially during the season of most rampant growth between March and July.

Drought. Summer is a time of almost certain drought when the plants have to be watered, between June and September. An automatic irrigation system supplied by your own rainwater, springwater, or purified sewage water will prove cheaper in the long run than paying a person to do the watering. Such an installation is familiar to most Italian plumbers, who benefit from the spin-off technology of the Italian horticultural industry.

Frost. The other most dangerous time for plants is the winter when temperatures can dip below -10c and frost can be a killer. A *limonaia* or an orangery is the traditional solution to this problem: a large glazed room facing south – or a small greenhouse – into which lemon trees and other tender plants in pots are wheeled for the winter. Otherwise individual plants must be wrapped in fleece, bubblewrap or hessian where they stand.

Winds. The arsenal of the Italian climate also contains withering winds, which need guarding against: the *tramontana* from Siberia – from the north-east – at its worst known as the *Bora* in Trieste. Steep hills and buildings in that quarter are worth noting as valuable protection. A shelter belt or a windbreak will also help: a wire or netting fence 5ft/1.5m or 6ft 6in/2m high, with a screen of shading fabric firmly attached, is the quickest and cheapest solution, preferably incorporating in its lee – to take over in the future – a row of hedging plants. The most robust of these would be the holm-oak or ilex *quercus ilex/leccio*, although bay *alloro, arbutus* (*corbezzolo*), *eleagnus ebbingei*, or a combination of these could be considered, and the cypress (*cupressus sempervireus pyramida-*

lis) planted close would be expensive but superb; excellent also around a tennis court, (make sure you get the grafted *d'innesto* pencil thin cypress and not the seedlings which branch horizontally).

> For an instant windbreak, a hedge of bamboo is recommended (get only *phyllostachys aurea*) known as *canne d'India;* an old favourite in Italian villa gardens. You need to dig a trench 20ins/50 cm in depth and width preferably by means of a minidigger (*scavatorino*), mix in a lot of humus and fertiliser (*concime*) and line both sides with an impenetrable vertical barrier 20ins/50 cm. Fibreglass *vetroresina* cut to size from the roll by your local hardware shop (*ferramenta*) is the best material for this. When confined in this way the bamboo becomes a neat, dense, constantly sprouting hedge, instead of a dreaded colonising monster thicket. It is self-mulching, the right height and of a cheerful green colour, swaying and singing in the breeze. It will not grow in heavy clay, needs watering the first year and responds to frequent fertilising. When grown on both sides of a broad path *phyllostachys aurea* creates a green shady tunnel.

Fire. Another hazard, fire, decimates hectares of Italian woodland every summer. Commonsense precautions are: to keep your garden clear of combustible dry undergrowth, refrain from lighting bonfires in the summer and be careful with barbecues and cigarettes.

Water. Heavy rainfall and flash floods are very common in Italy. Lanes become riverbeds, floods have been known to wipe out freshly planted groves. Storm drains must be provided. Heavy duty cast-iron grilles set into concreted gulleys must be placed at regular intervals on gravel access roads, and in front of houses and garages.

Insects. Insects in Italy are at least as virulent as they are in north America; stagnant water should be filled in – or stocked with Koi carp to eat up the mosquitoes. Italian country folk are puzzled by the English habit of growing creepers on their house walls. They attract insects and *animali*. This is particularly true of the wisteria (*glicine*) which hornets love and which is bad for asthmatics – and should with all its ilk be banished to the farthest reaches of the garden. You should surround the house with plants that repel insects such as:

○ The oleander (*oleandro*) is actually poisonous to animals as well as to insects.

○ The cypress, (*cipresso*) – the classic cupressus sempervirens pyremidalis mentioned above), has a pleasant smell for humans and birds but not for insects. Its wood was prized as a moth repellent for wardrobes. Originating from Afghanistan, it loves the arid conditions at the base of a house wall exposed to the sun and it grows into a neat aromatic evergreen column, which only needs occasional clipping.

○ Cotton lavender, *santolina* – needs clipping.

○ Lemon verbena Lippia citriodora (*cedrina*) seems to die in the winter, but grows back in the summer with intensely aromatic leaves to over 8ft/2.40m.

○ Rue (*ruta*).

○ Curry plant *helichrysum italicum*.

○ Artemisia.

○ Rosemary (*rosmarino*) a plant whose life is lengthened to 30 years or more by annual clipping, is excellent as topiary, growing to the height of a person it is ideal on either side of a kitchen door, being an essential ingredient of sauces and roasts, also good ground cover for escarpments (*scarpate*), for which the creeping version, *rosmarinus prostratus* is recommended.

Another plant to avoid in the garden is the umbrella pine (*pinus pinea*) which as well as attracting the toxic processional caterpillar plays havoc with terraces with its roots. Further precautions against insects – fill and point all cracks in brickwork, stonework, remove all loose piles of rubble, where scorpions might lurk – and spray all surfaces with insecticide.

Animali. Animals to guard against are porcupines (*istrici*), wild boar (*cinghiali*), roebuck (*caprioli*), pine martens (*faina*). Porcupines will dig out and eat any bulbs or rhizomes – lilies, iris, tulips, narcissus etc. Wild boar will rootle and wallow destructively. Roebuck love feeding on roses, flowers and any tasty young shoots. All can be kept out by a stout fence of rabbit wire, or chain link. 5ft or 6ft 6in/1.5m or 2m high. But the pine marten (*faina*) is a mysterious loner, which climbs on to roofs and dislodges tiles in search of eggs, often at dead of night. Feral cats on the other hand are to be welcomed for their elimination of mice, rats, and other vermin. Bats are beneficial for their consumption of insects, but their bite can be lethal and they frighten people, so should be discouraged by screening off their entrance holes to attics, sheds and cellars. Snakes are also frightening; mostly they are harmless long green grass snakes (*serpi*), but adders (*vipere*) which are short and dark are occasionally found. They love sunning themselves and hiding in piles of stones. Country house-holders are recommended to keep viper serum in the fridge as an antidote to bites. *Il siero anti-vipera* can be acquired at the pharmacy (*farmacia*). But the best protection against snakes is to point or grout all cracks and hiding places, get rid of all piles of stones and bricks and beware of all gaps or spaces beneath decking; also lay ashes and grit to deter slugs and snails.

Prying Eyes and Thieving Hands. Prying eyes are a psychological discomfort, which can be screened off by a double layer of bamboo slatting (*cannicci*) or preferably by evergreen plants or trees. The variety and ingenuity of the screening used on the Ligurian Riviera shows what can be done for the preservation of privacy at close quarters – much of it being *pittosporum tobira*, which thrives there. As for thieves and vandals, even in apparently law abiding areas, there is always the first time. In the countryside, near Siena, for example an Italian couple who had proudly planted a new olive grove found that their olive saplings were disappearing at the rate of four or five a night, and there was nothing they could do about it. Similarly terra-cotta pots of lavender or jasmine in village streets are a temptation to passing kleptomaniacs and have to be chained firmly in place. Tools have to be locked up in cars and sheds. 'Not like in the old days when you could leave your... ' is a sentiment as common in Italy as any-where else. Stout wire netting fencing around your whole property is your best defence.

Noise. Noise can be muffled by evergreen thickets – Italian neighbours are characteristically noisy, they are part of the music of the country – but the sound of roads, motorways, or factories is a form of pollu-tion which could become unbearable. The only really effective barrier against noise is a mound of earth three metres in height (to test this go to the old Roman amphitheatre at Roselle near Grosseto.) This remedy should be considered before any landscaping operations take place (such as digging out the pool). With careful forethought hundreds of cubic metres could be redeployed for this purpose that would otherwise go to waste.

Gardening Glossary			
Abete	fir tree	*Melo*	apple tree
Albicocco	apricot	*Mirto*	myrtle
Alloro	bay (laurel)	*Mortella*	myrtle
Arancio	orange tree	*Nespolo*	medlar, loquat
Argilla	clay	*Noce*	walnut
Arnesi	tools	*Nocciolo*	hazel
Badile	shovel	*Oleandro*	oleander
Boschetto	grove	*Oliveto*	olive grove
Bosso	box	*Pacciamatura*	mulch
Calce	lime	*Paiolo*	pail
Carciofo	artichoke	*Pala*	shovel
Carriola	wheelbarrow	*Pero*	pear tree
Cedrina	lemon verbena	*Pesco*	peach tree
Cedro	cedar	*Potare*	to prune
Cesoie	shears	*Pratino*	lawn
Cipresso	cypress	*Pino*	Pine tree
Corbezzolo	arbutus (strawberry tree)	*Pineto*	pine grove
Cotogna	quince fruit	*Querce*	oak
Cotogno	quince tree	*Rastrellare*	to rake
Falce	scythe	*Rastrello*	rake
Falcetto	sickle	*Rovere*	oak
Fico	fig	*Sabbia*	sand
Forbici	scissors/secateurs	*Sabbione*	coarse sand
Forca	pitchfork	*Secchio*	bucket
Fragole	strawberry	*Spuntare*	to trim
Frutteto	orchard	*Topinambur*	Jerusalem artichoke
Grappolo	bunch of grapes	*Tufo*	soft sandstone

Lampone	raspberry	Uva	grapes
Leccio	ilex, holm oak	Vanga	spade for digging
Lentisco	lentisk	Vite	vine
Limonaia	orangery	Viti	vines
Limone	lemon	Vigna	vineyard
Mandarlo	almond	Vigneto	vineyard
Mazza	sledgehammer	Zappa	hoe, mattock
Melagrano	pomegranate		

TRAVELLING AND TOURISM IN ITALY

Most foreigners retiring to Italy aspire to travel widely within their adopted country. Italy will never disappoint travellers, as it has everything in terms of landscapes, antiquity, culture, coasts, cuisine and climate that you could ever wish for. Evidently the Italians feel the same about their own land. Of the 28% of Italian pensioners who took a holiday in 2005, only 6% crossed the Italian frontier for their break, while the remainder took their holidays within Italy. Of the younger generations, twice as many took their holidays in Italy as went abroad.

Most Italians therefore take their holidays in Italy, in places that have been popular for generations around the lakes, up in the mountains, at the spas, and especially on the coastal areas including the Italian islands: large (as in Sicily) and small (as in the Tuscan archipelago). Italy has 8,000km of coastline, so there is plenty of space for everybody. Foreign package tourists are channelled to the tourist hotspots and purpose-built seaside places, where ugly buildings and indiscriminate developments are on a scale large enough to be utilised by the operators of mass tourism. If you want to find the best places, the trick is to go where the Italians go. As far as their coastline is concerned. Italians prefer to holiday where there are *pensiones* and small hotels, or they will rent a villa or modern apartment, rather than stay in a high-rise hotel or resort. Writer Harris Freedman who moved to Umbria five years ago, waxes lyrical about travelling in Italy:

Where I live near Castiglione del Lago is pretty much central Italy. I can drive for two hours either side of here and get to the Mediterranean on one side, or the Adriatic on the other. I can drive to Rome and get a ferry to the Pontine islands, or to Tuscany and visit the islands off the Tuscan coast. There are still lots of places in Italy I want to see. I am surrounded right here in Umbria by three dozen cities such as Assisi, Spoleto, Cortona, Chiusi, Arezzo, which between them contain most of the treasures of Western civilization.

Italy has such an array of possibilities for travel and tourism within its own borders that it can be a problem choosing. The state train service Ferrovie dello Stato is excellent and amazingly cheap. There are internal Italian budget flights such as those operated by Volare (www. volareweb.com, currently in administration, but still functioning) and there are ferries to the Italian islands, and long distance coaches for intercity travel. These options will not always allow you to explore the hidden corners of the Italian countryside, for this you may need your own vehicle. You can of course save on accommodation costs by touring with a caravan or motor-home, but Italians are so hospitable that you would be depriving yourself of a range of delightful encounters in inexpensive, local accommodation in charming residences, *alberghi* (inns) and *agriturismi* (farmsteads).

Travel by Train

The Italian railway system, *Ferrovie dello Stato* (FS), runs one of the cheapest railway services in Western Europe. This is more remarkable than you might think, considering the substantial reforms that were made to services during the last two decades, which resulted in a greater network of inter-city lines and a generally modern, fast and reasonably reliable service. Unlike the UK and North America, branch lines reach the most remote areas, with connecting buses that will get you to the most obscure spots. Despite the heavy subsidies handed out to the rail network, the railways still run up a huge deficit.

Tickets, Timetables and Special Fares. There are usually long queues for tickets at main stations. There are automatic ticket machines, especially at larger stations. It is compulsory to validate all tickets by inserting them in the yellow machines on the platforms, which clip and stamp them. Failure to punch your ticket can make you liable for an on the spot fine.

There is a complete national pocket timetable (*Il Pozzorario*), which can be bought at stations and newspaper kiosks or you can look on the Trenitalia website www.orario.trenitalia.com. The FS website is www.fs-on-line.com and you can avoid queueing by getting regional train information and booking tickets online at www.trenitalia.com. The Trenitalia website also shows current promotional fares such as a Rome to Naples high speed fare for 25 euros and the Happy Train last minute train fares from 10 euros which you can select on a regional basis and book a week or less in advance. Very cheap international tickets (*tariffe speciali)* are sold under the tag 'Smart Price' on the Trenitalia website (www.trenitalia.com) and include from €15 Italy to Nice (*Riviera* trains), Italy to Paris from €25 (*Artesia* trains) and Italy to Austria from €29 (*Allegro* trains). These are usually overnight trains and the prices quoted are just for seats; sleeping compartments are extra. The Italian superfast trains are the *Pendolini* (leaning trains) now exported to many other countries. Confusingly for Brits, high speed services in Italy are called *Eurostar Italia*.

The *rapido* and *IC* (Inter-city) trains are invariably the fastest and most expensive internal trains, stopping only at the major cities. For these a supplement (*supplemento rapido*) is required according to mileage. Remember that the best prices are usually for tickets bought in advance, as tickets bought on the train are subject to a surcharge. Reductions are available to children under 12 and people over 65. The Milan to Rome *rapido* train takes under four hours, with an onward link to Naples. You can also get a Eurostar train from Milan to Rome (650kn) at very cheap fares if you go at night.

The *interregionale, espresso* and *diretto* trains are the next fastest, and more reasonably priced, stopping at most large towns. Lastly, and to be avoided wherever possible (unless you are hoping to enjoy the leisurely pace of Italian rural life) are the painfully slow *regionale/locale* trains which seem to stop at every small village and country backwater imaginable.

There has been a no smoking policy on all Italian national trains since 2004.

STATION SIGNS AND PHRASES

Al Binari/Ai Treni	to the platforms/trains
Arrivi/Partenze	arrivals/departures
Biglietteria	ticket office
Deposito Bagagli	left luggage
Entrata/Uscita	entrance/exit
Orario	timetable
Sala d'Attesa	waiting room
Sottopassagio	underpass
Vietato l'Ingresso	no entry
Andata/Andata e ritorno Firenze	single/return to Florence
Il primo/l'ultimo/il prossimo treno	the first/last/next train
A che binario?	which platform?
È questo posto libero?	Is this seat taken?
Dove siamo?	Where are we?

Buses

Italian cities are dotted with bright orange town buses weaving chaotically through the traffic as Italian motorists resolutely refuse to acknowledge the function of bus lanes. Italy has more buses than any other European country but no national bus company. This means a proliferation of companies, some providing local and others long distance services known as *urbano* (town) and *extraurbano*. (inter-town) respectively. Some companies e.g. www.saj.it run both local and national networks. Bus tickets are fairly inexpensive (though more expensive than train tickets) and are not obtainable on town buses or trams but from tobacconists (*tabaccherie*) which have the black 'T' sign displayed, from ticket offices at the bus termini (*capolinea*) and from some news-stands, tobacconists, lotto windows etc. Tickets should be cancelled at the ticket machine once you are on the bus. Tickets can be bought on inter-city buses, after hours.

There are a number of ticket types, including single tickets (*corsa semplice*), morning or afternoon tickets also known as half-day tickets (*biglietti orari*) and season tickets (*abbonamenti*) of varying length. A season ticket can include use of bus, tram and subway routes (*intera rete*) if necessary. Each city has its own day/week(s) or month passes for local transport, details of which you can usually find on the municipal website. The website www.busstation.net is an excellent site with links to bus companies all over Italy.

Although travelling by train is preferable, especially between large cities, the buses and coaches are a reasonable alternative for shorter trips and can be especially useful during train strikes.

International coach services from Italy include Eurolines (www. eurolines.it) and Stam. Information on bus systems throughout Italy can be found at viaggiare.cerca.com/automezzi_pubblici/centro.html.

Taxis

Italian taxis are either a cheerful canary yellow in colour (like the New York cabs), or white and are more expensive than London cabs. This is partly due to the list of hefty surcharges that are imposed for countless extras including excess luggage, night trips and rides to the airport. Often the meter becomes irrelevant for longer journeys (e.g. 50km to an airport), and it is advisable to negotiate a price in advance rather than recklessly jumping in the cab and finding the price outlandish later.

Air

The Italians indulge in internal flights far more than the British, though not as much as North Americans. This is partly due to the distances that separate Italy's most important cities, principally Milan and Rome (flight time about 50 minutes). Alitalia, the national carrier, and a clutch of lower cost and charter airlines fly to most of the major cities throughout mainland Italy, Sardinia and the smaller islands. Internal flights used to be pretty expensive but the last seven years have seen the evolution of no frills airlines (*voli no frills*) in Italy, operating on both the domestic routes, and also inter-Europe.

National airline Alitalia has regular *offerte speziale* including weekend and day-return tickets, but individual discounts on regular fares are offered only to young people and students. There are also reductions for groups, while children under two years pay 10% of the adult fare and children aged two to twelve pay half fare. Pensioners do not get any individual reductions, but they probably have the greatest flexibility for the special offers. The other large Italian carrier, Meridiana (www.meridiana.it; ☎020 7839 2222), owned by the Aga Khan, has transmuted into a lower cost airline (e.g. €9 plus €40 taxes and other charges for a single fare from Bologna to Palermo). Meridiana also flies inter-Europe. A website claiming to find the cheapest fares from anywhere to anywhere is www.lowcost.com. Other websites that claim to find the smallest fares for your chosen journey include: www.bestfares.com, www.priceline. com, and www.bigliettaerei.it. A useful web page for everything to do with air travel in Italy is viaggiare.cerca.com/in_aereo/.

A number of small airlines sprang up in Italy following the opening up of the skies to the free market, these include the following.

Useful Contacts

Air One: www.air-one.it, regional Italian network.

Air Dolomiti: www.airdolomiti.it, regional Italian network.

Alisarda: flies between main Italian cities and Sardinia.

Alpi Eagles: www.alpieagles.com, regional Italian network.

Azzurra Air: www.azzurraair.it. Rome to Bergamo.

Ryanair: www.ryanair.com. Rome to Alghero, Venice & Verona.

Transavia: www.transavia.com. Amsterdam to Genoa & Venice.

Ferries

There are regular ferry connections between the mainland of Italy and the islands. Large car ferries run from the ports of Genova, Civitavecchia and Naples to Sardinia and Sicily. There are also ferry connections from the mainland to the smaller Tremiti, Bay of Naples and Pontine islands. The ferries also make international trips from the mainland to Malta, Corsica, Spain, Greece, Turkey, Tunisia, Egypt and Israel. Fares are reasonable although you may have to book well in advance, especially over the holiday season in the summer months. In the winter the number of crossings is greatly reduced. In Italy the tourism office and travel agents can provide information, which can also be found on the website: www. traghettionline.net or www.informare.it which is a comprehensive guide to all Italian ferries, with timetables and booking online. Alternatively, refer to the websites of the individual ferry operators.

Carole Means and her husband live in Apulia from where they make frequent visits to Sicily:

We've been on holiday almost everywhere in Italy and we love Sicily. We tend to drive from our home here in Apulia and get the ferry across the Stretto di Messina. As soon as you land off the boat you are made to feel incredibly welcome. There are also flights to Palermo from Bari.

Getting to Sardinia. There are frequent ATI, Meridiana and Air Sardinia flights from Italian mainland airports to Cagliari, Olbia and Fertilia (for Alghero and Sassari). The sea ferries arrive from Italy, Sicily, Tunis, Corsica and France and are run by Navarma, Tirrenia, Trenitalia and Sardinia Ferries. For high season in the summer, bookings have to be made two or three months in advance.

Tourist Accommodation

If you do not want to arrange a rental in one spot so that you are free to move around a region, the following accommodation options may be useful:

Hotels (Alberghi) and Guest Houses (Pensioni). Hotels are classified according to quality standards based on cleanliness, service etc., which are given a star rating from one to five. The more stars, the higher the price. If you stay during the low season or stay for longer than two weeks, you may be able to secure a lower rent. Cheap hotels with one or two stars in large cities are often used for long-term accommodation. An up-to-date list of hotels can be obtained from the *Aziende di Promozione Turistica, Ente Per il Turismo Uffici I.A.T.* (tourist information offices) in the main cities.

Bed and Breakfast. Another enjoyable way of experiencing Italian hospitality and bijou lodgings is to stay in a B&B. A useful organisation with a wide range of choice from simple to luxury style B&Bs is Italian Bed and Breakfast (www.Italian-bandb.it). On their website you can search by region or province and the degree of luxury or not that you require.

Religious Guest Houses. Orders of monks and nuns may sometimes offer hospitality in their communities. Many of the monasteries are in fabulous settings, so this is worth exploring as an alternative kind of travel tourism, particularly as they are open to all. Usually just bed and breakfast is offered, but some communities may also offer an evening meal. The rates are usually very reasonable. A typical example is the Benedictines of the Tuscan monastery *Abbadia di Monte Oliveto Maggiore* who offer bed and breakfast for €25. There are a couple of guides that are useful if you can track them down via Amazon.com: *The Guide to Lodging in Italy's Monasteries* (Eileen Barish 1999) which details about 400, and the less comprehensive *Bed and Blessings* (June Walsh 1998). A global guide to religious community guesthouses *Itinerantibus in Toto Orbe Terrarum* (To Wander About the World) by Don Giovanni Munari is also available.

Agriturismo. Agriturismo is heavily promoted in Italy and there are thousands of farms nationally, which welcome guests. For the farmers it is a way to supplement their incomes and bring tourism business to the backwaters of the countryside, The formula varies a little from region to region but the basic set up is that guests get to stay on a working farm that provides one or more daily meals. Stays can be for a couple of nights, a weekend, a long weekend, a week or more. The meals provided can be a revelation as the ingredients are locally sourced, and often a speciality of the region (e.g. cheese, wine, cured or fresh meat and poultry etc.) is included. Some agriturismi have gourmet classification for their food; others welcome dogs with owners, and some advertise connoisseur wine cellars. The way to find what you want is to pick a region and then look at what is on offer. There are also last minute offers for agriturismi, offering bed and breakfast for €25/30 per person per night, especially in low season.

Information about *Agriturismos* can be obtained from the local tourist office and the website www.tuttoagriturismo.net which lists them by region and province. There is also a magazine *Tutto Agriturismo*, published every two months.

FAIRS, FEASTS, FESTIVALS AND PUBLIC HOLIDAYS

Keeping track of Italy's countless fairs, feasts and festivals from the internationally renowned to the village-based, many of them with origins lost in the mist of time, and some with obviously, pagan, Christian or medieval roots (or a fusion of these), could be a full-time occupation for anyone living in Italy.

Many villages hold annual summer festivals; typically they last several days, or a week and involve outdoor entertainments and feasts cooked outdoors in the village square. Some village festivals revolve around local crops such as the Cherry Festival of Celleno in Lazio, or the bizarre *Carnevale d'Ivrea*, which involves mass fruit hurling. For the truly bizarre look no further than the *Festa dei Serpari* (Snake Festival) of Cocullo, L'Aquila, which involves draping a 900-year-old saint with hundreds of (live) wild snakes wrangled from the local undergrowth. Festivals range from the elegant masks and mummery of the (revived) *Venice Carnevale*, to the brutal pig and poultry slaughtering festivals and feasts of the countryside, and from the bizarre exploding cart of Florence, to the floral festivals dating back to Classical times in Sicily. There are too many of them nationally to be listed here, so only some notable ones are given below. You can find out about any such events in your vicinity from the local tourist office, provincial website or even the local grapevine (or should that be grape wine festival?).

FESTIVALS IN ITALY

Date	Where	Festival	What
January 6th	Piana degli Albanesi, Sicily	*Epifania Greco-bizantino* (Byzantine Epiphany)	Custom begun by Albanian refugees in the 15th century
1st half of February	Agrigento, Sicily	*Sagra del Mandorlo* (Almond Blossom Festival)	Songs, dance, costumes, fireworks. Traditional folk festival (orig. ancient Greek?)
February/ March in the 2 weeks before Lent	Venice	*Carnevale* festival of costumes and masks often portraying well known historical and theatrical figures.	Aristocratic festival from Medieval times, repressed by reformers of 18th/19th century. Revived in 1981. (Carnevale from carne vale i.e. goodbye to meat)
Last Sunday in Lent and Shrove Tuesday	Oristano, Sardinia	*La Sartiglia* Ring jousting tournament.	16th Century. Spanish origin. Knights on horseback race and collect rings from wayside posts on to their lances
Easter week	Assisi, Umbria	*Calendimaggio* Medieval Easter Celebrations.	Flag waving, archery, costumes
Easter Sunday	Florence, Tuscany	*Scoppio del Carro* (Explosion of the Cart)	Mechanical dove launched from cathedral tower on wire during High Mass to ignite cart of fireworks in square below. Accounts of origin differ.

1-4 May	Cagliari, Sardinia	*Sagra di Sant' Efisio*	One of the biggest and most colourful processions in Italy. Thousands of traditionally costumed pilgrims follow the Saint on foot, in carts and on horseback
2 May	Asti, Piemonte	*Palio San Secondo*	700-year-old ceremony with procession and horse racing in Medieval costume.
7 May	Bari, Puglia	*Sagra di san Nicola*	Historic procession in costume
15 May	Gubbio, Umbria	*Festa di Ceri* (Race of the Candles)	12th century religious procession of three, immensely tall shrines which are carried up to the church at the top of Mt. Ingino. Origin pagan?
May (last Sunday)	Sansepolcro, Tuscany	*Palio dei Balestrieri* (Palio of the Archers)	Crossbow contest with Medieval arms and costume
June (Corpus Christi)	Genzano, Lazio	*Infiorata* Flower Festival	Religious procession (orig. 18th century) along streets decorated with carpets of flowers arranged in intricate designs.
16/17 June	Pisa, Tuscany	*Luminaria di San Ranieri e Regatta*	The Arno is lit by 70,000 candles on the water and surrounding buildings for the patron saint of the city. The ceremony dates back to 1688. The following day a regatta is held on the river.
Sunday after June 22nd	Nola, Campania	*Festa di Gigli* (Lily Festival)	Allegorical towers carried along in colourful costume procession. Pagan/Christian orgin.
29 June	Genova, Liguria	*Palio Marinaro dei Rioni*	Rowing race in ancient costume.
End June/ first weeks July	Spoleto, Umbria	*Festival dei Due Mondi* (Spoleto Music Festival)	Renowned cultural event focusing on dance, poetry and music.
Feast of Corpus Christi (July)	Rome, Trastevere district	*Festa de' Noantri*	8 days of celebrations (folk dances, songs, carnival floats) culminating in a boat ride on the Tiber for the Madonna's effigy.
July/ August	Siena, Tuscany	*Palio*	Colourful Medieval pageantry and horse race in the Campo (main square) held amongst the representatives of the ancient city districts competing for the *palio* (banner)
September (first Sunday)	Arezzo, Tuscany	*Giostra del Saracino* (The Saracen's Joust)	Medieval jousting contest.

September (first Sunday)	Venice	Traditional Regatta	Gondola racing and water procession.
September (second Sunday)	Foligno, Umbria	*Giostra della Quintana*	Revival of a 17th century jousting contest
19 September	Napoli, Campania	*Festivale di San Gennario*	Religious ceremony and procession for city's patron saint.

Public Holidays

Note that on Italian national holidays (*feste*) offices, shops, banks, post offices and schools are all closed. Whether museums, parks, etc, are closed will vary from region to region:

PUBLIC HOLIDAYS

1 January (New Year's Day; *Capodanno)*
6 January (Epiphany; *La Befana)*
Easter Monday *(Pasquetta)*
25 April (Liberation Day; *Anniversario della Liberazione*)
1 May (Labour Day; *primo maggio)*
15 August *(Assumption; Ferragosto)*
1 November (All Saints'; *Ognissanti)*
8 December (Immaculate Conception; *L'Immacolata Concezione)*
25 December (Christmas Day; *Natale)*
26 December *(Boxing Day; Santo Stefano*)

The festival days listed below are held to honour each specific city's own patron saint. Shops and offices usually remain open on these days although it is as well to check with the local tourist board for specific information.

25 April (Venice, St Mark)
24 June (Turin, Genoa and Florence; St John the Baptist)
29 June (Tome, St Peter)
23-25 July (Caltagirone in Sicily, St James)
26 July (island of Ischia in the Bay of Naples, St Anne)
19 September (Naples, St Gennaro)
4 October (Bologna, St Petronius)
6 December (Bari, St Nicholas)
7 December (Milan, St Ambrose)

KEEPING IN TOUCH

Communications

It has never been easier to keep in touch with friends and family. Wherever you live, modern technology is making it possible to maintain regular contact without the vast telephone bills that this once generated. For the cheapest new way to communicate, which does not tie you to a landline and costs the same whether you call next-door or next country, you will need a broadband internet connection and the latest innovation VoIP (Voice over the Internet Protocol), though this may not be available depending on where you are in Italy. There are other options for communicating, which are detailed below.

If you are bemused by the technology, ask your niece, nephew, children or grand-children to help you get connected to the internet and show you the basics of using the internet and e-mail. Master this before leaving the UK (if you need to). Both Sir Tim Berners-Lee who invented the internet, and Bill Gates are now in their fifties, so this is no longer new technology and ignoring it will be a big missed opportunity to keep up-to-date with your family, friends and relations. In addition to avoiding huge telephone bills, use of the internet will greatly increase the efficiency and enjoyment of your life in Italy giving you access to all the information you want on every possible subject, and preventing you from feeling isolated.

Telephoning Using the Internet

To make an internet phone call you will need to rent broadband (£15-£20 per month), download the relevant software from Google, Skype etc., draw up a list of contacts on your computer, plug a telephone headset (cost about £5) into your computer and click on a contact's name. If they are online, they click to accept your call. You should either agree a time in advance when you will both be online, or see from your computer whether they are online. You can talk for as long as you like to anyone anywhere who has software compatible with yours. Hopefully you will have co-ordinated with friends and relations before leaving the UK about using the internet for telephony.

Internet telephony (VoIP or Voice over the Internet Protocol) is evolving and some providers enable callers to talk from a cordless phone anywhere in their house and garden without the need to switch on their PC. Some providers charge a monthly subscription fee (£5-£10 per month) or nothing at all. If there is no monthly subscription there will be tiny charges for calls to landlines (typically 1.2 to 3p per minute) and if there is a monthly subscription (e.g.Vonage charges £9.99) the calls will be free. Providers in Italy include Skype, Tiscali and Vonage. All providers at present charge for calls to mobiles.

Having Friends and Family to Stay

The chances are, when you retire to Italy you will have friends and family coming to stay on a fairly regular basis. It is important for you to buy the house that suits you, rather than being obsessed with any potential visitors. Estate agents may try to sell you a larger house than you can afford citing regular family usage and visitor space as a selling point. There are alternatives to having a four-bedroomed house. Your guests and family can stay in a local agriturismo or bed and breakfast, or you may have outbuildings that you can convert to guest accommodation (and maybe let them out, when family and friends are not staying). Also, if friends and family visit for longer periods then it may be preferable for all, to have them living in separate accommodation on your land or nearby. Details of the types of rural accommodation in Italy are given above under *Travel and Tourism in Italy*. For information about renovating a building see *Renovating a Building* in the chapter *Your New Home in Italy*.

Another factor that may influence your visitor flow is accessibility. If you are not far from an airport which is on a no frills fare route, or near a train station the chances are that you will get more visitors, or more frequent visits than if you are in a remote country location.

PART-TIME WORK AND VOLUNTEERING

The majority of people who retire to Italy will be making the most of their freedom from the constraints of paid employment to indulge their passion for seeing art or other activities; others may find it harder to give up all work, or will be hoping to do something on a part-time or occasional basis, to help fund their life in Italy. Typically, older people prefer to work for themselves, as consultants, or to offer a service from their homes such as teaching English, holistic massage, freelance writing and translating, design and so on. Englishwoman Freddi Ferrigno, who moved with her husband to Brindisi in Apulia was approached by neighbours to teach English to them and their children:

I became an unofficial English teacher when neighbours and friends starting asking me to teach them English and help their children with English homework. Italians are very aware that it is advantageous for their children to speak English. I was asked to work at a local English school too, even though I have no TEFL qualifications. For my own sake as much as theirs I would get a qualification if I were going to be an official teacher in a school.

Rather than go through the rigmarole of setting up a company, they can simply register as a Sole Proprietor with the local chamber of commerce and obtain a VAT number from the tax office, and incorporate any income earned from their commercial transactions on their personal income tax form. For a freelance consultant, the formalities are even fewer: you do not need to register with the chamber of commerce, but you do need a VAT number from the local tax office. Another potential source of income is renting out spare accommodation or offering bed and breakfast. This is becoming more common amongst foreigners and is often done on an unofficial basis. You have to feel your way about offering accommodation as it may be a jealously guarded source of income for locals, and there is a lot of competition in some areas.

Renting Out Your Property

Renting out your Italian home is not necessarily a certain source of income as Carole Means, who runs a property consultancy in Apulia (www.apuliabella.com), explains:

It is less easy to rent out property here than it was, since Ryanair reduced flights to Bari/Brindisi from two to one a day. This means that the number of tourists to the region was reduced by a 1,000 a month. The flights are unlikely to stop altogether though, as lots of Italians come here too, to see their relatives.

Houses are usually let to foreigners (mostly Britons and Americans). There is a glut of properties in some areas and standards of maintenance and facilities and equipment are usually high. If you don't want to pay an agent then you will have to advertise the property, deal with enquiries, formalise arrangements with clients, meet and greet them, and deal with any problems that may arise during the rental period. The best way to build custom may be word of mouth. If you are planning to let out your empty home, while you travel for long periods in summer then you will not be able to dispense with an agent to manage and keep an eye on things. Agents charge from 20%-40% of gross rental income and for advertising the property on their internet site or catalogue. High season weekly holiday rents vary from €350 for a simple self-catering apartment up to €6000 for a luxury villa with a swimming pool.

Volunteering

Volunteering in Italy can be a good way to integrate into your local community, or to pursue a personal interest in conservation, environmental protection, social concerns, history, nature, or to make you feel better about yourself. One of the most needed kinds of community volunteering is the care of the very elderly, disabled or the very young; however these could be tricky for foreigners without the requisite knowledge of Italian but if this is your field of interest then the local religious organisations or church will be able to help, or you can contact your nearest *Centro di Servizio per il Volontariato* whose address you can find on the website of the *Fondazione Italiana per il Volontariato* (www.fivol.it), or in the local telephone directory. *Misericordie d'Italia* (www.misericordie.org) is one of the oldest charity organisations and was founded in the 14th century to help the poor. It has 700 branches and over 670,000 volunteers in Italy.

If you have the appropriate skills and aptitude, expat websites need volunteer editors to help with putting together articles and information on the website and moderators who 'police' the online discussion forums and ensure that contributors conform to the code followed by that website (i.e. no personal insults, swear words etc). In March 2006 Expats in Italy (www.expatsinitaly.com) was inviting editorial volunteers to contact the website; other websites with forums include www.italymag.co.uk. Or you could write online articles for websites on Italy such as www.ciao-italy.com.

You could be on safer ground volunteering with a local historical or ecological organisation many of which organise workshops, training courses and programmes of manual volunteer work, often outdoors and often in glorious places.

One volunteer project permanently reliant on volunteers, is *Il Cimitero Acattolico* (Protestant Cemetery) in Rome founded in 1748 as a final resting place for Protestants from northern Europe who could not be buried in consecrated (i.e. Catholic) burial grounds. The remains of many foreigners' (over two and half thousand of them) are interred there, including those of Keats and Shelley and the Scottish writer R.M Ballantyne. For sixty years the Rome Protestant cemetery has been cared for by a foundation formed from the diplomatic missions of all the countries whose nationals are buried there, but increasingly it seems, diplomatic staff are unwilling to shoulder the responsibility. The cemetery attracts thousands of visitors a year and is well worth preserving for its historical interest alone. Any volunteers willing to help maintain the grounds, fundraise etc. could try contacting the British Embassy in Rome. The Protestant Cemetery of Florence (last resting place of Elizabeth Barrett Browing amongst others) is similarly afflicted by neglect, and volunteers wanting to help there can contact The English Cemetery, Piazzale Donatello 38, 50132 Firenze or email juliani@tin.it.

If your interest is the environment and nature conservation then organisations such as LIPU (www.lipu.it), the Italian bird protection organisation have volunteer programmes for all ages. The *Lega Ambiente* (www.legambiente.com), the Italian environmental organisation has over 1000 local groups in Italy and thousands of volunteers of all ages help protect the environment or go on courses (e.g. an archaeological conservation course at Pompei) through them. Past summer activities have included repairing hiking paths and removing litter from beaches. Another well known environmental organisation is *Italia Nostra* (www. italianostra.org) which has many local groups and needs volunteers for all kinds of projects from campaigning against measures that threaten the environment to maintaining local parks and historic sites and the similarly widespread *Pro Loco* (For the Region).

Personal Finance

CHAPTER SUMMARY

- It is advisable to maintain a bank account in the UK as well as opening one in Italy if you still have property or income in the UK.
- The Italian Post Office offers all banking services, except wired bank transfers. It also offers internet banking.
- If you are living permanently in Italy, you can have an offshore savings account and get interest tax-free. Some offshore banks offer a dual currency (e.g. euros and sterling) cheque account .
- Most offshore banks require you to maintain a large minimum balance and charge an annual fee.
- You must not go into the red with your bank account in Italy without a prior arrangement as it is a criminal offence to write a dud cheque (*assegno a vuoto*) and you may be banned from having an Italian bank account for several years at worst, or fined at best.
- If you have a pension lump sum due to you on retirement, it will be taxed in Italy if you are resident there. You can avoid this by taking the lump sum while you are still UK resident.
- Italy abolished inheritance tax in 2001 making tax planning simpler compared with other countries such as France and Spain; but you are liable for 3% transfer tax (based on the cadastral value of the property).
- Britons who buy property in Italy are advised that for inheritance purposes their property (movable and immovable) will follow English inheritance law. In order to avoid any possible later confusion it is strongly advised that you have a will registered in both Britain and Italy.

BANKING

Opening an Account

Anyone who is considering living in Italy on a long-term basis will need an Italian bank account. Accounts are available for foreigners with non-resident and resident status, though anyone buying a property to live in Italy may need to wait for their *residenza* (residence permit) before being able to open their resident's account. The only option if you are not yet in possession of this is to enlist the assistance of an influential Italian who may be able to persuade a bank manager to let you have a resident's account pending the arrival of the paperwork. Alternatively, if the institution you currently bank with has a branch in Italy near where you will be living, you can ask for a letter of introduction that may smooth and quicken the process of opening an account. If you cannot open an Italian bank account before receiving your residenza you will have to manage with Eurocheques, cash and credit cards until you receive it.

Once an Italian bank account has been set up the customer receives a *libretto di assegni* (cheque book) and he or she will be able to cash cheques (*incassare un assegno*) at their branch. When paying for goods and services by cheque a *carta di garanzia* (cheque guarantee card) is obligatory. For larger purchases a bank draft (*assegno circolare*) is normally required.

Couples can opt for a joint account (*conto corrente cointestato*).

Using an Italian Bank Account

The majority of expatriates do not normally choose to transfer all their assets into their Italian bank account. There are sound reasons for this related to the higher bank charges in Italy, and Italian tax considerations. The consensus seems to be that you should maintain an account outside the country (either 'at home' or offshore) and transfer money as needed to Italy. Credit and/or debit cards linked to accounts outside the country can be used to make purchases in Italy. If UK citizens do maintain accounts in the UK it is essential to inform the British tax authorities and the bank that they are resident abroad in order to prevent double taxation.

When calculating the amount of funds needed in your Italian account you should err on the side of generosity as there are various ways you can be caught out. For example there are charges levied per cheque written, and the gas and electricity companies may automatically adjust your standing orders after the bi-annual meter readings. Banks do pay a small amount of interest, usually two or three per cent, on current accounts in credit, but this is cancelled out by bank charges. If one is unfortunate enough to issue a bouncing cheque (*un assegno a vuoto*), albeit by accident, it can lead to legal problems, being disbarred from holding any bank account and even to having your name gazetted in the local press, so doing this should be avoided at all costs. On the other hand pre-arranged overdrafts are usually possible.

Bank and Credit Cards

All banks issue debit cards for purchasing goods and services and for use in ATMs (called *Bancomats* in Italy). Credit cards are not hugely popular in Italy. They come with a small monthly management fee, and have an annual fee. Many small shopkeepers are averse to credit cards as it costs them to process the transaction (even though this cost is usually factored into their prices). This is why in Italy you can nearly always haggle successfully for a discount if you are paying in cash. There is also a type of payment card that is recharged from your account (*una carta prepagata ricaricabile*), which is popular with Italians as it is like carrying cash around but in a handier way, though there are the usual Italian credit card operating charges. The Italian Post Office also provides a full range of credit/debit cards with its banking services (www.poste.it/bancoposta/cartedipagamento).

It is rarely a problem finding a bancomat machine, even in towns of 1000 inhabitants there is usually one. They have drawbacks, which include regularly running out of money; the worst times for this are before and just after a public holiday. Note that as in the UK, if you use a bank card to withdraw money from an ATM that is not part of your bank's network, charges apply.

Important Points to Consider About Banking

○ If you are moving abroad there are several possibilities, some of which it is possible to do conjointly, such as having a bank account in the UK, and also in Italy.

○ You can keep your current account in the UK (you will need to do this anyway if you still have property and income in the UK)

○ If you are selling up and moving permanently to Italy, you can open an offshore account through UK high street banks and building societies. Most require a large minimum balance to be maintained and charge an annual fee but there may be advantages (see below).

○ You can open an account in Italy with a local branch of an Italian bank. Alternatively HSBC banks are particularly popular with expatriates because of the number of countries where they operate and the process of referral they operate between their branches.

○ You need a local bank account in Italy to gain access to important services such as utilities. You will probably also find it useful to have an Italian cheque book to use in rural areas where acceptance of credit/debit cards is not universal.

○ It is best to open an account in Italy with a bank that has a lot of branches, as this will be useful if you travel around.

○ Most UK High Street banks will charge you to access your money outside the UK. Many people do not realise this until they start withdrawing cash from ATMs abroad.

○ Nationwide is popular as it does not charge its current account holders for accessing their money at ATMs abroad.

○ Some UK banks conceal commission charges for accessing your account abroad within a loaded exchange rate.

○ The Italian post office (*Poste Italiane*) has a banking department that offers almost all the same services as a bank (except wire transfers from an overseas bank) but is cheaper. Non-residents and residents can both open an account with a cheque book, credit card and use of ATMs. The post office has just launched its version of Internet banking, *Banco Posta Impresa Online*.

Italian Banking Costs and Charges

○ Interest is paid on current accounts quarterly, and ranges from a typical 0.5% to 3.50% introductory bonus rate (Ing Direct's Conto Arancia internet account).

○ Most transactions made through a current account are charged for and there is also usually a charge for each cheque book, and for processing cheques and direct debits. Some banks allow you so many free transactions a year before charges kick in, while others relate the charges to the average balance maintained. Internet operated accounts may not have bank charges at all, so it pays to shop around or consider using the Italian Post Office banking system (see above).

Important Points about Cheques

○ Cheques require endorsement on the back before they can be paid into an account.

○ Note that even crossed cheques (*assegni sbarrati*), can be endorsed to a third party up to a limit of €10,350; a fact which is potentially a boon to fraudsters. This is probably why few people in Italy use personal cheques, even with a guarantee card (*carte di garanzia*). You may however need cheques to pay local tradespeople.

○ You can make a cheque non-transferable to a third party by writing *non trasferible* on the back.

○ To obtain cash at a bank counter, you have to fill in a form, or write out a cheque made out to self (use either *me medismo* or *m.m.* for short). Usually, this can be done only at your own branch. The words on a cheque must be written in Italian using all lower case letters and without spacing between the words. The date should be written in numbers (day, month, year) with a dot between each part.

○ You cannot stop a cheque in Italy if you change your mind. Cancelling a cheque in Italy is a police matter, and is for lost or stolen cheques only.

Transferring Funds from Abroad into Italy

For retirees and expatriates paid in their home country, transferring funds to Italy is necessary on a regular basis. By using the same bank at each end of the transfer the process can be speeded up, which is a good reason for using a larger bank. However, nowadays the system has been greatly improved and Swift transfers that go directly to your local branch rather than via the head office of the bank in Milan, Rome, etc. are one of the best ways to transfer money. Online banking services from banks such as Citibank and HSBC allow customers to submit transfer instructions such as this 24 hours a day through their computer and can be very convenient for expatriates with internet access. Also useful for those with internet access is the electronic payment facility xetrade of www.xe.com which 'works seamlessly with your existing bank accounts' and claims to be one of the cheapest methods on offer. Other banks have telephone banking services, which can be just as convenient, though the cost of international phone calls to deal with them, especially when the lines are busy and you get put on hold, can be much higher.

Lastly, if the bank cards issued by your bank outside Italy carry the Maestro symbol and your Italian bank accepts Maestro payments, you can draw out money into your Italian bank account whilst sitting in the manager's office. Both the issuing bank and Italian bank can limit the amount of cash you can draw down at any one time. The issuing bank will place a limit on how much you can charge to your card in a specified time period and the Italian bank can have what is known as a floor limit, which limits how much they are allowed to accept via a single Maestro payment.

With these options in mind, it behoves the prospective foreign resident to base the selection of an Italian bank account and bank on what services are available, not just the charges levied and the nearness of the branch to your place of residence.

Choosing a Bank

Despite the problems within the Italian banking system in general, some banks do enjoy a better reputation than others in their dealings with foreigners. These include: *Istituto Bancario San Paolo* based in Turin, with 500 branches nationwide, and *Banca Toscana* (424 branches) and *Banca Intesa* (4,000 branches) which are more familiar with the banking needs of expatriates. Some of the smaller, privately-owned banks may also be worthy of closer acquaintance: in particular, *Credito Emiliano* (Milan, Rome and central Italy), has a policy of encouraging clients from the foreign community.

Useful Contacts

American Express Bank: Piazza San Babila 3, 20122 Milan; ☎ 02 77901; fax 02 76002308.

Banca Intesa: via Monte di Pieta 8, 20121 Milano; info line in English in Italy 800 02 02 02; from abroad ☎ 02 4832 2222. 4000 branches.

Banca Nazionale dell'Agricultura (BNA): Direzione Centrale, Via Salaria 231, 00199 Rome.

Banca Nazione di Lavoro: Direzione Generale, Via Vittorio Veneto 119, 00187 Rome.

Banca Toscana: www.bancatoscana.it. 424 branches in 9 regions: Toscana, Umbria, Le Marche, Lazio, Abruzzo, Lombardia, Liguria, Emiglia Romana and Molise.

Chase Manhattan Bank: Via M. Mercati 39, 00197 Rome; ☎ 06 844 361; fax 06 844 36220. Piazza Meda 1, 20121 Milan; ☎ 02 88951; 02 88952229.

Citibank: Via Bruxelles 61, 00198 Rome; ☎ 06 854 561. Foro Bonaparte 16, 20121 Milan; ☎ 02 85421.

Credito Emiliano: Via Emilia San Pietro 4, 42100 Reggio Emilia; ☎ 0555 5821.

Credito Romagnola: Via Zamboni 20, 40126 Bologna.

Istituto Bancario San Paolo di Torino: Via della Stamperia 64, 00187 Rome; ☎ 06 85751; 06 857 52400. Piazza San Carlo 156, Turin; ☎ 011-5551.

Istituto Monte dei Paschi di Siena: U.S.I.E. Sett. Serv. V.le Toselli 60, Siena.

National Westminster Bank: Via Turati 18 20121 Milan; ☎ 02 6251; fax 02 6572869.

Unicredit Banca per la Casa: Via Orefici 10, (zona centro), Milan; ☎ 02 8545651; fax 02 85456508; www.bancaperlacasa.it. National mutual credit bank that bought out the mortgage business of Abbey National Bank Italy in 2003.

Offshore Accounts

Offshore banks are based in places where the tax rules are different and can be exploited when there is a legal opportunity to minimize tax liability. They have advantages and disadvantages. Amongst the former is the fact that they can be operated in two currencies. For instance if you are living in Italy, you could open an account which provides a euro cheque book and debit card, but you could also maintain the facility of paying UK bills in sterling. This would be useful if you are no longer able to maintain accounts in the UK (i.e. you are no longer resident there).

The disadvantages include the fact that you may (depending on the bank) have to maintain a large minimum balance and there are annual charges. Offshore product providers include, Alliance and Leicester International, Lloyds TSB Overseas Club, Abbey Gold and NatWest/ Royal Bank of Scotland Advantage International. Among the items to compare when considering offshore banking are the annual charges, the permanent minimum balance required and the facilities offered with the account.

The European Savings Directive came into force on 1 July 2005 and means that tax is now deducted at source from the next interest payments. This does not affect the rate of tax for those already declaring their worldwide income but it has caught a few offshore account holders who were happy to ignore the tax rules or were ignorant of what they were. If offshore savers do not accept deduction of interest at source, they will have to opt for having their interest paid gross and participating in 'an exchange of information' and have details of their interest passed to the tax authorities of the country in which they are resident. The latter option is the route currently recommended by some leading tax advisors as it will avoid the possibility of paying too much tax.

All the major British high street banks and some building societies offer offshore banking. Customers of such accounts are not normally liable for UK taxes, but they may be required to pay tax in the country where they are resident. Unless you are a financial expert you should get independent advice from someone qualified to analyse the advantages of offshore banking in your particular circumstances.

Offshore No Notice Savings Accounts

Abbey International: ☎01534-885100; www.abbeyinternational.com.

Alliance & Leicester Int: www.alil.co.im/offshore.

Anglo Irish Bank IOM: ☎01624-698000; www.angloirishbank.co.im.

Derbyshire IOM: ☎01624-663432; www.Derbyshire.co.im.

Nationwide International: ☎01624-696000; www.nationwideinternational.com.

Northern Rock Guernsey: www.northernrock-guernsey.co.gg.

Portman Channel Islands: ☎01481-712004; www.portmanci.com.

Tax Advisors

Blevins Franks: ☎+356 21 347 347; www.blevinsfranks.com.

Fry Group: ☎01903-231545; www.thefrygroup.co.uk.

Towry Law: ☎01344-828000; www.towrylaw.com.

UK Companies/Trusts

This is an immensely complex area that also requires expert advice and it is usually linked with tax planning and asset management. You can buy Italian property in the name of a UK company or trust but this means it would be locked into a vehicle that has some advantages but is not suitable for the majority of second home buyers. Unlike in some countries, Italian law recognizes that a Trust can be regulated by non-Italian laws, but expert advice may be needed in this area. An offshore structure may be useful to anyone whose assets total more than a million pounds, as in this case, financial advantages should outweigh the high cost of setting up and maintaining an offshore structure.

Advantages/Disadvantages of UK Companies

o It is a fairly simple matter to transfer the shares of a UK company to say, another family member

o There is no requirement to involve an Italian notary in transferring shares to another party

o If you are not an Italian resident, the shares come under the UK tax regime because they are a UK company. This means that if they are willed to a surviving spouse, that person will not normally have to pay inheritance tax.

o The UK company will be taxable in the UK for capital gains. There may be additional tax liabilities should you liquidate the company or distribute the net sale proceeds.

o Potential buyers are normally put off by the idea of buying shares in a company and will probably want the property transferred to their name, which means liquidating the company, which is expensive and carries tax liabilities.

Useful Addresses for Expatriate Financial Planning

Blackstone Franks LLP: Barbican House, 26-34 Old Street, London EC1V 9HL; ☎020-7250 3300; www.blackstonefranks.com. Specialists in the expatriate financial sector.

Brewin Dolphin Securities: Cross Keys House, The Parade, Marlborough, Wilts. SN8 1NE; ☎01672-519600; fax 01672-515550; e-mail info@ brewindolphin.co.uk; www.brewindolphin.co.uk. Services include international portfolio management with offshore facility for those domiciled or resident outside the UK.

Hansard Europe Ltd: Enterprise House, Frascati Road, Blackrock, Co. Dublin, Republic of Ireland; ☎01 278 1488; fax +353 1 278 1499. Hansard has products aimed at residents of EU countries with regard to tax and life assurance regulations. www.hansard.com.

Smith and Williamson: 2 Athenaeum Road, Whetstone, London N20 9YU; ☎020-8446 4371; fax 020-8446 7606; www.smith.williamson.co.uk. A UK chartered accountant, experienced in dealing with most tax matters relating to expatriates and non-UK residents.

UK PENSIONS AND BENEFITS

Pensions and Benefits

As already described in the *Basics* chapter in *Preparations for Departure* if you are already receiving a UK pension, you should make arrangements to have it paid directly into your Italian bank account before you leave the UK. The UK State Pension is payable in full anywhere in the European Economic Area. Note that Pension Credit is not payable outside the UK. UK War Pensions can also be paid in full to people living permanently outside Britain.

If you are retiring to Italy before the official retirement age, you can get a UK State Pension forecast by completing form BR19 available from a Jobcentre Plus (or download the form at www.thepensionservice.gov.uk/resourcecentre/br19/home.asp). If you are already living abroad contact HM Revenue and Customs in Newcastle for form BR19 (or download it) and send the completed form back to HM Revenue and Customs.

Note that nearly all other UK derived social security benefits cannot be paid to those who are living permanently outside the United Kingdom. Instead you will be able to claim local benefits and social assistance on the same terms as Italian citizens from their social services. Most of these benefits are related to health and wealth (or lack of them). Further details of Italian medical benefits and E forms 106 and 121 which give you access to Italian state healthcare if you have paid National Insurance in the UK, are given in the *Healthcare* chapter.

Things to Know About UK Pensions and Italian Tax

○ If your pension is derived from British Armed Forces or the Government it will be taxed in the UK and will not be taxed in Italy.

○ All other types of UK pension paid in Italy, are taxed in Italy, not the UK.

○ If you have a pension lump sum that is paid to you on retirement this will be taxed in Italy. You can get round this by taking your lump sum while you are still a UK resident.

ITALIAN TAXES

There are numerous taxes in Italy and so only the main ones that expatriates will be most likely to come across will be covered below. As the tax regulations change regularly, it is worth checking frequently on the current situation. Information is available on the internet though self-employed expatriates earning income in Italy are well advised to employ an accountant with experience of working with expatriates in order to avoid double taxation. You can spend up to 183 days a year in Italy and still be regarded by the tax authorities as resident in your home country. *The Informer*, an English language website (www.

informer.it) for expatriates in Italy is a goldmine of advice on tax issues and goes into much more detail than is possible here. The taxes expatriates might incur are:

Imposta sul reddito (**IRE**). This is levied in a format most people are used to, i.e. it is a progressive tax that increases with the amount you earn. US citizens in particular are likely to consider the rates very high. However, Italians get a lot in return for their taxes in the form of pensions, health care and other social security benefits and the rates are not the highest in the EU. Tax rates begin at 23% and go up to 43% for high earners. Employees have the taxes deducted at source every month by their employer based on an estimate of the year's tax – any necessary adjustment will be made early in the following year. Self-employed workers operate under a complicated system whereby some taxes are paid at source and some in arrears – expert advice from an accountant is recommended.

Imposta regionale sulle attività produttive (**IRAP**). This is a corporate tax that is charged to every business no matter how small. The rate is decided by the region in which the business is located. IRAP also includes health contributions. It is a tax on services and goods produced, on the difference between the value realised after specified production costs (except labour costs) have been deducted. The basic rate of IRAP is around 4.25%, but as with ILOR there is a reduced agricultural rate (3%). The rate for banks, insurance companies and other financial services is approximately 5%. IRAP was once levied directly into the National Treasury but is now a regionally payable tax, so local rates can vary.

Imposta sui redditi delle persone giuridiche (**IRPEG**). This is a corporate tax levied on S.r.l. and S.p.A. type companies; not generally applicable to self-employed workers.

Imposta sul valore aggiunto (**IVA**). This is VAT (value added tax) and is levied on all sales, whether retail or wholesale, and even by consultants and other businesses who do not sell an actual product. There are three rates of 4%, 10% and 20%, the standard rate being 20%. Most foodstuffs are taxed at 10%. For other goods including most clothing, shoes, records, cassettes and certain alcoholic goods the rate is 20%.

Social security contributions. Whilst these are not really a tax, they amount to approximately 10% of income.

Many of the other financial benefits that expatriates may enjoy are all counted as part of their income and their value will be taxed and added to the tax liability.

2006 INCOME TAX RATES (IRE)	
Income	**Tax rate**
€0 to €26.000.00	23%
€26.001,00 to €33.000,00	33%
€33.001,00 to €100.000,00	39%
over €100.001,00	39% + 4% ('solidarity contribution')

Other Taxes

Apart from the main taxes listed above there are a multitude of other taxes payable by those living in Italy, which include:

- Rubbish disposal (*nettezza urbana*) and water rates (*acquedotto comunale*). These are usually based on the floor area of the property. House owners with their own independent water supply such as a well or spring are exempt from water rates. Note also that for second houses these charges are higher. This is to ensure that the better off pay more tax.
- Car (or other motorised vehicle) tax.
- TV licence fee.

Tax Evasion

Tax evasion in Italy is a popular topic of conversation and supposedly occurs on a grand scale, mainly amongst the self-employed. Though Italians reputedly do it, expatriates should consider the implications of doing it themselves and getting caught – being put in an Italian prison, deportation, or the financial burden of playing catch-up with the tax authorities. It has been estimated by the tax inspectors' organisation, *Il Servizio Centrale degli Ispettori Tributari*, that 83% of the self-employed category declares an annual income of less than £4,000. The *Guardia di Finanza*, (a.k.a. *i Finanzieri*, the tax police) feel obliged from time to time, when facing the enormity of the problem, to indulge in advertising campaigns to remind the public and themselves that they are there to root out the culprits. The Finance Ministry has been making progress in catching tax evaders, especially as far as high income earners are concerned. Foreigners become taxable as residents if they are in Italy for 183 days or longer and technically all their worldwide income is taxable.

Deciding to pay one's taxes gives rise to its own set of problems, particularly if one is in business or self-employed, as the system is constantly being amended. Unfortunately, new taxes are often brought in without the old ones being cancelled. This induces a permanent state of chaos in the tax system so that it is extremely difficult to ascertain which taxes one is actually liable for. However, it is undoubtedly better to pay some taxes rather than none at all. It is probably unwise to proceed without the services of an accountant (*commercialista*) preferably obtained through personal recommendation.

There are other peculiarities regarding the Italian tax system: unlike Britain where the tax office will chase you to fill in a tax form, in Italy it is up to the individual to present him or herself at the *Intendenza di Finanza* (local tax office) to fill in a standard tax form (known as a *modello unico* 740) and be given a *codice fiscale* (tax number). A *codice fiscale* is needed in not just in order to work, but for various transactions such as property and car purchase, rentals and bill payments.

Owing to the complexity of taxation it is strongly recommended that you take independent, expert financial advice before moving to Italy as well as after arrival. A list of such advisors in the UK can be obtained from the Financial Services Authority (25 The North Colonnade, Canary Wharf, London E14 5HS; ☎020-7676 1000; www.fsa.gov.uk).

The estimated amount of both income and business taxes are payable in two tranches in May and November. There are big fines for non-payment and under estimation of the amount due. Late payment is also penalised with fines.

WILLS AND INHERITANCE

Wills

The easiest and most effective policy regarding the disposal of his or her estate for foreign citizens resident in Italy is to make a will that follows the law of their own country. If a will involves the dispersal of property both within and without Italy, it is advisable to consult a lawyer (*avvocato*) with experience of both your own country's and the Italian legal systems to avoid legal complications later on. In this case, you may find that it is simplest to make two wills, which deal with non-Italian and Italian assets separately, rather than trying to combine the two. If you wish, you can make an Italian-style will, but unless you have taken Italian nationality during your time in Italy, this will be executed in accordance with the law of your home country. Non-Italian wills also avoid the Italian system of *Legittima*, common to most Western European countries, which gives those directly related to the deceased an absolute right to a share in the estate, regardless of the wishes of the deceased as expressed in the will. Remember that to validate an Italian will you will need to obtain a certificate of law from your consulate, which will state that the will is being made under the terms of your own country's law and includes a provision for the free disposition of property. Any good lawyer will be able to organise this for you.

A lawyer should charge about £150 for an Italian will, which can be handwritten (*testamento olografo*) and checked by a lawyer to see that it satisfies legal requirements. A public will (*testamento pubblico*) is a more formal (and expensive) document, which has to be drafted by a notary, and its contents are disclosed to other parties.

What Happens if You do Not Make an Italian Will

If you have an English will pursuant to your Italian properties, and no Italian will, the inheritance law of the nationality of the deceased is the one that is applicable. If you inherit an Italian property from a British relative who is a British citizen you will need to engage an Italian lawyer to transfer the property in Italy, in accordance with the English will. This involves the avvocato legalizing the English will through various procedures in Italy. Even if you have both an English and an Italian will as mentioned above you still cannot avoid legalizing the UK will in Italy to make it work under Italian law. This is a complex area needing special legal advice as it is theoretically not essential to have an Italian will, but many property owners and lawyers feel it is more secure to do so and a lawyer will explain the particular legal permutations that apply to your situation.

Useful Addresses in the UK

Claudio del Giudice: Avvocato and Solicitor, Rivington House, 82 Great Eastern Street, London EC2A 3JF; ☎020 7613 2788; e-mail delgiudice@clara.co.uk; www.delgiudice.clara.net.

The International Property Law Centre: Unit 2, Waterside Park, Livingstone Road, Hessle, HU13 OEG; please contact Luca De Giorgi, Italian Avvocato, on ☎0870-800 4591 (e-mail lucadg@maxgold.com); or Stefano Lucatello, Italian Solicitor on ☎0870-800 4565 (e-mail Stefano@maxgold.com); fax 0870-800 4567; general e-mail internationalproperty@maxgold.com; www.internationalpropertylaw.com.

John Howell & Co: The Old Glassworks, 22 Endell Street, Covent Garden, London WC2H 9AD; ☎020-7420 0400; fax 020-7836 3626; e-mail info@europelaw.com; www.europelaw.com.

Funerary Formalities and Afterwards

Dying abroad complicates its attendant matters slightly, especially if near relations are not on the spot to deal with the formalities of arranging burial or cremation. It is therefore advisable to make your wishes concerning the matter i.e. what form of burial you want and where, known in advance, and preferably also ensure they are written into your will. Note that burials in Italy must take place within 48 hours of death.

All deaths must be registered with the local *sindaco/municipio* (town hall) at the *ufficio stato civile* within 24 hours. The attending doctor issues a death certificate, though you will need an international death certificate if a body is to be transported back home. You can also register the death overseas of a foreign national with their respective embassy or consulate and get a death certificate from their own country so that the death can be registered in the home country as well as in Italy.

Even though this is not obligatory, there could be advantages to doing this, which may not be apparent at the time. The embassy or consulate will charge for registering a death and issuing a certificate of death. The British Embassy also offers bereavement advice and can provide a list of Italian undertakers (www.britishembassy.gov.uk). Cremation, particularly in the north of Italy, is fairly common, although practically every Italian comune has its own cemetery in which all residents are entitled to be buried free of charge. There are also British cemeteries in large cities like the one at Staglieno in Genoa.

The British Embassy warns that transporting a coffin for burial back to the UK by air is an expensive business – to North America it is of course, even more expensive. Freight charges depend on weight but the minimum cost is about £2,000; prolonged storage will also add to your costs. The body will have to be collected once it arrives home, and some Italian funeral directors have contacts in other countries, who will see to it that the body is safely delivered to its final destination. The UK company Golden Leaves (www.goldenleaves.co.uk); 0800 8544 48) offers funeral plans which include repatriation of the deceased's remains from Italy for burial in the UK. An alternative might be to have just your ashes returned home, which is much cheaper. Courier companies should be able to handle this if a friend or relative cannot do it.

Italian Probate

There are certain procedures to be followed to establish probate in Italy. It may be necessary to assemble documentation, organise certified translations of documents and secure the services of a local notary to transfer title to the beneficiaries, at the Land Registry. Although Italian inheritance tax was abolished in 2001, there may still be a need to pay foreign taxes if the owner was born and domiciled in the UK. Specialist accountancy advice may be required. Even though there is no inheritance tax in Italy, there is still a legal requirement to lodge a *Dichiarazione di Successione* (Inheritance Tax Declaration), where property is part of the estate, within one year of the death of the deceased. This is part of the procedure for transferring title of ownership at the Land Registry.

If the deceased's estate includes a bank account there are lengthy and usually expensive formalities to go through, with slight variations depending on the bank, in order to secure the release of the funds to the beneficiaries. The formalities are meant to guard against fraud.

Surviving Spouse or Partner

Presumably you will have considered what the situation would be if your spouse should die after moving to Italy. It may well be that the survivor would want to return to the UK to be closer to family and friends: provision should be made for this at the outset, perhaps by arranging life assurance which will cover the costs of returning home. In a forced situation these costs could be much greater than those involved in the original move out.

Healthcare

CHAPTER SUMMARY

- There is a noticeable north/south divide in the provision of state health services. In the north, public health services are what you would expect from a highly developed country; elsewhere in the country they may be adequate but many in the south fall below the expected standard.

- On the plus side Italy has more doctors per head of the population than most other OECD countries (4.1 per 1,000 compared with 2.9 average).

- Anyone who leaves the UK to live abroad is no longer automatically entitled to free treatment with the British NHS.

- If you are of official retirement age and are living permanently in Italy, you are entitled to the same health benefits as an Italian pensioner. However, you may still want to take out private insurance if you consider the regional facilities are inadequate for your needs.

- Medical visits and out-patient care are usually free for pensioners below a certain income limit. The least well off benefit most. Others make a token contribution.

- Anyone registered with the SSN gets entirely free In-patient, chronic disease and emergency treatments whatever their financial status. However outpatient treatment, specialist referrals and prescriptions all operate on the co-payment principle.

- Italy is now focusing on the problems associated with ageing and aims for better provision for the elderly. The government is encouraging responsibility at commune level. This means providing social-medical facilities locally, so the elderly can maintain optimum health, and continue active links with their own community.

THE HEALTH SYSTEM IN ITALY

It would be a salutory lesson perhaps, for those who are accustomed to moan about the British NHS, to be sent for treatment in an Italian National Health Service (Servizio Sanitario Nazionale, SSN for short) hospital in Sicily for instance. They would be guaranteed never to complain again. In common with other systems under state control in Italy, the state medical system is liable to cost the government (i.e. the taxpayer) a fortune (100 billion euros), 8.4% of GDP (only Switzerland, Germany and the USA spend more) and employs 1,280,000 people (4.2% of the national labour force) and still, at some hospitals, particularly those run by religious foundations, or in the south, no linen or personal care is provided; relatives have to see to these and other daily non-medical needs of hospitalised family members.

There are 1,300 state hospitals providing 350,000 beds. The largest hospitals operate as so-called 'trusts', have financial autonomy and enter into contracts with the Italian NHS. They receive their funding after annual agreements on the rate of charges. Despite the erratic standards of Italian state hospitals, Italy has no shortage of dedicated, well trained and compassionate doctors, especially (but not exclusively), in private clinics. Carole Means, who has lived in northern Italy, and now lives in Puglia is enthusiastic about Italian doctors:

There was an item on the news yesterday claiming that 2.5% of all deaths in Italy could be attributed to medical negligence or malpractice. On the other hand many Italian doctors are excellent and efficient. You cannot fault their bedside manner; they make you feel they are not just your doctor, but your friend.

In fact Italy has a higher number of doctors per head of the population than any other OECD country (4.1 per 1,000 compared with an average of 2.9 per 1,000). Italy also has a clutch of world-renowned specialists including a Nobel prize winner (Daniel Bovet) and a singing heart surgeon with a string of hit records as well as medical successes under his gown (Enzo Jannacci). On the other hand, Italy has fewer nurses per 1,000 head of the population than any other OECD country (5.4 in Italy, compared with an average of 8.2). So simultaneously with some of the best doctors in Europe, Italy possesses some of the worst hospitals for a rich nation, with long waiting lists for treatment, haphazard in-hospital personal care, and inadequate facilities.

That said, state hospitals in the north of Italy are much better run than those in the south, which also has its good ones, but not very many. If you are going to buy property in the South make sure that one of the good state hospitals is nearby. Kate and Mel Holmes did this when they bought a property in Calabria:

One of the reasons that we chose Trebissace to live is that it has a good hospital. True, it is basic and not very comfortable and you have to get your friends to bring fresh clothes and food for you, but that is usual. There is no waiting here. If you need to see a specialist it is the same day or near enough. For instance, a friend of ours here had a heart attack. It was discovered that he needed a bypass operation. He was in and out of hospital and convalescing before a friend of ours in England, with the same condition, had even got an appointment with a specialist.

Italian residents often prefer not to chance their luck in the state system unless their local state hospital has a good reputation. Both nationals and expatriates tend to insure themselves privately for healthcare in case they need basic care, let alone long-term, expensive hospitalisation (see *Private Healthcare* below) Note that a list of local national health centres and hospitals is available from your local health office (*Azienda Sanitario Locale*). If you need a doctor that speaks English, embassies or consulates should be able to provide a list of English-speaking (private) doctors in your region. You can also search for a practitioner via the website of the Italian doctors and dentists association, FNOMCeO, the *Federazione Nazionale degli Ordini dei Medici Chirurghi e degli Odontoiatri* (www.fnomceo.it), but these will not be English-speaking.

When purchasing private healthcare it is essential to read the small print to ensure that the coverage is as complete as possible and covers all your possible future requirements – exclusions can be extensive. Paul Wolf of Innovative Benefits Solutions (www.ibencon.com) says, 'There are no bargains out there, you get what you pay for'.

Main Points About the Italian State Health System (Servizio Sanitorio Nazionale SSN)

o In 2004 the Italian health ministry executed reforms in the way the health service is run. Control and part of the costs are being increasingly devolved, in phases to be completed by 2013. Poorer regions will receive top up funding from a national fund.

o The Ministry of Health coordinates the activities of IRCCS (*Istituto di Ricovero e Cura a Carattere Scientifico)* which embraces sixteen private and public hospitals that are designated centres of research. Gerontology, including the illnesses of the third age are receiving a larger focus as befits the largest growing sector of the population.

o At local level you deal with a USL (*Unita Sanitaria Locale*) now renamed ASL (*Azienda Sanitoria Locale*), though many people still refer to them as USLs. There are 200 USLs/ASLs responsible for 50,000 to 200,000 head of the population each.

o Every citizen and foreign EU citizen living in Italy has to register in person, at the ASL and receive a personal health card (*tessera sanitaria*). A controversial new electronic health card (see below) was piloted in Abruzzo in 2004 and introduced on a wider basis in 2005.

o USLs/ASLs can provide the name and address of a local general practitioner (*medico di base/famiglia*) and they organise and coordinate in-patient/out patient hospitalization (but not emergencies).

o Unless you are over 65 and in receipt of a pension from an EU country, disabled or chronically sick you pay a contribution for prescriptions, laboratory analyses and visits to a specialist (fees are between €2 and €4 for prescriptions and €13 and €36 for consultations). These fees are set by the various regions.

o Almost all dental treatment is private. Only 6% of dentists in Italy work for the SSN.

o If you wish to consult a specialist gynecologist or eye doctor, you do not need a referral from a GP; you can go directly to the specialist.

o It is obligatory for children under 14 years to be seen by a paediatrician rather than a general practitioner, but where there is a shortage of doctors (e.g. in the south) this may not always be the case.

o The amount you pay for prescriptions is related to the category of drug that you are prescribed as well as your personal circumstances (see above). Drug categories are: group A – strong drugs for chronic disease; group B – drugs with 'therapeutic meaning'; group C – drugs not classified A or B; group H – drugs offered in hospitals. A and H are 100% free. Pensioners over 65 do not usually pay prescription charges.

- The cost of prescriptions is similar to France, but less than in the UK.
- For other medical services (nurse, chiropodist, physiotherapist) you can get a referral from your general practitioner. Normally you will have to pay for home visits from a nurse or doctor.

Italian Electronic Health Card

Beginning in April 2004 with a pilot scheme in one region, the Italian health service began issuing e-health cards with the aim of monitoring health care spending on specialists and the correct issuance of prescriptions as part of the National Healthcare Expenditure Monitoring System (a.k.a. TS System). The TS System includes the National Health Card, a new Prescription Form (e-prescriptions) and a dedicated network, which will enable all healthcare facilities in Italy to file electronically the data relating to each service that is delivered to each patient. The card is supposed to improve communication between health care professionals and deliver better services to patients as well as enabling financial resources to be used most effectively. The card was piloted in Abruzzo in 2004, followed by Umbria, Emilia Romagna, Veneto and Lazio and is being introduced in other regions progressively.

Issues have been raised by privacy groups in Italy regarding the potential for an individual's electronic medical files to become available to unauthorized personnel, but the Ministry of Health claims that adequate legislation and data security measures are in place to prevent this.

Dentists

In Italy, 94% of dentists work in the private sector and the remaining 6% are public (i.e. national health) dentists. Doctors are allowed to practice dentistry in Italy, but increasingly, dentistry is a specialist profession with separate university degrees and training. Occasionally a dentist forms part of an SSN clinic. You can ask for *il dentista pubblico* at the local ASL. On the off chance there is one in your area they will be based in a national health hospital or in a state health centre managed by the ASL. Private dentistry is extremely expensive, and the number of Italians seeking dental treatment has declined for that reason. A dental specialist is a *specialista dei denti*.

Preparation for Accessing Italian Healthcare

If you are going to be in Italy for a visit exceeding three months, you should, before you leave the UK, ask the Department of Work and Pensions (☎0191-218-7777/7367; www.dwp.gov.uk), for the reciprocal health agreement forms which allow you to access Italian healthcare: these are the E121 if you are a pensioner and E106 if you have retired before the state retirement age. You then register at the ASL/USL (see below). You will need to take with you your E106 or E121, your passport and proof of your UK address. These forms exempt you from paying Italian social security contributions as you are still attached to the UK system.

A foreign individual who is resident in Italy permanently and has no UK address, should register at the local ASL/USL health insurance office (address can be obtained from the local *provincia* website or town hall). If you have not reached retirement age you will also have to make contributions (if you are not eligible for an E106). These contributions amount to €387.34/£267 a year and provide for a range of health and social security benefits for the contributor and his or her dependants. UK pensioners living in another EU country will be entitled to the same healthcare benefits as a citizen of that country. The alternative to plugging into the state stystem is to go completely private and take out commercial healthcare insurance. This is a route followed by many foreign residents but in some areas may not be totally necessary as public and private healthcare overlap and in some areas, public healthcare is of a very high standard and is mostly free. See sections below for more details.

Medical Treatment for Non-resident Foreigners

Foreigners who are non-residents, even though they are from elsewhere in the EU will only receive doctor/hospital treatment if they pay first and then apply for reimbursement. British expatriates working in Italy while continuing to pay UK national insurance contributions will be covered if they have applied for form E101 or E106 (depending on their length of stay). Maximum cover is for two years.

Anyone just visiting Italy should apply for an EHIC (for details of how to get a European Health Insurance Card see below) which covers emergency treatment only, or they, or the person looking after them, will have to choose between returning to the UK for free treatment or paying up front to go to an Italian hospital. Charges could run into thousands of pounds for treatment of serious medical problems including surgery and drugs, accommodation and food and intensive care. Note that anyone requiring unexpected emergency treatment will still be treated without paying first.

The EHIC

In the initial moving period, or on reconnaissance visits, or while on a speculative visit to Italy to look at property, you will not be covered by the Servizio Sanitario Nazionale, and in such cases, you should take out private travel insurance. It is also possible to obtain mainly free, treatment under a reciprocal agreement, which exists between some EU countries. To qualify for such treatment you need an EHIC (European Health Insurance Card) formerly known as the E111 or E-one-eleven. The form T6 *Health Advice for Travellers* available in post offices, contains the application form for the EHIC or you can download it at www.dh.gov.uk/travellers, or contact the Inland Revenue, National Insurance Contributions Office (International Services, Longbenton, Newcastle upon Tyne, NE98 1ZZ; ☎0191-225 4811; international services helpline ☎0845-9154811; fax 0845-9157800; www.inland-revenue.gov.uk/nic/intserv/ose.htm).

If you pay any charges, keep the receipts and apply for reimbursement at the *Azienda Sanitaria Locale*. If the doctor gives you a prescription, take it to the pharmacy and show your EHIC to the pharmacist. Some medicines will be free, for others you will be charged the standard, non-refundable fee.

Accessing Italian State Healthcare

Access to the Italian national health service is at local level via the ASL. ASLs are the interface between the user and the public services. Their responsibilities include the public day hospitals, which provide general medical consultations, x-ray, blood-tests and the coordination of home nursing facilities. To be automatically eligible for the benefits of the Italian health service you must be over 65 and in receipt of a pension from an EU country and resident in Italy. This entitles you to use the health service on the same basis as retired Italian citizens. If you are not of official retirement age when you move to Italy, you can arrange voluntary enrolment in the SSN (cost €387.34 annually) until you reach retirement age, when you will then become eligible for the mostly free pensioner services. The alternative is to take out private health cover. By law, you are obliged to do at least one of these things, so that you are medically covered. If you enrol with the SSN voluntarily, cover is automatically extended to family members. For voluntary enrolment you need a valid residence permit (see *Residency Regulations* section) and a *codice fiscale* (fiscal code).

Using the Italian Health Service

Medicina Generale. Italy has 54,000 general practitioners, most of whom belong to the Italian Federation of General Practitioners, FIMMG (www.fimmg.org). Once you are officially resident in Italy and have registered with a general doctor at the ASL, you can visit the doctor in his *ambulatorio* (surgery) as and when you need to. Most doctors operate on a first come, first served basis so you don't need to make an appointment, but ideally you should arrive as early as possible. If you need to see a specialist, the doctor gives you a referral (*impegnativa*), which you take with you to your appointment.

Specialista. For the specialist there will be a cashier (cassa) where you may be required to pay a small amount (see *Main Points* above), before receiving any treatment. Specialists are usually hospital-based but may also be in the local health centre. There is a rather complicated relationship between the public and private health sector, which means that some private doctors are accessible to national health patients at their private consulting rooms. A specialist can also recommend spa treatments (*le cure termali*) at reduced cost (the maximum reduced cost: €50).

Drugs and Medicines. The SSN's profligate spending on pharmaceuticals is exceeded in Europe, only by the French health service and prescribing habits are being monitored for efficiency via a new prescription form. If you need drugs or medicines, the general doctor will make out a prescription (*ricetta*), for you to take to the pharmacy (*farmacia*). Pharmacies are outlets for medicine and medically-related items only. Prescription charges apply at a reduced rate if you are registered with the state health service. They are set by the region and are normally €2 to €4. There is a whole list of exemptions (the chronically sick, organ donors, victims of crime, war, terrorism, work accidents etc) and the least well off. If you take prescribed medication on a regular basis you should find out the generic (as opposed to brand) name of the drug from your doctor before leaving the UK, as brand names vary globally.

Ospedali. If there is an urgent need for admittance to a hospital this will be done by the treating doctor at the *pronto soccorso*. A patient can also be admitted to hospital on the authorisation of the *Guardia Medica*, out of hours service (see below). If the need is not urgent then a GP will issue the application form for hospital treatment at a hospital of the patient's choice. Hospital treatment costs are normally 100% covered by the SSN.

State Hospitals, as already said here, vary widely. The current wave of health reforms aimed at reducing central funding of the SSN, increasing the regions' responsibility for their own health services, and streamlining of operations through new technology, has yet to create an equality in health provision throughout the country. While doctors and treatments may be efficient, the shabby décor, lack of basic facilities and absence of personal care endemic in most state hospitals, seem to worsen the in-patient experience. Wards may contain either six or three beds. You can have a single room if you pay a daily supplement of €65-€75. If you want to go to a particular hospital in another city for specialized treatment you can request this under the National Health, but usually such hospitals (i.e. those in the north) have long waiting lists. If you want to jump the queque, you will normally have to pay for private treatment.

In state hospitals all in-patient treatment (including medicines and drugs), is free. For out-patient treatment including day case operations, consultations, medical tests etc. you pay a small charge. You have to be referred for outpatient treatment by your GP.

Each hospital produces a list of services and amenities (*Carta dei Servizi*), which includes details of visiting hours, meal times, where the public phones are in the hospital, the whereabouts of the nearest bancomat, not to mention copious rules and regulations about keeping the room tidy and not blocking corridors with your friends and relations. Although food is usually provided, it does not mean it is desirable and you may want to have food brought in.

Continuing to Use the UK NHS While Living in Italy

During visits to the UK, Britons can also continue to use the British National Health Service for the first three months while they are living in Italy, provided that they are still registered with the Department for Work and Pensions in Britain. However, this dispensation is only while they remain technically UK resident. Once they have become an Italian resident, if they have not reached retirement age: they will have either applied for an E106, or be paying Italian social security contributions, in order to be able to use the Italian health service.

If you retire early (i.e. before the UK pensionable age) you must continue to pay social security contributions, but you will not be covered by Italian social security until you start contributing to their social security system. During this time you may continue to pay into the UK NHS System for a period of up to two and a half years, during which you can still receive UK National Health treatment, provided that your British National Insurance contributions are up to date, and you have obtained form E106 from the DWP in Newcastle upon Tyne, before you leave the UK. Special rules apply if you have an industrial injury or occupational disease.

The advantage of continuing to pay social security contributions in the UK for as long as possible is that they are much lower than in Italy. Eligibility for the E106 and how long it lasts is something of a fudged area and your best bet is to try to get as much clarification of your particular case with the DWP before you leave the UK for good.

EMERGENCIES/GUARDIA MEDICA

Emergencies

In life-threatening medical situations you should call the *Guardia Medica* (118) for free medical assistance. This is a 24-hour number to be used only for acute emergencies such as a heart attack. The emergency service provides an ambulance to take the patient to the nearest suitable hospital. 118 calls are free from landlines and mobiles.

Out of Hours Medical Assistance. You can also contact the Guardia Medica if it is not possible to contact your family doctor (at night or during holidays). For this you should not use the emergency number 118, but rather the local number; every town has a different one. You can discuss the problem on the telephone with a doctor and if necessary the doctor will visit the patient at home.

Pronto Soccorso. The equivalent of an ER, A&E or Casualty is known as *Pronto Soccorso* (or sometimes confusingly as First Aid), and is located at every hospital in the country. The service operates on a triage basis with each user being colour coded red (emergency), yellow (serious) and green (in no danger). Greens are not attended to until all critical patients have been treated, regardless of how long they have been waiting.

If your medical problem does not qualify as an emergency, payment will be requested.

Alternative Medicine and Natural Therapies/Le Medicine non Convenzionali e le Techniche Naturali

The most popular 'alternative' medicine in Italy is Chinese acupuncture, which has been a medically recognised therapy in Italy since 1997 and a useful and safe alternative to pharmaceuticals and their frequent side effects. In Italy only qualified doctors are allowed to perform acupuncture and there are 10,000 of them registered as practitioners. Acupuncture is the only alternative medicine to be prescribed, in suitable cases by the SSN, particularly for addiction problems. The token charge is up to a maximum of €36. More information can be obtained from the *Società Italiana di Agopuntura (SIA)*. Most Italian acupuncturists do not stock herbal medicines, as by law doctors cannot sell direct to patients and few pharmacies stock herbal compounds, and if they do, they are very expensive. The Milan company *Lao Dan* (www.laodan.it) is one of the few Italian companies producing Chinese herbal medicines in Italy to rigorous standards using only plants from known sources and at standardized strengths.

A Bergamo herbal pharmacy *Farmacia Guidetti* (www.farrmaciaguidetti@yahoo.it; ☎035 237 220) sells teas, herbal medicines and other herbal products on the internet). If you take herbal medicines regularly, it may be cheaper to get them sent to you from home, or to stock up when you visit the UK or even France, as they are a lot cheaper outside Italy.

Osteopathy (*osteopathia*) is rarely practised in Italy; Chiropractic (*chiropratica*) is slightly better known. The costs of herbal medicines and alternative treatments/therapies are not covered by the state health service.

PRIVATE MEDICAL CARE

There has been a huge growth in private medical facilities in Italy over the last decade; the majority of them in the north of the country. The number of Italians who are covered by private medical insurance has also increased from 20% to about 30%. Most of the insurance is bought by Italians living in urban areas, and again, largely in the north. If you are on a low income and a pensioner, everything under the state system is either free or almost free. EU foreigners, living in Italy and under official pension age, can make voluntary contributions to the Italian system, or they can take out private health care insurance. Private health insurance for those in their 50s and 60s can cost hundreds of pounds a year, yet all emergency treatments, treatments for chronic illnesses, and in-patient state hospital operations are free for residents under the health system. You are likely to find that you will be well looked after from the medical perspective whether you are a private or a public patient. Vince and Freddi Ferrigno cancelled their private health insurance not long after arriving in Brindisi in Puglia; Freddi explains:

There is a new local hospital, which is modern and up-to-date. It is very efficient, calm and clean. We get the same national health service rights as Italian pensioners which means we pay token charges such as €2 for a prescription and €15 for a scan. We had private health cover to begin with, but we cancelled it as we find we don't need it here.

Only well off pensioners on larger family incomes (above €36,151.98/£25,000 gross) have to pay contributions for x-rays, bloodtests etc required, but these are capped at a fairly low rate and the clinic will supply a rate sheet. What private health insurance will give you is a hospital room to yourself with en suite bathroom, bedside television and decent food. Your medical treatment will be comparable, though you almost certainly won't have to wait for your operation. In the south of Italy state medical facilities are acknowledged to be patchy and in some cases poor.

Whether you decide to invest in private medical insurance will probably depend on where you live and what facilities are available there. If you require regular check ups for your own peace of mind then you will have to get private treatment as the SSN has priorities other than prevention programmes; (apart from childhood vaccinations). There is also the likelihood that you will need dentistry at some point. This is very expensive in Italy and you should check if your policy covers this.

Private Health Insurance Providers

AXA PPP Healthcare: ☎01892-612 080; www.axappphealthcare.co.uk.

British United Provident Association (BUPA): ☎01273-208181; e-mail info@bupaintl.com; www.bupa-int.com. BUPA International offers a range of worldwide schemes for individuals.

Exeter Friendly Society: ☎01392-353535; e-mail sales@exeterfriendly. co.uk; www.exeterfriendly.co.uk.

Goodhealth Worldwide (Europe): 5 Lloyds Avenue, London; ☎0870-442 7376.

CARE IN THE HOME AND RESIDENTIAL CARE

Care in the Home

Provision for the care of increasingly frail elderly people is a subject of much current debate in Italy where the number of *anziani* (aged persons) is set to increase to a third of the population. Traditionally seniors have provided invaluable grandchildren babysitting and childminding services and in return they could expect to be looked after by their children in their frailer years, often living in the same house with them. While this may still be true in some parts of Italy, lifestyles in the north particularly, have changed to the point where caring for elderly relatives is not an option for many people leading busy modern and fragmented lives. In the countryside, elderly people are often left behind when the younger family members leave to make their fortunes in the towns and cities.

The basic principal is that the elderly should be kept active and able (*autosufficiente*) for as long as possible and then assistance should be provided at whatever level is needed from home help (*assistenza domiciliare*) and meals on wheels (*I pasti a domicilio*) to help someone remain living in their own home rather than full-time long-term care in an institution. In reality, your options depend on which region you are resident in and even then, the least well off and most disabled and vulnerable of the over 65s get the most benefits. There is considerable disparity in provision between rich and poor regions. Innovations in 2001 and 2002 saw some regions including Liguria introducing a voucher system aimed at the elderly, which could be used to 'buy' home help, transportation or a home carer. This handout is means tested. The poorest (with incomes less than €8,300 per year) make no personal contributions although their town of residence has to supply 20% of funding, while those with incomes from €8,300 up to €13,000 and over €13,000 have to come up with a personal contribution of 35% and 50% respectively. The amount of the voucher depends on the level of dependency.

Regional Spending on Care of the Elderly

o The region with the highest spending on the elderly (defined as over 65) in 2003 was Trentino Alto Adige at €466 per capita, and the lowest was €19 in Calabria.

o The share of total social resources expenditure spent on services for the elderly is highest for Campania (40% of expenditure) and only 12% in Calabria. The highest average share is found in the North (30%+) while in the south and islands it is less than 10%.

o The southern regions tend to give more vouchers and cash while more residential care is provided in central and northern regions.

o The maximum incidence of residential care provision was 61% (Valle d'Aosta) and the minimum was in Basilicata and Molise.

Range of Social Services Assistance for the Elderly

Le Case di Riposo. These have bedrooms with one or two beds and a bathroom per two persons and are designed to cater for self sufficient or partly self-sufficient elderly people for an indeterminate period of time. There is usually a restaurant, cultural and creative activities and a day centre/room. Help with personal hygiene, laundry and basic health care are all provided. Every *casa di riposo* has to be authorised by the Region or Comune, which control the regulations under which it operates.

The cost of staying in a casa di riposo is borne by the social services of the region with a personal contribution from the customer, which is based on means. The cost includes board, food, heating, maintenance, laundry and medical care. Useful websites for case di riposo include www. casediriposoitaliane.com and www.windowweb.it/guida/medicina/case_riposo_anziani.htm, which will help you locate the nearest.

Le Case Albergo. A type of apartment block with communal facilities such as club-room for communal breakfast and pooled services such as laundry and cleaning. Suitable for single or married pensioners who want to be independent yet live in a community where there are communal spaces and where amusements are laid on for everybody.

Le Case Protette. These provide sheltered housing for aged people needing general assistance and whose own family cannot care for them. They can leave their own home temporarily or on a permanent basis to live in sheltered housing. Doctor, nurse and therapist attention is provided on the spot, and personal care, laundry and the needs of daily life are taken care of. There is a communal restaurant and recreational and cultural activities are laid on. There are one or two beds to a room.

Costs are paid partly by the comune and partly by the user. To find out what *case protette* are available locally, contact the Assistente Sociale of the comune where you are resident.

I Centri Sociali Anziani/**Pensioners Clubs.** Many comunes have pensioners clubs, which are mostly self-generating and run by their various memberships. Depending on the ages of the members, some are very active in the community helping out at local schools and on school buses, in the parks and museums, helping with the festivals and with transport for the disabled. They also organise various cultural, recreation and sporting activities for themselves as a group activity.

L'Assistenza Domiciliare/**Home Help.** This service can be provided for those who are not totally self-sufficient but who, with regular help, can stay living in their own homes. Assistance with personal care, domestic chores and paperwork, and 'chaperoning' on visits to the doctor or personal appointments are all part of the service.

Sources of home helps include the comune and the ASL (often in conjunction with a private organisation).

Il Servizio di Accompagnamento/**Companion Service.** Accompanying and companion service provided to people who have difficulty walking and getting around. Can be called on for instance if travelling on urban public transport. This service is usually provided by the local volunteer organisation.

I Pasti a Domicilio/**Meals on Wheels.** This service is provided to people who are on very low incomes (*con gravi problemi economici*), or those who are sufficiently autonomous to live at home but who are unable to prepare meals on their own. Precooked or hot lunches and suppers are brought to the house.

This is a means tested service supported by the comuni.

Soggiorno di Sollievo/**Therapeutic Holiday.** Depending on where you reside in Italy, some comuni organise two-week stays for self-sufficient anziani to stay in special climatic zones (mountains, spas) with medical personnel in attendance. You may also be recommended this by a doctor. There is usually a charge, and depending on your financial circumstances this can be minimal.

RETURNING TO THE UK FOR TREATMENT

One point to bear in mind is that once Britons have retired to (i.e. are permanently resident) in another country and are attached to that country's social security system, they are no longer entitled to use the British NHS free of charge. If they decide to move back to Britain permanently and re-enter the British social security system they can start to use the British NHS again on a no charge basis.

Of course, free treatment is available in the case of any accident or other medical emergency suffered while on a visit to the UK (under the EU reciprocal health agreement), but routine treatment cannot be claimed free of charge.

LOCAL HEALTH ISSUES

Italy has similar health issues, including high rates of the so-called industrialised country diseases, to those found in other developed countries. The anomaly in Italy is that it has the highest mortality rate in Europe in diseases of the heart and lungs amongst the 15-29 age group. The much vaunted healthy Mediterranean diet, which has until now assured not just longevity but accompanying good health to a large part of the aged Italian population, could be undone in the next generation by the soaring rate of childhood obesity. Italians have far fewer children and spoil them; mainly it seems, by over indulging their appetites.

As regards other main hazards to health: according to Amnesty International, Italy has a very high incidence of domestic violence against women, but much of it goes unreported. Italy also has one of the highest rates of road accidents (usually caused by speeding and reckless driving), and very high incidences (at enormous cost to the health service) of occupational diseases, a legacy of many bad working practices and conditions, which were commonplace until quite recently.

Creepy Crawlies

Forget the largely imagined hazard of snakes. They are all harmless in Italy, except for the light brownish, zig-zag patterned viper, which is venomous (not deadly) and will slither away from you at top speed, if you don't accidentally step on it first. The best protection is to wear ankle boots (not sandals) when walking in the countryside, and look before you sit on the ground. There are also scorpions in Italy, but you would be unlucky to be stung by one (they hide under large stones and in wall crevices) if you don't go looking for them. Far more important is fending off the mosquitoes, which plague summer nights. Burn mosquito repelling candles and spirals, spray yourself with insect repellent and keep your arms and legs covered with clothing with elasticated wrists and ankles if possible. Keep your bedroom window closed at night. There are also plants that help to keep mosquitoes away (see *Gardening*)

If you hear howling at night, you will probably be hearing the conversation of Italy's wolves that roam freely in the central part of Italy and in the mountains of the north. They do not usually attack humans, but 6% of the prey of Italian wolves is domestic animals. Shepherds have large sheepdogs for their flocks' protection.

Italy claims to be rabies free after random testing of wild and domestic animals in the alpine regions, where the last outbreak occurred, came up negative. This is due to a concentrated programme of baited-vaccination throughout the Alps.

MENTAL HEALTH

Mental illness and problems with mental well-being can affect anyone during the course of their lives. However, expatriates with high expectations of retirement can suddenly find themselves overwhelmed by feelings of isolation once they have moved abroad, and find it difficult being so far away from loved ones that they previously saw often and whose support they relied on. Additionally, life-changing events such as bereavement or a marriage break-up are usually hard to cope with on your own, and may be even harder if you feel isolated in a foreign country with no support network around you.

There is no need to despair. There are sources of help for all kinds of problems within the expatriate community on internet forums, English-speaking help organisations, that you can contact for face-to-face support (depending where you are) and counselling. You can join one of the English churches in Italy. The website www.europe. anglican.org gives their locations and contact details. If your Italian is good you can deal more easily with Italian medical and social services. In the first instance contact your GP. You can also visit your local *Consultorio Familiare* of which there is a nationwide network to advise those having difficulties in coping with their daily lives.

Ways to Keep Your Chin Up

○ **Contact your local expat group.** Either look on the internet and find a specialist support group, or join an expat forum, or contact a local expat group on the internet and arrange to go to a gathering.

○ **Contact the local *Voluntariato*.** Every community has a volunteer bureau. In areas where there are a lot of English-speaking residents, these may be run by English-speakers.

○ **Get out more.** Join a local village club, take up a sport or volunteer for archaeological, conservation work. If you don't feel you can cope with humans try offering to help with an animal charity or local animal rescue centre.

○ **Join an Italian class.** If you can't speak Italian, now is the time to begin. If you speak a little, now is the time to improve.

○ **Take a hobby or interest to the next level, or develop a new interest.** There are some ideas in the *Quality of Life* chapter, or just see what goes on locally.

○ **Gardening.** If you don't already garden, start now. Gardening can be a great mental soother (see *Gardening* in *Quality of Life*).

○ **Take up one of the mind and spirit disciplines.** Yoga is one of the best known and it is not all about being as bendy as India rubber. There are yoga groups in Italy and places you can go to for yoga weekends. Just type 'yoga italia' into your internet search engine and you will be able to find the nearest. Tai Chi is also very popular. Also dancing classes.

○ **Talk to a stranger.** There is always someone you can talk to; strike up a conversation with a perfect stranger, and see what happens.

In extremis remember that you can always call the Samaritans (free within Italy) on 800 86 00 22 or call them in the UK from Italy (+ 44 8457 909090).

Alcoholism & Addictions

Italy is a country where regular drinking of alcohol is part of the culture. Although the benefits of drinking red wine in moderation have been extolled by the medical profession, it is also a fact that it is all to easy to get carried away when wine is being pressed all around you. Unfortunately, there is a well-known tendency for those living an expat lifestyle to socialise, which while an essential ingredient of a happy retirement, may involve a lot of liquor consumption, this may build up a tolerance to alcohol, or in some cases, a slide into alcoholism. The other causes of alcoholism may be loneliness, or a devastating bereavement. The Italians take alcoholism very seriously and have draconian traffic laws against drink-driving. The Italian version of AA is *Alcolisti Anonimi* (www.alcolisti.anonimi.it) on whose website you will find the address of the nearest support group.

If you have other health damaging addictions such as drugs and tobacco, or even gambling, contact your local ASL who will put you in touch with the nearest *Centro per la Cura delle Dipendenze* (Dependency Treatment Centre) or ask for the *Servizio Tossicodipendenze* (called also SERT or I Sert.T) which will provide medical help and support to those suffering from dangerous substance addictions.

Crime, Security and the Police

CHAPTER SUMMARY

O Crime rates vary considerably around Italy. Typically, villages have minimal crime, whereas some resorts and cities have high levels of burglary and violent crime; while the South of Italy is the infamous centre of organised crime.

O The regions of Italy with the highest crime rates are Lazio, Puglia and Campania.

O Generally, major crime and organised crime are not a problem for foreigners living in Italy, but petty crime can be. The Italian police estimate there to be 1000 gangs working central Rome, snatching bags and picking pockets, in the streets and on public transport.

O Isolated properties are particularly at risk of being burgled so extra security precautions are needed including a resident housesitter if possible.

O Insurance companies usually have a list of security requirements such as window shutters that have to be installed before they will insure your home.

O If you are unfortunate enough to be burgled, it is a condition of insurance policies that you must report thefts to the police within 24 hours.

O Insurance policies are renewed automatically, so if you do not want to take on the previous owner's insurance then you have to actively cancel it.

O The latest scam: beware anyone who pays by cheque for a larger amount than you agreed, then claims it was a mistake and asks you for an immediate refund of the excess. They are just trying to fleece you before their bogus cheque bounces.

CRIME

Overview

Most European countries have high crime rates, and Italy is no exception. However, whereas in Britain the increase has been in theft and malicious offences against property, particularly cars, in Italy nearly three-quarters of all crime is drug-related. The three areas with the highest crime rates are Lazio, Puglia and Campania. The last two in particular have shown a spectacularly rising crime rate based on the statistics for reported crimes of theft and robbery in recent years.

Violent organised crime in Italy is so infamous it needs no introduction. There are Mafia black spots where murder is a regular occurrence, though there are fewer vicious kidnappings where traditionally, the perpetrators have the charming custom of sending the odd ear or finger of the victim to the family as an *aide-mémoire* to pay the ransom. Fortunately, most expatriates will never knowingly come face to face with mafia crimes as Mel Holmes, who moved to Trebissace in Calabria in 2000 explains:

> *There is a saying around here that if a town is controlled by the mafia, it is a safe place because the mafia would not allow anything to go on that attracts bad attention. The streets are so safe that people allow their children to walk outside on their own at night, knowing that they are almost as safe as in their own houses. We feel a thousand times safer here than we did in the UK. Having said that, if I won the lottery I wouldn't come here and build a million pound villa, because that might be inviting mafia attention. But ordinary folk like us can live completely unaware of the mafia's existence.*

In fact, although kidnapping occurs, predominantly in Calabria or Sardinia, instances have fallen to one every few years (in the 60s and 70s, it was up to sixty a year).

Apart from Mafia violence in well-recognised areas, there is little street violence, such as muggings and brawls, which happen far less than in many European countries. This may be connected to the fact that widespread drunkenness, which proves the catalyst to much crime in the UK, is not apparent in Italy. Indeed the Italians look with consternation upon the hooliganism of drink-inflamed British football supporters. Also little-known in Italy are the type of crazed gunmen found in North America, who blast away a few dozen complete strangers in an orgy of gunfire. Private arsenals, except for hunting rifles, are a rarity (except of course amongst the Mafia). Until recently, serial killings and crimes against children were a rarity in Italy, but sadly these types of crime are on the increase – or they are being reported more frequently as in other countries.

A new crime wave that has erupted in the last few years is connected with the influx of refugees and immigrants from Albania – the Albanian Mafia are reputed to be more ruthless than the indigenous groups. Most large towns have a contingent of Albanian Mafia along with Romanians and Serbs. According to local police chiefs the Albanian criminal element is much more aggressive and ruthless than other foreign criminals and they are simply murdering the Italian, African and Arab competition out of the way.

Petty Crime/Microcriminalità

The Italian police estimate there to be a 1,000 gangs working in central Rome alone, snatching bags and picking pockets in main areas of the city and on urban transport. Pickpockets especially, operate in the streets and at the main tourist sites in the cities (mainly Rome, Naples and Florence), on trains and buses, in museums and autostrade filling stations and in campsites. They operate on foot or on mopeds with the pillion rider doing the snatching, and are known in Neapolitan slang as *scippatori* (snatchers). Danger spots are: Naples city centre and station area, Rome's public transport services connecting the station with the Vatican, and Palermo in Sicily. Gangs of juvenile pickpockets, called *slavi* or slavs, from former Yugoslavia, have always been a problem at places like Rome's Termini station.

There are some police countermeasure success stories: petty crime has been eliminated in central Bari for example by patrolling Carabinieri. On the other hand Central Naples is proving a much greater challenge. In danger areas the only way to be sure of not being robbed is to adopt sensible precautions:

- Refrain from wearing jewellery and watches.
- Don't carry cameras or videocameras.
- Keep car doors locked while driving in cities.
- Don't carry large sums of cash.
- Keep credit cards and cheque books separate and secure.

By contrast, some rural areas in such places as Umbria, Tuscany, the Marches, Emilia Romagna, Piemonte, Friuli, Molise, where the old local cultures prevail, are nearly crime free. You are told that the only crimes there are committed by outsiders. In places like Buonconvento (Tuscany) you can confidently predict, still, that a wallet lost in the street will be handed in to the local police station (the Carabinieri) with its money intact.

Organised Crime

Organised crime in Italy is a veritable state within a state. Based in the South its tentacles spread throughout Italy – and abroad. It is nicknamed the octopus – *la piovra*. The *Mafia* or *Cosa Nostra* in Sicily is bigger, more calculating, and structured than the more chaotic and opportunistic outfits in the toe and heel and ankle of Italy: the *Camorra* in Campania, the *Ndrangheta* in Calabria and the *Sacra Corona Unita* in Puglia. Brave magistrates and policemen have struggled to quell the phenomenon. General della Chiesa of the police *carabinieri* was assassinated by the *Mafia* in 1982 and Giovanni Falcone and Paolo Borsellino ten years later, these latter two heroic magistrates are now commemorated in the name of Palermo's international airport.

Gangland warfare inside the Camorra resulted in 100 murders in Naples during 2005.

THE POLICE

It is unfortunately the case in Italy that the police have a dismal record in beating crime – around three-quarters of all crimes committed in Italy go unsolved. To be fair, the lack of effectiveness is often due to the difficulty of finding witnesses brave enough to testify. This is mainly because the bulk of crime occurs in the far south and Sicily – in other words Mafia territory.

For historical reasons, Italy has four main, separate police forces. Liaison between the forces has traditionally been difficult, but the situation has improved in recent years with more cooperation taking place. Most usefully, there is a division of territory allowing the state police (*Polizia di Stato*) to be the main operators in towns and the *Arma dei carabinieri* (para-military police), everywhere else including rural areas. The provinces also run their own police forces called *Polizia Provinciale* or *Polizia Municipale*. The official police forces are:

I Carabinieri: the paramilitary *carabinieri* are the largest force, numbering nearly 86,000. They have been striving in recent years to shake off their thick image and academic entry requirements have been raised. Nowadays they are generally personable and helpful. Carabinieri have dark blue uniforms (designed by Giorgio Armani) with red stripe and matching peaked cap. Accessories include white belts with matching cartridge holder and holster. Caribinieri police stations are known as *la caserna* or *la stazione dei carabinieri*. The carabinieri are responsible for stopping motorists in contravention of traffic regulations and administering on-the-spot fines.

La Polizia di Stato: there are a few thousand fewer Polizia than Carabinieri. Their uniforms are lighter blue than the Carabinieri and have a deep pink stripe. They also have a riot squad section (formerly known as the *celere,* for their green uniforms). *La Polizia* have a reputation for uncouthness and being rather trigger-happy. Their plain-clothes section have been mistaken, on occasion, for armed robbers. A police station is *una questura.*

La Guardia di Finanza/I Finanzieri: These are the customs police who can trace their origins back to the eighteenth century. Their force level is half that of the Carabinieri. They wear light grey uniforms and dark green berets with a yellow badge. Their already poor reputation reached its nadir when their former head, Generale Raffaele Giudice, was jailed for corruption on a multi-billion dollar scale, but has marginally improved since. They are responsible for investigating fraud, particularly organised crime fraud, amongst other things. When leaving an Italian bar or restaurant it is obligatory to carry your till receipts for 100 metres after leaving the premises in case *i Finanzeri* wish to inspect it, as a check on whether restaurant owners are fiddling their VAT.

I Vigili Urbani: These are the local municipal police forces. They are normally dressed in navy blue, with white jackets and a matching helmet. Of all Italian police they are the least professional. Like the carabinieri, they can stop and fine motorists. They are responsible for checking residence permits, investigating planning infringements and other local matters. In Rome their on-going feud with the *Polizia di Stato* provides regular street entertainment for local citizens.

There are additional police groups in Italy including the coast guard, prison police (*polizia penitenziaria*), the forest police (*corpo forestale dello stato*) and commercial security guards such as the armed ones in combat gear that patrol the Rome metro. Note that outside towns and cities it is generally the carabinieri who will come if you call out the police, whereas in towns you will get the *vigili urbani*. The police emergency numbers are 112 or 113. Theft being one of the most common crimes in Italy, the chances are that sooner or later you will require the police to make out a stolen goods report (*la denuncia*). If they are unwilling to do this you will have to insist as you need a *denuncia* for insurance purposes. It is best to go to a *comando dei carabinieri,* or *questura,* in person.

SECURITY MEASURES AGAINST BURGLARS

Precautions Against Burglars

Although Italy has a bad reputation for petty crime, it is mostly confined to the cities. However, even in rural areas, securing your home is important and it is always advisable to lock your house, even if you are only going to the local shops, as in a few hours a competent burglar can empty a house and drive away with all your possessions, which the police (carabinieri) are unlikely to recover. A few inexpensive timer switches linked to house lights and radios and TVs so that they go on and off intermittently, and a 'beware of the dog' sign on the gate (whether you have a dog or not) can help deceive potential opportunistic burglars by making the house seem occupied and protected.

Insurance

Another important consideration is the insurance requirements – no insurance company will settle a claim if the property is not secure. Most insurance firms insist on:

○ An external door, which should be strong either made of steel (*porta blindata*) or have a steel-rod mechanism. Some policies insist on two locks on external doors.
○ Windows to have internal lockable shutters with iron cross-bars fitted. Bars on all windows and doors less than ten metres from ground. Grilles can be fitted externally which allow for open windows in the heat of the summer and prevent intruders.

You can also have an alarm fitted and this too will reduce your insurance premium. There are several different systems available and there is even one that can monitor your property from another country although this is costly.

Insurance Agents. If you are living in Italy permanently then it is easier to arrange your home insurance with a local agent. Axa, Generali and Winterthur are the largest companies in Italy and they are most likely to have a representative in your nearest town, so you can deal with them face to face. If you are pre-retirement but have bought a second home in Italy, even though it is meant for retirement later on, it is probably sensible to take out insurance with an agent from the UK that specializes in second home abroad insurance (i.e. for homes that spend longish periods unoccupied). Firms in the UK include Schofields (www.schofields.ltd.uk) and Copeland (www.andrewcopeland. co.uk)sitemap/house-insurance-italy.html.

House-sitters

For temporary absences for a month or more, it is a good idea to employ housesitters who, unlike a caretaker, would be expected to stay on the premises at night. For your own peace of mind you could invite friends to stay or employ trustworthy locals perhaps recommended by the local priest or doctor.

Lucy, an expatriate widow with a large villa near Florence, who was vacating her property for a month's holiday in Australia was delighted when her local priest found two university students who were only too glad to house-sit as they needed peace and solitude to study. The payment they received was a welcome bonus. Their only duties were to care for two dogs and three cats thus ensuring their employer could go on holiday assured her home was protected.

Owners of holiday homes are often glad to have reliable people stay for free in their houses during the winter in return for some kind of useful work: chopping and stacking wood, garden clearing, looking after animals, painting and decorating etc. The owners then relax knowing their house is secure and heated.

SCAMS

Just because you have moved to Italy, doesn't mean that you are out of reach of fraudsters and scam artists trying to divest the gullible of their money and enrich themselves with minimal effort. The advent of foreigners owning property abroad and the open market of the EU has resulted in similar types of scams operating in many different countries; the international scam has never been more active. An area of current vulnerability is with internet-based transactions. Doorstepping is not entirely out of fashion though: as in the UK beware of unannounced callers who claim to be from utilities companies, and who demand access to your home; you should always ask for proof of identity and if you are at all suspicious then do not let them in. Likewise, if you are introduced socially, or cold-called by someone offering financial advice or investments you should check into their background.

If you want to find out if something is a scam you could check out the website www.scamvictimsunited.com which is full of cautionary tales.

Investment Frauds

'Financial services' type fraud occurs quite often in Spain and recently in France: The Dordogne in France, is currently reeling from the effects of a previously convicted (in the UK) fraudster who operated in and then fled the Dordogne taking investors' cash with him. He offered retirees in the Dordogne the chance to invest in a genuine *Société Générale* fund. Exploiting a loophole in French banking practices, which allows the recipient of a cheque made out to a bank to pay it into a personal account by signing it on the reverse, he thus paid investors' money into his own account. The same technique could be employed by a fraudster in Italy, which has similar banking practices to France.

According to the authorities whose job it is to battle fraud, bogus investment schemes are on the rise. Punters may be offered worthless or non-existent shares by a crooked share dealer usually based overseas, who contacts potential victims by phone. Usually he (it is normally a he) is charming, English and well spoken. One of the main sources of these financial parasites is Spain, and they are extremely adept at mimicking how genuine businesses operate. Yet others entice their target prey to invest in fine art, wines and rare gems.

Overpayment of Property Rental/Purchase Price Frauds

There is also a scam that is plaguing property owners who advertise their homes or self-catering accommodation for letting. The fraudster makes an arrangement to rent your property, sometimes by booking it on the internet. They will probably arrange to rent for several months, which amounts to a lot of money. They then send you a cheque for double the amount you have requested. It is at this point that alarm bells should go off, as who on earth overpays their rent? The fraudster then explains that they have made a mistake and asks you to refund the overpayment (which could be thousands of pounds). Of course the cheque they have sent you is fraudulent; their aim is to get money out of you fast, before their cheque bounces. They are aided by the rather slow Italian banking system. To be on the safe side you should make sure a cheque has been cleared, but preferably do not accept cheques at all, but insist on a bank transfer via the SWIFT system. Note that the same practice of overpaying and requesting a refund, can be applied to other transactions such as buying and selling of goods. Do not be caught out.

Online Payment Fraud

With the growth of internet selling including from small ads on expat websites there is plenty of opportunity for fraud. How do you know that if you pay the money you will get the goods? For some the answer is to use an escrow account where a third party holds the money in order to protect both buyer and seller. Do not use an online escrow account unless you know that it is genuine, as most of them are scams. One that is genuine: www.escrow.com.

Do's and Don'ts

o **Do** try to deal only with buyers and sellers who live locally and who are willing to meet you face to face.
o **Don't** ever wire money to a distant seller using Western Union or any other instant money wiring service.
o **Don't** pay the money into an escrow account suggested by the other party. If you want to go down this route make sure that you yourself nominate an account that you know is genuine; but better still, avoid escrow accounts completely.
o **Don't** ever give out personal financial information (such as bank account numbers).
o **Do** trust your instincts. Most fraud relies on its victims being gullible or greedy, and sometimes both. If a deal sounds too good to be true, then it almost certainly is.

Returning Home

CHAPTER SUMMARY

○ Many of those moving abroad do not plan their retirement finances before departure and overspend on property purchase and renovation. They are then forced to sell up and return to the UK.

○ Trailing spouse syndrome is another cause of returning, where one partner is much keener on moving to Italy than the other and who subsequently finds it impossible to settle down. The couple may then return home to save the relationship, or one partner may return on their own.

○ If you return to the UK you should contact HM Revenue and Customs and request form P86 or download it from their website. This is the form for re-entering the UK tax system if you have been resident abroad.

○ Pensioners who have returned to the UK through financial hardship may be able to claim UK benefits such as Pension Credit aimed at pensioners on low incomes.

○ If you rent out your Italian property after moving back to the UK and you are tax resident in the UK you will still have to declare your rental income to the tax authorities in Italy and the UK.

○ Longer lets of property in Italy give the landlord/owner a lot less leeway than short lets.

○ Although capital gains tax (INVIM) was abolished in Italy in 2002, there is a tax which operates in a similar way on *plusvalenza* (literally 'plus value') up to 30% on property sales that occur within five years of purchase.

REASONS FOR RETURNING

According to the Office of National Statistics of the 190,000 British people who move abroad each year, many will return home. Failing health and intimations of mortality make people homesick and want to return to the old familiar UK. Some widows (it is still the case that the majority of surviving spouses are women) feel that if middle-aged children start having to spend a lot of time visiting them in Italy for care duties arising from frailty or serious illness, they would return to the UK, and most say they would do so before they reach this stage. Financial strain is often a cause as is the difficulty of abandoning the habits of a lifetime and living like the locals in Italy for ever.

Common Causes of Returning

o Not enough research and preparation.
o Unreal expectations.
o One partner is not in harmony with the other about moving.
o Financial problems.
o Illness of one partner.
o Homesickness.
o Death of a spouse or partner.

No Escaping From Problems

Some people decide to leave the UK as a way of escaping problems they may be having in their lives. Expectations may be too high of how moving abroad can change a life around. They may be disappointed to find that they and their problems are inseparable and that they cannot change their lives until they themselves change. Changing yourself usually requires shedding emotional baggage and altering the way you think and perceive the world the around you. In some ways, it would be better to start this process before leaving the UK. You could then move abroad as the next step. You might then be less likely to give up and come back to the UK.

Rose Tinted Glasses/No Preparation

A considerable number of people have decided to move to Italy on the basis of spending a holiday there. Having had a memorable week or two admiring the stunning beauty and treasure trove of Italy and meeting picturesque locals, they suddenly think how wonderful it would be to live there permanently, forgetting that all the mundane details of daily life would be just the same in Italy (probably worse because of the bureaucracy). The hot weather, which seemed so perfect for dining outdoors at night, is not so brilliant when you are rushing about your daytime chores, or sitting baked in your car. In fact, the lack of rain is a severe problem in parts of southern Italy where water can be turned off for hours at a time during summer. It is as well also to remember that every country has its issues, which drive its populace mad. In the case of the Italians this can result in multiple manifestations of workers *in sciopero* (on strike) at the same time, which may not affect country dwellers unduly, but they are very inconvenient for city folk. Oh, and there is the minor problem of hardly anyone in Italy being able to understand your English. When the rose tinted glasses are removed the vision does not match up to the reality and returning to the UK seems to be the only solution.

Before moving abroad ask yourself why? Why would living abroad be better than taking your holidays there. What would change in your life if you moved abroad? Once you have made up your mind to retire to Italy, then you should research what living in Italy on a day-to-day basis entails in practical terms and work up to retiring there gradually.

Trailing Spouses and Relationships

This is a common expatriate problem, where moving abroad suits one half of a couple much better than it does the other half. Once out in Italy the strain in the relationship begins to show as one partner begins to resent that they were forced into the move, feels isolated and cannot cope without their network of friends around them. Of course it is possible to make new friends but if you don't speak Italian you will be cutting out half your potential acquaintances and in your day-to-day

life in Italy this can cause untold frustration. Couples will either decide
to part, or they will return to the UK to try to save the relationship.

It is very important that both partners are in harmony about the
wish to retire abroad and that they discuss their aims and expectations
in advance of making the move to Italy.

Financial Pressures

Retiring abroad is not cheap: property purchase, renovations, transporting personal effects, buying a car, trips back and forth to the UK,
mean that the first part of your retirement is hugely costly. What happens after that depends on how well you have done your calculations. A
large number of expatriates get carried away with the property aspects
of living in Italy and buy a house that they have to beggar themselves
to renovate. Unable to live comfortably in Italy they are forced to sell
up and move back to Britain.

It is essential when you move abroad to have done your retirement
financial planning before you leave and have a substantial emergency
fund that is not part of your budget for moving but is for unexpected
expenses only. That way you will have a much better chance of
surviving the initial hit of the move financially. After that, expenses
will even out on a year-to-year basis and you should be able to budget
more accurately from experience.

TAX, SOCIAL SECURITY & HEALTHCARE

Whether you move back to the UK as a result of things not working
out, or because a partner has died or you have parted from them, or
for any of the other reasons that expatriates decide to return home,
there are practical and financial implications. Before you return to the
UK you should go through all of your financial affairs including bank
accounts, pension schemes and other income and consider the effect
the return to the UK will have on your financial situation. If you have
offshore accounts, you can continue to use these but when you move
back to the UK, i.e. become UK resident, you will have to declare
them and pay tax to HM Revenue and Customs on any interest.

HM Revenue & Customs

When you arrive back in the UK you should request HM Revenue and Customs form P86 or download it from their website (www.hmrc.gov. uk). According to HM Revenue & Customs 'this form should be completed if you have come to the UK for the first time or after a period of absence.' After you have completed the tax form you should return it to the local tax office (consult HMRC if you do not know which this is). You will need to know your UK National Insurance number as this is requested on the form.

You will need to keep proper financial records from the time you return to the UK and remember that tax returns in the UK have to be in by 30th September if you want the tax office to work out the figures for you, or January 31st if you are doing the sums yourself.

Pensions and Social Security

You need to contact the Department of Work and Pensions (www. dwp.gov.uk) as soon as you arrive back in the UK in order to switch payment of your pension to a UK bank account. Follow up any telephone calls to the DWP with written confirmation.

Pensioners on low incomes and with limited savings may qualify for income-related state financial assistance on their return to the UK. Benefits include Pension Credit (towards weekly income) and Housing Benefit (help towards rent). You can enquire about these from the DWP on your return. They are not usually payable outside the UK.

Useful Contacts for Pensioners

Benefit Enquiries: ☎0800 88 22 00.

Help the Aged: www.helptheaged.org.uk.

Pension Assessment: ☎0845 3000 168.

Pension Credits: ☎0800 99 1234.

NHS Direct: ☎0845 4647; www.nhsdirect.nhs.uk.

Winter Fuel Payments: ☎08459 151515; www.thepensionservice.gov.uk/ winterfuel.

Healthcare

Worsening health combined with financial pressures is a frequent cause behind expats returning. As already said, state healthcare in Italy is patchy: the supply of decent Italian National Health hospitals is mainly in the north, forcing many to take out expensive private health insurance. Pensioners are entitled to free prescriptions and medical tests, consultations and treatments (but not dental care) in the UK; while in Italy, the better off make a contribution (except for in-patient treatment). There is also the fact that as the health of one partner worsens, the other one often finds the strain easier to handle by returning to where there is a family support network. As health worsens, there may also be a wish to see the UK again.

Once resident again in the UK you can use the British National Health service without charge by registering with your nearest GP or healthcentre.

Healthcare Useful Contacts

Care Homes: www.nursing-home-directory.co.uk (by areas).
Retirement Homes: www.bettercaring.co.uk.

LETTING YOUR ITALIAN PROPERTY

Many people only rent out their second home or retirement home occasionally to people they know, or privately through placing small ads in the UK. Short-term lets of holiday homes protects the owner from tenants who might become problematic if they do not want to leave. If the right conditions are not observed, and the tenants refuse to leave the property, there will be major legal costs involved in evicting them. Short-term holiday lettings are also preferable if you think you might want to sell up in Italy in the near future. For holiday lettings:

○ The property should be fully furnished.
○ The rental should be for no more than three months.
○ The tenants should have a principal residence elsewhere.
○ There should be an agent, or someone you trust on the spot to keep an eye on things while the property is rented out, so that you can concentrate on organising your re-entry to the UK.

Holiday Letting

This is usually done from spring to autumn. Renting is a useful way of recouping some of the cost of restoration and it is also wise not to let your property remain unoccupied for long periods especially for security reasons and insurance cover. The income you can expect will vary according to the degree of luxury offered, and whether the let is in the high season (July and August) mid-season (June and September) or low season (April, May and October). Rentals range from £300 for a one-bedroom apartment, to upwards of £6,000 for a luxury villa for one week in the high season. These are the prices that owners have been commanding in recent years, however with thousands of Britons investing in holiday homes around the world there may be a lot of competition from equally picturesque, but far cheaper alternatives in Bulgaria, Turkey, Montenegro and so on.

If you decide to rent out your property, be it a villa, farmhouse or apartment, there is no shortage of holiday rental companies that can be approached – the Italian State Tourist Office can provide a list or check out websites such as www.estate.net.

Considerations Before Renting Out

Before you place an advert for your property in a newspaper or magazine you must make sure that you meet all the requirements that make your house/apartment a suitable rental.

- A swimming pool is fairly essential in the countryside.
- If your property is near a major city or place of interest you can charge more rent.
- Well-equipped kitchen.
- Provide bed linen and towels.
- Have a cot and highchair for young children.
- Central heating or another form of adequate heating.
- Washing machine/dryer (laundry room).
- Place to hang washing.
- TV, video, radio, CD player.
- Bicycles, badminton, table tennis etc.

o Garden space with private corners for guests to sit.
o Barbecue area – eating area suitable for up to 12 diners, equipped with crockery, cutlery – fridge for cold drinks.

With holiday letting you are free to make your own rules e.g. period of rent, deposit and number of occupants.

> You will be liable to pay tax on your rental income in Italy; and long-term rentals over a month should be registered with the authorities. Some comunes require all guests whatever their length of stay to register. This is a requirement of Italian bureaucracy which some comunes will not waive.

Advertising Your Property

If you decide to act as your own agent there are many ways you can advertise your property. The publications in the UK which contain holiday rental classifieds from homeowners in Italy are *The Sunday Times*, *The Sunday Telegraph*, *The Observer*, university alumni, and other niche magazines such as *The Gay Times*. Another possibility is to rely on internet agencies such as VRBO (villa rental by owner) or Owners Direct. You must provide a well produced brochure with internal/external photographs, information on the attractions, the facilities and shops etc., a map, contact details, and clear instructions about the cost, paying the deposit and balance. When you have had a satisfied client – then word of mouth will be your best advertisement.

Agents

If you don't have much time to do the renting yourself you can decide to use an agent or agents, who deal with the clients and sort out any problems affecting the visitors during their stay. The agent charges commission of 20-40% of the gross rental income and has a catalogue/brochure or internet site. If you are considering renting, contact the rental company the summer before you want your renting to begin. Letting agents turn down as many as nine out of ten properties that are sent to them. Needless to say, it is of the utmost importance to employ an agent who is conscientious, efficient and honest and comes recommended.

> You do not have to have a special licence to set up as a holiday rental agent in Italy and some have gone bust owing their customers thousands of euros.

A company that has been trading for a number of years and can show you other villas and apartments on their books is the best bet. It is usual to sign a contract with the agent and this is renewed annually. The services of the agent should include:

- Meeting the guests – handing over the keys.
- Tour of the property and how main appliances work.
- Arrange for cleaners and linen changes between rentals.
- Arrange for a gardener and for the pool to be cleaned.
- Give guests contact phone number for emergencies.
- Check property occasionally when not rented during contract period.
- Arrange for payment, deposit etc.

Because of the immense competition in renting it is possible that all your vacancies in your villa, farmhouse or apartment in Italy will not be filled. At best you can expect 20 weeks especially if your property is of a high rental standard and with good staff. However, geopolitical problems and changing fashions can have a devastating effect on a rental season. At the moment Italy is extremely popular because of its abundance of history and art treasures combined with good food and *simpatico* people.

SELLING ON

When you buy a property in Italy – it could be that you are considering living there for the rest of your life. On the other hand you may be buying the property as a business venture and intend to restore it and then sell it on. It may be that life in Italy did not live up to your expectations and you want to sell and leave, whatever the reason you must ask yourself some questions:

- What is the state of the property market?
- It is a good time of year to sell?

O Should I get more than one valuation?
O How do I find a reliable estate agent? Where will I find one that speaks English. Should I consider sole agency?
O Do I need to change the interior or exterior of the property to improve its chances of selling?
O Shall I sell the property myself?
O Where shall I advertise my property?
O Who can give me advice about the legalities of selling a house in Italy?
O What reasons do I give prospective buyers for selling my house?

There are advantages to selling the property yourself:

O You do not have to pay commission.
O You have already been through the buying process and can advise any interested parties what to do.
O You can explain the layout of the property and clearly explain about the water, gas, electricity and telephone, which will facilitate the purchase.
O It may be that your staff i.e. cleaners, gardener, handyman/care-taker etc. would be glad to remain in employment at your property. This provision would be very welcome to most buyers.

Note that if you have thoroughly restored your property, even if you have spent a fortune (or more especially if you have) and it looks immaculate, unless you paid a bargain price for it, you will probably not recover all the money you have spent. To maximise your chances of getting the best price it is a general rule that a good time to sell your property is in spring. However, a lot of purchasers like to see the property in the winter. This is a good idea because by seeing it at its bleakest, they know what to expect.

It is a good idea to get at least two or three valuations. You can also look at similar properties for sale and set a realistic price. If you ask too much you will price yourself out of the market. The valuation should take into account that buyers might ask you to drop the price; you don't want to deter them because your price is not negotiable (*trattabile*).

Tax on Plusvalenza

Although capital gains tax (INVIM), was abolished in Italy in 2002, there is a tax which operates in a similar way on *plusvalenza* (literally 'plus value') and is levied at 30% less deductions for some costs (see below). It is applied to property sales that occur within five years of purchase.

Plusvalenza (literally 'plus value') is the difference between the declared purchase price of a property, and the declared sale price, minus deductions for renovation and notarial fees. This means that if you expect to sell the property within five years you should plan ahead so that you minimise the tax on the plusvalenza. You should ensure that the declared price on the conveyancing documents when you buy is as high as possible.

Estate Agents (Agenzie Immobiliari)

It might be beneficial to use the estate agent who sold you the property as he will be familiar with it. If this is not possible or desirable, there are lists of Italian estate agents on the internet including www.grimaldi.net, www.arpnet.it, www.casa.it and www.findaproperty.com. All estate agents must be registered and have a document attesting to their legality. An estate agent must have a signed authority from the owner and come to an agreement whereby either the estate agent has sole control over the sale; or, seller has the right to deal with other agents and private individuals.

> ### Sole Agency
> N.B. The benefit of a sole agency agreement is that the percentage is usually lower. If however you sign an estate agent's authority without stipulating that you have the right to find your own buyer then you still have to pay the agent's commission even if you sell the house yourself.

Selling Through an Estate Agent

Always scrutinise any contract and make sure you understand what you are signing. Contracts will specify the estate agent's commission and this is not paid until completion although sometimes the commission is paid at the *compromesso* stage. Agents' fees vary; the rate of commission can be anything from 3-8% depending on the area and the market. The cost is usually shared between the vendor and the buyer. If you are selling a property include the estate agent's fee in the price; if the estate agent used another person to procure a buyer then it is up to the estate agent to share the commission.

Before putting your house on the market it is important to make sure that the exterior and interior are up to a high standard. The interior should be bright and clean. The kitchen and bathroom should be modern and of the best quality. It is not necessary to spend a fortune on designer products as it is unlikely you will recover the amount spent. The price of buildings in Italy is based on the link between the cost per square metre times the area m2 e.g. 300m2 @ 1,000 euros per m2 = €300,000.

Your estate agent will advise you about any improvements that would attract buyers. He will be up to date with buyers' preferences. If you are forced to sell your home and it is not fully restored, this should be reflected in the price. The house should also come with any planning permission needed for renovation and an estimate for the cost.

Selling Your Own Property

If your home is in a good location and is very desirable and you have set a realistic price, then it is possible that you will have no problems selling it yourself. Good advertising is the best guarantee that you will sell. Access to a computer means you can place your advertisement with various agents who specialise in overseas property such as www.knightfrank.com, an international agency with associates in Tuscany and North America and www.piedmontproperties.com, a specialist in marketing villas in the Monferrato and Langhe regions of Piedmont.

A useful publication is *Ville e Casali* (www.villecasali.com) a national property and decoration magazine in Italian. The classified property advertisements are listed in both Italian and English.

A 'For Sale' (*vendesi*) sign at the entrance to your property can be useful, if only as a signpost indicating the location of the property. An advertisement put into newspapers or magazines is also a must. Italy is now attracting buyers from America, Canada, Australia and European neighbours. Italians too are also buying property, mainly restored as holiday homes. In fact they are buying back what was once theirs.

It is a sensible to compile all the documents, guarantees etc. that pertain to your property. Certificates such as *il certificato di abitabilità*. This is to certify that your house meets the standards required. Any architectural drawings (*planimetria*) are useful, and a list of local plumbers, builders and electricians. The guarantees for the boiler and information on the gas *bombola* and where to locate the pump for the water are important.

When selling your home yourself you will need the services of a notary (*notaio*) to give you sound legal advice, prepare the contracts and conduct the completion. It is your choice whether you engage the services of an estate agent or sell the house yourself. If you give an estate agent exclusive rights – you get a guarantee of quality and service. The agent's commission takes care of the costs of advertising the property and he or she will have personnel to pay who deal with telephone calls, letters and the preparation of documents for the *notaio*. An estate agent will also use forms supplied by the organisation of Italian Estate Agents (*Federazione Italiana Mediatori Agenti d'Affari*) F.I.A.M.A.A. If you give an estate agent sole rights he will be more committed to advertising and do his utmost to get you a buyer.

Must Do List for Arrival Back in the UK

o Open a UK bank account as soon as possible so that you have access to funds for daily expenses without paying unnecessary charges.

o Contact the HM Revenue and Customs (www.hmrc.gov.uk) for a P86 form or download it from their website in order to reinstate yourself in the UK tax system.

o Keep proper financial records from the time you arrive back in the UK as these will be essential for your self-assessment tax form.

o Contact the Department of Work and Pensions as soon as you arrive in order to claim your UK pension in the UK again.

o Register with your local GP or Health Practice so that you can use the NHS again without charge.

Case Histories

CAROLE MEANS

Carole, who is now 62, moved to Italy originally to work for Olivetti in Turin in 1988 as a technical writer of manuals in English; and her husband also had a job with the same company. They did not speak Italian, except for Carole's O level in the language. They bought a house in Umbria with the intention of retiring there. Finding the climate of Turin too cold for their liking they took early retirement and moved to Umbria in 1991. The severe Umbrian earthquake of 1997 destroyed their home. They had to start working again to replenish their losses, and in 2000 they bought a house 4 km from Ceglie Messapica (pop. 20,000) in the comune of Ostuni in Apulia.

What compensation did you get after your home in Umbria was destroyed?
We lost everything except some furniture, which we salvaged from the ruin. There was no insurance payout, as it was not possible to insure houses with Italian insurance against earthquakes in Italy prior to the 1997 quake. Soon after 1997, the government brought in a new law making it obligatory for house-owners in a seismic zone to insure against earthquakes, because they did not want the expense of compensation.

We rented somewhere nearby to live. The alternative was to stay in the emergency portakabins provided by the regional authorities; some people were still living in these five years later. Because we took care of ourselves we received no compensation from the state. We didn't think it was worth waiting for them; we wanted to get on with our lives, so we went back to work.

What kind of house did you eventually buy in Apulia?
We had to buy a house which was already renovated as we did not have
the resources to do up another house. Our house is in the country and
has an acre of land with olive and fruit trees, which we harvest ourselves. We sometimes sell the olives.

So are you retired now for the second time?
Well let's say that until recently we were working very hard, but we can
calm down a bit now as we've survived everything that happened to
us in Umbria. I would say I am now semi-retired. My husband is less
retired than I am.

So what have you been working hard at?
We help people who want to buy property in Apulia find what they are
looking for. My husband searches out properties for people of the type
that they specify they are interested in and acts as a property consultant.
We have a website www.apuliabella.com for this and other services we
can provide. Before that we promoted tourism in the area as we knew
lots of people who had tourist accommodation they wanted to let.

Is it easy to let holiday property here?
It is less easy than it was, since Ryanair reduced flights to Bari/Brindisi
from two to one a day. This means that the number of tourists to the
region was reduced by a 1,000 a month. A lot of Italians come here
too, to see their relatives.

Presumably you are fluent in Italian?
Yes, my husband Kevin and I usually speak to each other in Italian
as it seems more natural to us after all this time. My daughter lives in
Umbria and her children were born in Italy and speak only Italian so
when we are together as a family we usually speak Italian or half English half Italian sentences to each other.

How popular is Apulia with expats?
When we moved here, I think we were the only ones. Then there were
a couple of newspaper articles on the Trulli dwellings unique to Apulia,
and the expat boom here took off in 2004. Then in 2005 there was

the SIPPS fiasco when people thought they were going to be able to put foreign property into their pension pot; lots of people had already bought properties here before the government changed their mind. Someone suggested a figure of 1,000 expats living here. It's not quite like the Dordogne though; you can walk down the street without hearing any English spoken.

We hear a lot about the Italian State Health Service, along the lines of: when it's good it's brilliant and when it's bad, it is very bad indeed. What do you think?
There was an item on the news yesterday which claimed that 2.5% of all deaths in Italy could be attributed to medical negligence or malpractice. On the other hand many Italian doctors are excellent and efficient. You cannot fault their bedside manner; they make you feel they are not just your doctor, but your friend.

What about the Italian bureaucracy?
It absolutely tries your patience to the limit. It always takes a minimum of a day to get a single piece of paper. I have been in an office where the person in front of me, an Italian, was told to come back the following day to collect some paper or other. After he had left the room, the official calmly stamped the piece of paper and put it in a drawer. How perverse is that, not to give the paper immediately. Thank goodness that my husband and myself have a *permesso di soggiorno* that is for life. We always go to the post office or bank at lunch-time because here, that is the quietest time.

What do you do for recreation?
We've been on holiday almost everywhere in Italy. I love Sicily. We tend to drive from here and get the ferry. As soon as you are off the boat you feel welcome. There are also flights to Palermo from Bari. My main interest is in seeking out new restaurants to recommend. As my husband loves eating this works out well. The food in Italy is so wonderful and different in every region because they keep their own recipes. You can only get spaghetti Bolognese in Bologna.

CAROLE ORAM

Originally from Hartlepool, Carole Oram moved to Italy in June 2005. She is 49 and Brian, her partner is seven years older. Carole was a practice manager for a group of GPs and Brian worked for Nestlé as a food technologist. We asked Carole:

What made you choose Italy for retirement?
I think for us it was the way events turned our lives. We were both in other relationships but had known each other for many years as friends. Brian's wife died and I was divorced. Brian had the chance to retire and take his pension. We realized that you never know what is round the next corner, so we decided to seize the chance to live for today and open an entirely new second chapter of life for us both.

Did you speak Italian before you arrived in Italy?
We started to learn it while we were in the UK but had little time to put into it. We take private lessons weekly and last year we did a two-week intensive course locally. It is very hard work learning it.

How would you describe your location?
We live in the hills about 7 km above Lisciano Niccone, north of Lake Trasimeno in Umbria. 5km of 'white road' separate our house from the main road to the village so we are very remote. The house is in a forest of holm oaks, although there are some olive groves around us and rough farmland grazed by sheep and white cattle of the chianina breed.

How did you set about finding your home in Italy?
We started a wish list and then looked to see which items on it we could tick. We then thought about the pros and cons, trying to be practical and objective and not get swept away with the romance of it all. Realistically, this resulted in a compromise. We loved the location, even though most locals and visiting family and friends think we are totally mad. We don't regret anything so far and love our little casa with all its warts. We used a relocation company Brian French and Associates to locate a property and they were incredibly helpful.

How far are you from 'civilisation' and airports?

Our nearest airport is Perugia (45 minutes). Pisa and Rome are both two and a half hours by car Florence half an hour less and Forli (airport) one and a half hours.

What's the property like?

It is the only renovated part of a very old (500 years) farmhouse. The piles of stones around us are the remains of other buildings. It had been a rental house and was habitable with power, bottled gas, central-heating (which we can't afford to use). I think it could best be described as a place that had previously been fixed quickly to make a fast buck. We have a raised meadow opposite where the swimming pool is and we have negotiated use of a patch of land for a vegetable garden.

So is there is a lot of renovation needed?

The main thing was a new insulated roof. After that, we did lots of cleaning and decorating and made alterations to the shower room attached to the guest bedroom. We are making do with the existing kitchen and other shower rooms but in time we plan to refurbish these. We thought of buying one of the derelict buildings outside and renovating it as a holiday let, and we may do this in the future. At the moment we have enough to work on without beginning the complicated process of getting permission and planning consent and the difficulty of locating source materials. After all, we wanted to retire, not work that hard.

Any unforeseen problems?

We are having to wait ages for a landline telephone installation. This is because of the chaotic Italian systems. Before we completed on the property deal we investigated the time needed to get a phone here and we were assured three months max. We have had a series of dates and excuses and had to go to an Italian solicitor who finally got them to start work. We know of Italians in nearby villages who have had to wait a year. We have no idea how much it is going to cost as quotes have ranged from €1800 - €3000.

What about the other utilities?
We needed a better source of water, so we had a new well sunk. We now have spring and well water. Electricity seems to be reliable. Bottled gas is extortionately priced and getting even more expensive. We have heard that there are grants for solar power and pellet burners. We had a wood burning stove installed which also vents two additional rooms, which helps as the winter is very cold.

And the paperwork?
Registering for the *permesso di soggiorno* is an experience. Time, patience, a sense of humour and remembering that you are not in the UK anymore are essential. I found the way to look at it is this: the Italians have their systems and you must simply work with them.

Are you registered with the state health service?
Yes. Once you have the permesso di soggiorno it is easy to register. We understand there are nominal charges to pay though we haven't paid anything so far, as we haven't used the service yet. It is easy to see a private practitioner, English-speaking doctors contact details and rates are available on websites.

Is it easy to make friends?
We are lucky enough to have met many people and the rules are quite simply different here. It seems that everyone in the expat community is more open to make new friends. You are all in the same boat with a very large thing in common and we have a great social life. We socialize with expats including Dutch and Americans as well as the locals. The Italians are crazy, warm and for the most part helpful, and they have a different perspective on life, which is after all why we came here in the first place.

What do you like most about Italy?
Hey I could write a book for you. Italy and Italians are so diverse. It's beautiful, it has brilliant wine, food, art and culture. It has cheap trains that are easy to use and hill top towns of the most amazing interest. It has seasons. Most of all it suits the needs of myself and my partner at this time in our lives.

HARRIS FREEDMAN

Writer Harris Freedman was originally from New York but lived in central London for 16 years and took British nationality. He is now 64 and lives near Castiglione del Lago overlooking Lake Trasimeno in Umbria. He moved to Italy in 2001 to a 17th century farmhouse and lets out three self-contained apartments, which are part of his house, plus a fourth apartment that is separate.

What made you choose Italy for retirement?
Writers never retire. I wrote the screenplay for the film *Broken Thread* which is due for release this year. I knew I wanted a slower pace of life after being a city person, and Italy was one of the places I thought might be suitable. Besides, I have a great love of Italy going back 35 years.

How did you go about making the move?
After I had decided I was going to move from England, I brought my car over and came through France into Italy. The plan was to drive around to find an area where I would like to live, then rent somewhere in it, then find a property to buy. But life isn't like that.

What happened?
I went into a realtor's and ended up seeing 50 properties in 30 days. On the penultimate day the realtor said to me 'There's this house I've got, it's not quite what you say you want, but the location is unbelievable.' I went to see it. The track was overgrown, the place was completely unkempt, it needed masses of work but as soon as I stepped out of the car I knew this was it. It was a farmhouse with a 360° view including two lakes, rolling hills and seven or eight towns in the distance. It was March 2001 when I went back to the UK to sell up there. When I came back to Italy in November 2001, I rented an apartment in Perugia (the capital of Umbria), for ten months while the house was being made habitable. I went back to living like a student in a small apartment with just my books and music and the lively city for amusement. It was fantastic.

Did you speak Italian before you moved to Italy?
No. I learned it when I arrived. I spent four months going to basic Italian classes in Perugia; after that it got too difficult driving back and forth to the house, which is about 40 minutes from Perugia, so I gave up classes and just carried on learning through talking to Italians.

How do you find Italians?
They are fantastic if you deal with them on a personal level. The bureaucracy is diabolical. I got so desperate that I called up the mayor and dealt with him personally. It worked. Everything got sorted very quickly; nothing much would have happened otherwise. In Italy, it's all down to personal contacts. If you deal with the Italians, look them in the eye. People are responsible here. If you really need something done; it will be. On another level you find yourself wondering 'how does Italy function?' People are always late and they say 'yes' to you because they don't want to say 'no'. The trick is to know when 'yes' means 'no'.

What do you like best about living in Italy?
Sunshine, clean air; Umbria is the lungs of Italy, it is one of the least industrial and most beautiful regions. I like the lifestyle, the food, which is simple, always freshly made and delicious wherever you are in Italy. You never have the same food in another region; each has its own cuisine. All the sauces are different. I love the rhythm of life here, though obviously it speeds up as you go north and into the cities.

Are you still exploring Italy or travelling much?
Where I live near Castiglione del Lago is pretty much central. If I drive for two hours either side of here I get to the Mediterranean on one side and the Adriatic on the other. By train I am only an hour from Rome and one hour from Florence. I can drive to get a ferry to the Pontine islands off the coast of Rome, or to the Tuscan coast and take a ferry to islands off the Tuscan coast. I still have lots of places I want to see. I am surrounded right here in Umbria by three dozen cities such as Assisi, Spoleto, Cortona, Chiusi, Arezzo, Perugia, Orvieto, Montepulciano, which when you include nearby Rome and Florence contain most of the treasures of European civilisation.

Don't you miss the big city buzz?
I go back to London maybe four or five times a year and spend three or four days or a week there. I often fly to Paris from here (Rome). It's not a problem.

Do you think you will stay in Italy for the rest of your life?
Well you can never be bored here. There are an enormous number of cultural festivals: all kinds of music and the arts. There are probably 100 of them just in Umbria. If anyone wants to come and see for themselves, I rent out apartments in my house. You can check them out on my website www.fontegallo.it

MEL AND KATE HOLMES

Mel and Kate Holmes moved to Calabria in southern Italy in 2000 after Mel took early retirement from teaching in South Wales. He is 59 and Kate is younger. They have bought two houses, both situated in historic centres. One is ten minutes walk from the sea, and the other is 5km inland. They have bought and sold another house in Italy, in between buying the two houses they now own there. Mel and Kate also run an advice service (www.calabrianholidays.co.uk) for people who think they might like to live in Calabria, but according to Mel 'it is more of a hobby than a business'. We asked Mel:

Why Italy?
When I was a teacher I spent my holidays touring in Europe and of all the countries I visited, I liked the atmosphere of Italy best.

How did you end up in Calabria; it's a bit off the expat map isn't it?
Originally, we planned to find a place on the Adriatic coast of Le Marche. We found an apartment we liked, but the seller procrastinated so we decided to go touring further in Italy with the car. We reached Calabria and liked it, so we decided to look for a property to buy. We asked local estate agents and locals about properties for sale. They were not used to dealing with foreigners trying to buy property and so it took a long time, which we had plenty of. For a while we were the only Brits in the area, but since then we have

encouraged a few others to follow suit. There are half a dozen of us living here now.

Where in Calabria are you?

The house on the sea is in the old city of Trebissace, and our other house in 5km away in Villapiani. We are on the Ionian Coast, which is undeveloped at present. The thing about the historic towns here is that they are living cities, not just resorts. However, there is the likelihood of a new airport being built at Sibari, 15 minutes away, though in Italy these things take years to happen. The local hospital was 23 years in the planning before it was built. However, the infrastructure is definitely being upgraded around here with better roads and more supermarkets and hotels being built, and the number of banks has increased from two to six. The local authorities are trying to build up more tourism here. I would say it is a good time to invest in seaside property here while prices here are still reasonable.

Do you live in Calabria year round?

No, because we want to be British. We pay our taxes in the UK, so we spend the requisite number of days in the UK to qualify for tax residency there. We prefer to be tax resident in the UK as it is easier.

You mean than dealing with the Italian bureaucracy?

In the south, you have Italian bureaucracy, only slower. People here don't queue. If the official sees someone he knows, he waves them to the front. You can spend half an hour queuing in the bank or post office.

How is your Italian?

We didn't learn before we came, but we brought tapes with us. We pick it up as we go along. I learnt a lot of Italian words from dealing with builders. I can get by. The thing about Italians is that they are genuinely delighted if you try to speak Italian. I don't think the same can be said of the French.

What's the best way to buy a house in Italy if you don't speak Italian?

We used a legal proxy. This can be any professional person such as a teacher, doctor etc. We used an English teacher who is bilingual. We advise other

Brits wanting to buy property in Italy to do this so that you have someone on your side who understands the documents they are signing.

What type of properties are available in Calabria?

You can get ruins for €10,000 to €15,000 but you spend as much again on renovations. For €22,000 to €30,000 you can get a studio apartment. Other property may not be as cheap. For instance you can't buy farmhouses here like you can in other parts of Italy because they still have farmers living in them. You can occasionally find country houses for sale, but these are expensive. We have a garden at our house in Villapiani but it is quite small, 250 sq m with fig, citrus fruit and olive trees. Apartments and houses in old towns are a possibility. You could buy one house to live in and buy a seaside apartment as an investment or for holiday rentals.

What about the medical facilities? We hear that state hospitals in the south can be very basic?

One of the reasons that we chose Trebissace to live is that it has a good hospital. True, it is basic and not very comfortable and you have to get your friends to bring fresh clothes and food for you, but that is usual. There is no waiting here. If you need to see a specialist it is the same day or near enough. For instance, a friend of ours here had a heart attack. It was discovered that he needed a bypass operation. He was in and out of hospital and convalescing before a friend of ours in England, with the same condition, had even got an appointment with a specialist.

Calabria is mafia territory isn't it?

There is a saying around here that if a town is controlled by the mafia, it is a safe place because the mafia would not allow anything to go on that attracts bad notices. The streets are so safe that people allow their children to walk outside on their own at night, knowing that they are almost as safe as in their own houses. We feel a thousand times safer here than we did in the UK. Having said that, if I won the lottery I wouldn't come here and build a million pound villa, because that might invite mafia attention. But ordinary folk like us can live completely unaware of the mafia's existence.

What pleasure springs to mind when you think of your home in Calabria?
The smell in spring is wonderful, especially the citrus blossom.

VINCE AND FREDDI FERRIGNO

Vince and Freddi Ferrigno moved to a seaside villa near Brindisi in Apulia in 2003. Despite being half Italian Vince did not learn Italian while growing up in the UK as he was born just before the Second World War when it was not advisable to speak Italian. He is 68 and Freddi, his wife, is 66. Before they retired, Vince ran his own engineering company and Freddi was Personnel Director of a large company. She suffered badly from arthritis and asthma before she moved to Italy where both conditions have both become '100% better' after responding to the mild climate of Brindisi. We asked them:

It's obvious why you wanted to retire in Italy; why the Brindisi area?
Originally, we had planned to find somewhere around Ravello on the Amalfi coast as that is where Vince has distant family connections. However, we decided against this, as the climate did not suit my asthma and the steep hills made me breathless.

We wanted to find somewhere that had not been commercialised with all the trappings of a tourist area, and we did not want to find ourselves in a British community. Property is much cheaper in Apulia so we began looking here. We must have looked at 20-odd houses through a local agent.

What did you buy in the end?
We bought a modern villa with four bedrooms and a separate guest house. The villa is a few minutes from Brindisi, right on the coast between Casale and Apani. It cost about twice as much as we had planned to pay for a house, but as soon as we saw it, we knew it was the right one. The problem was that it had been empty and neglected for two years so we had to have a bit of refurbishing work done. There is a garden which goes all round the house with terraces on either side. It is quite big enough for us to manage. Originally we had hoped for more land, but now we are happy with what we have.

What about the local health facilities?

There is a new local hospital which is modern and up-to-date. It is very efficient, calm and clean. We get the same national health service rights as Italian pensioners which means we pay token charges such as €2 for a prescription and €15 for a scan. We had private health cover to begin with, but we cancelled it as we find we don't need it here.

And other facilities?

We can take a small ferry almost outside our house to Brindisi centre. Brindisi has a lovely old *centro storico,* and we love the old fishing port. We are keen golfers and there are two courses both within 40 minutes drive. Golf is our main recreation. Apart from that we love eating out. It's about a quarter of the price you would pay in the UK and the food is so healthy and wholesome. Ballroom dancing is also a big leisure activity here.

The airport at Brindisi is served by Ryanair and we wait until they have special offers and fly back to the UK. We have bought tickets for one euro each!

How is your Italian?

We did three-months of intensive courses before we came so that we had the basics and now we are learning as we go. I think we are improving all the time.

Any problems?

Well the bureaucracy is extremely difficult. We are just beginning to find our way around it. To begin with, it was a nightmare. If you don't pay your local property tax on time you get a fine of 60%! The taxes are quite high, about €800 property tax and the *spazzatura* (rubbish tax) is about €600 a year. The rubbish isn't collected from the house, you have to take it to the rubbish collection point.

Vince, you still have your British car, reregistered in Italy?

Yes, I am happy driving a right-hand drive on the right hand side of the road. I also like my automatic gears. It is very difficult to get automatics here; Italians are all boy racers who would be lost without their gear sticks. In retrospect though it was probably not a good idea to reregister a British car in Italy as it was a nightmare. Midway through the process we couldn't get any insurance as a British company wouldn't insure a car in Italy and the Italians wouldn't insure it because it didn't have an Italian registration. I probably should have just bought a car here; they are much cheaper in Italy.

What about making friends?
We have lovely neighbours including an English lady who arrived here when she was 18 and married an Italian. She is now 50. For the first few months after we moved here we didn't have to buy any fresh fruit and vegetables as neighbours brought these to us daily. One even brought us breakfast; I think she thought that we didn't have proper cooking facilities. The Italians are amazing.

Vince, what are some of the best things about retiring to Italy?
The marvellous climate with mild winters. The delicious food; people eat so healthily here. But best of all, the weather has done wonders for my wife's asthma and arthritis, and that is worth moving to Italy for on its own.

Complete guides to life abroad from Vacation Work

Live & Work Abroad